CD & DVD Recording For Dummies, 2nd Edition

KT-476-728

Sizing Up Today's DVD Media

Type	DVD-ROM Compatible*	Rewritable	Capacity per Side
DVD-R	Almost always	No	4.7GB
DVD+R	Almost always	No	4.7GB
DVD-RAM	Usually not	Yes	4.7 to 5.2GB
DVD-RW	Almost always	Yes	4.7GB
DVD+RW	Almost always	Yes	4.7GB

* Several generations of DVD-ROM players are on the market; generally, the newer the player, the more compatible it is with all four of these media types.

Strengths and Weaknesses of "Those Interface Things"

Type	Internal/External	Plug and Play?	High-Speed?	Max Devices per Cable
EIDE	Internal only	N/A	Yes	4
SCSI	Both	No	Yes	14
FireWire	External only	Yes	Yes	63
USB 1.1	External only	Yes	No	127
USB 2.0	External only	Yes	Yes	127

Mark's Common-Sense Installation Tips

- **Read the installation instructions!** Only the manufacturer's instructions can tell you whether to cut the blue wire or the red wire!

- **Prepare your work surface:** If you're installing an internal drive, prepare a flat, soft, well-lighted surface — several sheets of newspaper on a table work fine.

- **Take your time:** No one's looking over your shoulder with a stopwatch, so relax and follow the steps the right way the first time.

- **Keep those parts:** You're likely to remove small parts, so keep a bowl handy that can hold everything you remove. You need some of the parts when you reassemble your computer, and anything left over should be saved as spare parts for future upgrades and repairs.

- **Ask for help:** Got a hardware-knowledgeable friend or family member? Put 'em to work and buy 'em a meal.

For Dummies: Bestselling Book Series for Beginners

CD & DVD Recording For Dummies, 2nd Edition

Cheat Sheet

Clearing Drive Space: Unnecessary Stuff You Can Delete

- **Demos, samples, and ancient files:** Say goodbye to ten-year-old game demos, one-shot software installations you no longer need, and unnecessary documents you've created yourself.

- **Log files:** You can delete log files created by programs. As long as you don't need the information, you can safely get rid of things like virus-scanning files and disk diagnostic log files.

- **The contents of your Trash or Recycle Bin:** Don't forget to toss those files that are still tenaciously hanging on for possible undeletion.

- **Typical browser refuse:** You can toss out images, Web pages, and sound files that your browser stores in its cache to speed things up when you reload a page. Your browser should provide a method of deleting these temporary cache files.

- **Windows temporary files:** If you're running Windows XP, choose Start⇨All Programs⇨ Accessories⇨System Tools⇨Disk Cleanup to run the Disk Cleanup Wizard; the Wizard takes care of those tacky temporary files created by practically every Windows program ever written.

CD-ROM File Systems

Type	Platform	Long Filenames?	Suggested Use
Joliet	Windows	Yes	Recording for Windows
HFS	Macintosh	Yes	Recording for Mac operating system
Hybrid	Windows and Mac	Yes	Recording for both Windows and Mac operating systems
UDF	Windows and Mac	Yes	Recording for both Windows and Mac, DVD-Video discs
ISO 9660	All	No	Recording for any platform or operating system

Smart Tips for Buying Online

- **Never buy from an online Web store that doesn't offer a secure connection.** Look for the padlock icon on your Web browser's status bar before you enter your personal information and credit card number.

- **Beware of exorbitant shipping options.** If you can wait three or four days for your drive, choose the slowest delivery method and save your cash.

- **Watch for the words *refurbished* and *factory remanufactured*.** It may be cheap, but it's also used.

- **Avoid online Web stores that charge a restocking fee for unopened merchandise that you return.**

For Dummies: Bestselling Book Series for Beginners

CD & DVD Recording

FOR

DUMMIES®

2ND EDITION

CD & DVD Recording

FOR

DUMMIES®

2ND EDITION

by Mark L. Chambers

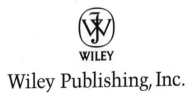

WILEY

Wiley Publishing, Inc.

CD & DVD Recording For Dummies, 2nd Edition®

Published by
Wiley Publishing, Inc.
111 River Street
Hoboken, NJ 07030-5774

About the Author

Mark L. Chambers has been an author, computer consultant, BBS sysop, programmer, and hardware technician for more than 20 years. (In other words, he's been pushing computers and their uses far beyond "normal" performance limits for decades now.) His first love affair with a computer peripheral blossomed in 1984 when he bought his lightning-fast 300 bps modem for his Atari 400. Now he spends entirely too much time on the Internet and drinks far too much caffeine-laden soda.

His favorite pastimes include collecting gargoyles, watching St. Louis Cardinals baseball, playing his three pinball machines and the latest computer games, supercharging computers, and rendering 3-D flights of fancy with TrueSpace — and during all that, he listens to just about every type of music imaginable. (For those of his readers who are keeping track, he has over 1,200 audio CDs in his collection.)

With a degree in journalism and creative writing from Louisiana State University, Mark took the logical career choice and started programming computers. However, after five years as a COBOL programmer for a hospital system, he decided that there must be a better way to earn a living, and he became the Documentation Manager for Datastorm Technologies, a well-known communications software developer. Somewhere in between organizing and writing software manuals, Mark began writing computer books; his first book, *Running a Perfect BBS*, was published in 1994.

Along with writing several books a year and editing whatever his publishers throw at him, Mark has recently branched out into Web-based education, designing and teaching a number of online classes — called *WebClinics* — for Hewlett-Packard.

Mark's rapidly-expanding list of books *includes Building a PC For Dummies, Scanners For Dummies, CD and DVD Recording For Dummies, Mac OS X Panther All-In-One Desk Reference For Dummies, PC All-In-One Desk Reference For Dummies, Mac OS X Panther: Top 100 Simplified Tips & Tricks, Microsoft Office v. X Power User's Guide, BURN IT! Creating Your Own Great DVDs and CDs, The Hewlett-Packard Official Printer Handbook, The Hewlett-Packard Official Recordable CD Handbook, The Hewlett-Packard Official Digital Photography Handbook, Computer Gamer's Bible, Recordable CD Bible, Teach Yourself the iMac Visually, Running a Perfect BBS, Official Netscape Guide to Web Animation,* and the *Windows 98 Troubleshooting and Optimizing Little Black Book.*

His books have been translated into 12 different languages so far — his favorites are German, Polish, Dutch, and French. Although he can't read them, he enjoys the pictures a great deal.

Mark welcomes all comments and questions about his books — you can reach him at mark@mlcbooks.com, or visit his Web site, MLC Books Online, at www.mlcbooks.com.

Author's Acknowledgments

In this, my fourth book on CD and DVD recording, I find that I'm again in debt to a number of great people at Wiley Publishing. I'm noticing a pattern here, and I must say I like it!

As with all my books, I'd like to first thank my wife, Anne, and my children, Erin, Chelsea, and Rose, for their support and love — and for letting me follow my dream!

No book would see the light of day without the Production team, this time led by project coordinator Adrienne Martinez — starting with my words and adding a tremendous amount of work, they've once again taken care of artwork, proofreading, and countless steps that I can't fathom. Thanks to each of the team members for a beautiful book.

Next, my appreciation goes to my editorial manager, Kevin Kirschner, and to my technical editor, Trevor Kay, who checked the technical accuracy of every word — including that baker's dozen of absurd acronyms that crops up in every computer book I've ever written. Their work ensures that my work is the best it can be!

Finally, we come to the Big Two who have worked on this project since the beginning. I promised Bob Woerner, my acquisitions editor, the fewest number of gray hairs possible: I hope that I succeeded! Despite what many folks think, *For Dummies* titles don't grow on trees. He was instrumental in launching this one. And this great title was guided by my latest project editor, Nicole Sholly, who checked the grammar and clarity of every word. This is my first book with Nicole in charge, and I very much hope it won't be the last. My heartfelt thanks to you both for another chance to put pen to paper — well, actually, fingers to keyboard!

Publisher's Acknowledgments

We're proud of this book; please send us your comments through our online registration form located at www.dummies.com/register/.

Some of the people who helped bring this book to market include the following:

Acquisitions, Editorial, and Media Development

Associate Project Editor: Nicole Sholly

Acquisitions Editor: Bob Woerner

Copy Editor: Virginia Sanders

Technical Editor: Trevor Kay

Editorial Manager: Kevin Kirschner

Media Development Manager: Laura VanWinkle

Media Development Supervisor: Richard Graves

Editorial Assistant: Amanda Foxworth

Cartoons: Rich Tennant (www.the5thwave.com)

Production

Project Coordinator: Adrienne Martinez

Layout and Graphics: Seth Conley, Andrea Dahl, Lauren Goddard, Michael Kruzil, Heather Ryan, Jacque Schneider, Melanie Wolven

Proofreaders: Andy Hollandbeck, Carl Pierce, Dwight Ramsey, Charles Spencer, TECHBOOKS Production Services

Indexer: TECHBOOKS Production Services

Publishing and Editorial for Technology Dummies

    Richard Swadley, Vice President and Executive Group Publisher

    Andy Cummings, Vice President and Publisher

    Mary C. Corder, Editorial Director

Publishing for Consumer Dummies

    Diane Graves Steele, Vice President and Publisher

    Joyce Pepple, Acquisitions Director

Composition Services

    Gerry Fahey, Vice President of Production Services

    Debbie Stailey, Director of Composition Services

Contents at a Glance

Table of Contents

Introduction

My first book on CD recording was published by IDG Books Worldwide in 1997 — it was called *Recordable CD Bible,* and I'm proud to say that it was one of the first consumer books on the shelves that covered all aspects of the art. Yes, in those days, CD burning was indeed an art form! Recording software was still expensive and hard to handle, with no wizards to guide you. Drives were ten times as expensive as they are now . . . and I'm talking about CD-R recorders only, because rewriteable CDs and DVDs didn't exist yet. It was all too easy to ruin a recording and burn a shiny, useless drink coaster. In fact, most computers literally weren't fast enough to deliver data to a recorder at the rate it demanded — I can vividly remember telling readers to drop their recording speed to 1X in many situations to avoid recording errors!

Everything has changed in the new millennium. Most PCs and Macs come with a recorder built-in, or you can buy one for pocket change. Recording formats, like UDF/packet-writing, and new hardware advances, like burnproofing, allow just about any PC to burn a disc without errors — not to mention that recording software has been refined to the point that it's virtually foolproof. (If all this sounds like I'm speaking in a foreign language, fear not: I cover it completely in the chapters to follow!)

If things are so easy and foolproof today, why did I decide to write a new *For Dummies* book about CD and DVD recording? Because the challenge is still there! It has just shifted from "the art of successfully recording *anything*" to "the art of using your recorder to its full potential." Today, a CD or DVD recorder can produce everything from superb-sounding audio CDs to DVD-Video discs that you can play in your home DVD player. More applications than ever are available for your recorded discs: digital photo albums, system backups, MP3 music discs, mixed data and audio CDs, and much, much more. I've written this book to introduce you to the entire range of discs that you can produce and how to create each of them like an experienced expert.

Also, the road to perfect recording still isn't perfectly flat. For example, if you're buying and installing a drive, you need all the information you can get. I give you an entire glossary full of terms, formats, and crazy acronyms that you need to understand. (Go ahead — flip to the back of this book and check it out!) Just because your recording software doesn't display all those configuration settings on the main menu any more doesn't mean that they're not there, and sooner or later, you need to know what all those settings do.

That's the reason I wrote this book: It's for readers who want to know everything about recording, from top to bottom! As in my other *For Dummies* books, I begin with the basics and lead you into advanced recording, with needed tips and tricks added along the way. I promise to stick to the English language, so you don't need an engineer or a computer programmer handy to decode anything. Like any *For Dummies* author, I get to be myself and use my sense of humor. This book is not your typical dry, dreary computer manual — I hope that this book is entertaining enough to read in the bathtub! (Just be careful not to drop it.)

What's Really Required

Forget the engineering degree and keep your wallet in your pocket (unless you haven't bought this book yet — if you haven't, please proceed to the cashier and support a computer-book author). I find that many folks have preconceived notions of what's needed to burn a great CD or DVD, so this gives me an opportunity to set things right. To wit, these are the requirements that you *don't* need for this book:

- ✔ A decade of experience with computers, recording, hardware, or even software.

- ✔ An entire bank account to spend on expensive software. Most software that I describe in this book either came with your recorder or can be bought as shareware for a few bucks — and some applications I cover are free for the asking!

- ✔ The latest drive on the market. If you've scavenged an older drive at a garage sale or eBay, you're in good hands. I cover information, tips, and tricks that apply to older drives and their idiosyncrasies.

If you haven't bought your CD or DVD recorder yet, this book will become your trusted friend in a hurry! I cover each of the features that you should consider, plus how to install and configure your new toy.

About This Book

Each self-contained chapter in this book covers a specific topic relating to your recorder. Although you can begin reading anywhere or skip chapters at will (for example, if you've already installed your drive, you don't need that chapter), but I think that reading from front to back makes the most sense — it's the whole linear-order thing, you know.

I've also included a glossary of all the computer and recording terms that I cover in the text, as well as an appendix with contact information for manufacturers of recorders and software.

Conventions Used in This Book

Like any other computer book, I have to ask that you type commands and click menu items from time to time. Luckily, *For Dummies* books have a set of conventions that can help keep things clear.

Stuff you type

If you have to type a command within Windows or the Mac operating system, the text appears like this:

Type me

Press the Enter (or Return) key to process the command.

Menu commands

Menu commands you should use appear in the following format:

Choose Edit⇨Copy

For example, this shorthand indicates that you should click the Edit menu and then click the Copy menu item.

Display messages

Whenever I talk about messages that you should see displayed on-screen, those messages look like this: This is a message displayed by a program.

In case you're curious about computers

I try to steer clear about much of what goes on underneath the suave exterior of your recorder — after all, computers are supposed to be getting easier to use, not harder. If you're like me, however, you sometimes like to know what makes something tick. Occasionally, you see sidebars that provide a little more technical background about what I'm discussing. Feel free to read these technical sidebars (or gleefully ignore them because I don't give you tests on this material afterward).

How This Book Is Organized

My editors demanded that I organize this book *somehow* — and because they have this contract thing I had to sign, I've divided the book into six major parts, with cross-references where appropriate. The book also has an index that you can use to locate a specific topic.

The six parts are described in this section.

Part I: Shake Hands with Your Recorder!

This part familiarizes you with your CD or DVD recorder. You find out how both types of optical media work, what to look for (and what to avoid) when shopping for a new recorder, and what you can do with DVD technology. I also have you installing your drive like a professional, even if you've never opened your computer's case before.

Part II: It's All in the Preparation

In this part, I discuss the preparations that you should take before you burn your first disc. I show you how to optimize your computer's performance, how to select the right recording software for the job, and how to select the right configuration settings for the type of disc that you want to record (settings like the format, the organization, and the file system).

Part III: Hang On — Here We Go!

Here's where things get *really* good — you advance to recording typical audio CDs and data discs with Easy CD & DVD Creator 6 (for the PC) and Toast 6 Titanium (for the Mac). These audio and data discs are the bread and butter of most home recording projects, and you find out to burn them by following step-by-step examples. I also show you how to use Drag-to-Disc, a program that can deliver effortless recording by using the drag-and-drop convenience of Windows.

Part IV: So You're Ready to Tackle Tougher Stuff?

I cover the advanced ground in this part as I show you how to create Video CDs, photo CDs, and DVD projects. I also demonstrate how to transfer your music from albums and cassettes to audio CDs. For that professional appearance, I show you how to print custom disc labels and box inserts, and I help you create a custom HTML menu system to spruce up your data CDs.

Part V: The Part of Tens

If you're a devoted fan of the *For Dummies* series, you should immediately recognize these four chapters — they provide tips and advice on recording, including troubleshooting tips, and software recommendations. Oh, and I also include my traditional chapter on Ten Things to Avoid Like the Plague — not to be missed!

Part VI: Appendixes

Here you can find a list of hardware and software manufacturers and a glossary of computer terms and unwieldy acronyms.

Icons Used in This Book

Consider the icons in this book as signposts pointing at particularly important stuff.

Whenever you see the Tip icon, it's sure to be accompanied by information that saves you time, trouble, or cash.

Look to the handsome sign of the Scavenger for information on buying or using an older recorder, as well as tips on using older hardware in general.

Like the sidebars in this book, the Technical Stuff icon indicates material that is entirely optional: It's for folks with computer curiosity.

Like a roadside warning sign, potential trouble is ahead. *Always* read the information next to this icon first to avoid damage to your hardware and software!

This information is the stuff that you would see in the *CliffsNotes* version of this book. It's highlighter material that reminds you of something important.

Because you're currently reading the Second Edition of this technological tome, you can expect updated descriptions and information on brand-new hardware and software . . . hence this attractive icon.

Where to Go from Here

I recommend that you read this book in linear order, but where you start depends on your knowledge (and whether you already have your recorder). To wit:

- ✔ If you're shopping for a recorder or you have yet to install your hardware, start with Part I. (That's also a good place to start if you're curious about how CD and DVD technology works.)

- ✔ If your recorder is already working, but you need help burning discs, start with Part II.

- ✔ In any other case, use the index, or jump straight to the chapter that holds the information you need. (Don't forget to check out the other chapters when you have time!)

I wish you the best of luck with your recording projects, and I hope that you find this book valuable. Be prepared to keep a spindle of 50 blank discs next to your computer!

Part I
Shake Hands with Your Recorder!

The 5th Wave   By Rich Tennant

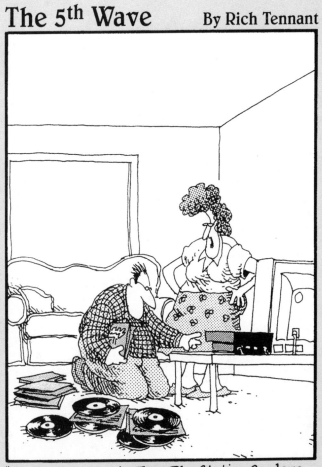

"I don't get it. The PlayStation 2 plays games, CDs, DVDs... Well, you keep looking for the tone arm and needle, and I'll page through the manual again."

In this part . . .

This part familiarizes you with your CD or DVD recorder. I go over reading to and saving from a disc and cover the differences between CDs and DVDs. You find out how these wonderful optical media work, what to look for (and what to avoid) when shopping for a new recorder, and what you can do with DVD technology. By the end of this part, I have you installing your drive like a professional (taped-up nerd glasses not necessarily included) even if you've never opened your computer's case before.

Chapter 1

Optical Storage: It's All in the Pits

*W*hen's the last time you really looked at a CD? I mean *really* stared at it, in rapt fascination? Believe it or not, CDs used to be enthralling!

CDs and DVDs are now both staples of the technical wonderland that you and I live in. Unless you're older and you were around long before 1980 — the days of disco, *Charlie's Angels,* and Rubik's Cube — you won't remember the lure of the compact disc. In those dark times, before the introduction of CDs, music lived on huge, clunky vinyl albums. Computer software was loaded on floppy disks. Movies? They were kept on videotapes. (Remember *those?*)

At first, this situation wasn't a bad one — at least until you kept these old-fashioned storage media for a year or two. Suddenly, you would find that those records had picked up scratches and pops. Computer programs were growing so large that they would span five or six floppies. And sooner or later, those floppy disks and movie videotapes could no longer be read reliably; after a mere 100 viewings or so, you would end up buying another VHS copy of *Enter the Dragon.* (Okay, so I'm a big Bruce Lee fan. Substitute your favorite movie instead.)

Like a circular knight in shining armor, the arrival of the CD heralded the beginning of the digital consumer age. I'm not kidding; I can remember an entire room of technotypes jumping with excitement just to *see* their first compact disc! (None of us could afford an audio CD player, and computer CD-ROM drives hadn't arrived yet, but it was great just to see a real CD.) In the beginning, audio

CDs brought us crystal-clear sound and the convenience of jumping instantly from track to track. Then, computer software suddenly fit on one CD, and the software could always be read reliably. With the advent of DVD, widescreen movies are accompanied by luxuries like alternative soundtracks and interviews with the cast and director. Would you go back to anything less?

In this chapter, I introduce you to the basics of compact disc and DVD storage: You don't have to know *all* this stuff before you jump into recording your own discs, but if you understand the basics of what's going on, you avoid mistakes. (Always be prepared.) I promise to tell you along the way about what you absolutely need to know. You find out how discs store information, video, and music as well as what's inside your CD or DVD recorder. I cover what types of media you can use and what you can store. Finally, I show you how to properly care for your optical pets. (You may not stare wistfully at CDs like I used to, but you still have to keep them clean.)

Always Begin with a Definition

In this case, let me start by defining the now-familiar term *CD-ROM* — short for *compact disc read-only memory*. (I've shortened this to *CD* throughout this book, which will save about 200 trees by the time I've finished.) This high tech description simply means that a CD stores information of some sort that your computer or audio CD player can read but can't write to (which makes the CD-ROM drive different from a hard drive, for example, which you can both read from and write to). In general, I use the word *disc* to describe both CD-ROMs and DVD-ROMs; they're both similar, read-only, and look very much alike.

Keep this in mind: Whenever folks refer to just a CD-ROM or DVD-ROM drive (without using the word *recordable*), they're talking about the drives that just read discs and can't record them.

Dig that crazy acronym!

I have to use a truckload of acronyms in this book. Luckily, each one has only one meaning, right? Almost! One strange exception applies: You may be wondering what DVD stands for, and as the mondo author expert, I *should* be able to tell you.

When DVD-ROM technology was first introduced, everyone agreed that it stood for *digital versatile disc read-only memory* because it could

store so many types of data. Although a CD can store music and computer files, it doesn't have the room for a full-length movie at the highest-quality level. DVD-ROM was the first optical media to hold all the different types of digital information we use today: lots and lots of data, an entire movie, or even super-high quality audio. Hence, the word *versatile,* and everyone seemed happy. (You find out how to cram huge amounts of stuff on a DVD-ROM in the section "Ready for stardom: DVD-R/W" later in this chapter.)

At some point, however, those first owners of DVD-ROM players who weren't acronym aficionados decided that DVD stood for *digital video disc* — and for a time that was true because DVDs were first used for only movies. This name situation leaves us in a quandary because more and more folks think *video* rather than *versatile*. Naturally, it doesn't matter a hoot because everyone just uses the acronym anyway, but it does make a killer trivia question!

The basic specifications of both audio CDs and data CDs (those discs you use in your computer) are the same; they're 12 centimeters in diameter and a millimeter thick, and they have an opaque top and a reflective bottom. Such is the Tao of the disc.

As you can see in Figure 1-1, however, the structure of a mass-produced disc isn't a single piece of plastic. It's made up of a number of layers, each of which has something special to add to the mix:

Figure 1-1:
And you thought that a CD was just a piece of plastic!

Protective plastic layer

Screen-printed or paper label

Aluminum film

Clear plastic layer

Smooth area, reflects light

Pit, does not reflect light

✔ **A label:** Commercially manufactured discs you buy in the store have screen-printed labels; these graphics are created from layers of ink applied one on top of the other (like that Metallica T-shirt you may be wearing).

What's that, you say? You don't have $2,000 or so to spend on a special CD screen printer? (Come to think of it, neither do I!) In that case, do what I do and use your inkjet or laser printer to create a fancy paper label, complete with the graphics and text you choose (more on this topic in Chapter 14).

"Do I really need a label?" To be honest, no. A disc you've recorded works fine without one. However, if you've ever dug through a 6-inch stack of unlabeled CDs to find that *Andy Williams Greatest Hits* disc you burned a month ago for Aunt Harriet, I *guarantee* that you will understand. If you don't need a professional look and you're not into appearances, just use a CD-marking pen and scribble a quick title on top. Most recordable discs have blank lines printed on them for just this purpose.

You can pick up one of these handy pens at any office supply store, but make sure that you buy a pen designed especially for marking CDs.

- **Opaque plastic:** You need something to protect the top of the disc. I suppose that you could use steel, but then a disc would weigh two pounds and cost much more. Therefore, the manufacturer adds a layer of scratch-resistant plastic.

- **Aluminum film:** Mass-produced CDs use a thin layer of aluminum that's covered with microscopic indentations called *pits*. These pits are arranged in a single, tiny groove that spirals around the disc, just like the groove on one of those antique record albums. (If something works, why mess with it?) However, the groove on a CD starts at the center and spirals to the outside of the disc, so it goes in the opposite direction.

- **More plastic:** Again, all that shiny aluminum has to be protected — however, in this case, the plastic must be crystal-clear (for reasons that soon become apparent), so the manufacturer adds another layer. Here's a hint about why this layer is clear: It has to do with the passage of laser light.

As I mention earlier in this chapter, this yummy sandwich is a cross-section of a commercial CD produced at a factory — the discs you record are different in one important way, which I cover in a minute.

DVDs are similar to CDs in construction, but, as I remind you from time to time, commercially produced DVDs can be double-sided (so you can flip them to watch the second half of a really long film, like *Das Boot* or *Gone with the Wind*). Therefore, they may not always have a label side, in which case the sides are marked around the spindle hole.

How Is Data Recorded on CDs and DVDs?

Consider just how audio, video, and computer files are stored on CDs and DVDs. Although these three types of information are different, they're stored in the same way: digitally. But what does that word really mean?

Programmers, technotypes, and hardware jockeys use the word *digital* when they're talking about *binary,* the language used by computers around the world. Unlike the imprecise languages spoken and written by mere humans, binary data is built from only two values — 0 (zero) and 1, which are often referred to as Off and On, respectively shown in Figure 1-2. (In fact, a computer is only a huge collection of switches, but that's another story.) Therefore, computer files, movies, and digital music are long lines of 0s (zeros) and 1s. If you sat next to a light switch for 100 years and flipped it off and on in the proper sequence, you would have the visual version of a digital song from a CD (and a bad headache along with incredibly sore fingers).

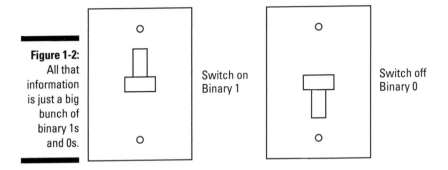

Figure 1-2:
All that information is just a big bunch of binary 1s and 0s.

Switch on
Binary 1

Switch off
Binary 0

Now that you're privy to the binary master plan, you can see how the absence and presence of light perfectly represents binary data — a room is either dark or bright. The geniuses who developed CD and DVD technology took this concept one step further! They had the great idea of using a laser beam to read the binary data stored on a disc, and that's where those pits in the aluminum layer that I mention in the preceding section take center stage.

Figure 1-3 shows how the binary data is read: When the laser beam hits a pit on the surface of the disc, the beam scatters, so most of it isn't reflected back: hence, darkness, which in this case stands for a 0 (zero) in binary data. If the laser beam hits one of the flat surfaces — they're called *lands,* by the way — the beam is reflected cleanly back, and the drive senses that reflected light. (Think of a 1 in binary.) And, ladies and gentlemen, that is why the business end of a disc shines like a mirror; the rainbow effect is caused by the microscopic groove that runs across the surface. Naturally, this process happens very fast (I talk about speed in Chapter 2), but that's really all there is to it.

Figure 1-3:
The surface of a CD or DVD, as read by your friendly neighborhood laser beam.

Laser strikes a pit, which scatters the light

Laser strikes a smooth area, which reflects the light directly back at the laser read head

Essentially, DVD technology works the same way — with a difference or two. A DVD-ROM can hold the approximate equivalent of seven CDs, and Figure 1-4 shows how: The pits on a DVD-ROM are much smaller and are packed closer together on the surface of the disc, and the drive uses a much more powerful laser beam to read them. DVD can also have multiple reflective layers. (That's the reason that data can be stored on both sides.)

Figure 1-4: Compared with a CD, the pits on a DVD-ROM don't have much elbowroom.

Believe it or not, the DVD specification standard provides for double-sided DVD-ROM discs that have *two* layers on each side, for more than 27 CDs' worth of storage space on a single DVD-ROM! However, these discs are so hard to manufacture that they're on the endangered species list, and I've never actually seen one.

It's All in the Dye

Consider the structure of recordable discs, which includes both recordable CDs and recordable DVDs. Remember the aluminum film that I mention in the section "Always Begin with a Definition" earlier in this chapter? Sounds permanent, doesn't it? Indeed it is, which is why you can't use commercially manufactured discs to record your own data; your recorder has to be able to create the equivalent of pits and lands in some other way. (Not even Bill Gates has a CD-R manufacturing plant in his house.)

Figure 1-5 shows the answer as well as a really bad pun. The CD-R (short for *compact disc recordable*), which can be recorded once, uses a layer of green or blue reactive dye under a smooth reflective surface of either aluminum or gold. The groove is still there, but until the disc has been recorded, the disc is perfectly empty. This dye permanently melts or darkens when hit by a laser beam of a certain frequency, which results in a pit. (As you find out later in the chapter, a number of DVD recordable formats are currently on the market, but things work the same.)

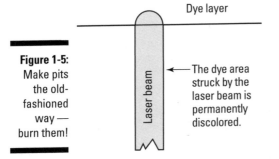

Figure 1-5:
Make pits
the old-
fashioned
way —
burn them!

Dye layer

Laser beam

The dye area struck by the laser beam is permanently discolored.

"Hang on, Mark — wouldn't the beam from my regular read-only CD-ROM or DVD-ROM drive cause problems?" Good question, but the designers of recordable CD and DVD drives have you covered. The laser beam that is used to read a disc is far less powerful than the beam used to record one. Therefore, when the beam from the laser in your CD-ROM or DVD-ROM drive hits one of these dark spots, the beam is swallowed like an apple pie at a state fair, so it acts just like a pit in a mass-produced CD. In fact, your read-only drive is completely fooled . . . it can't tell the difference.

Why all the different colors?

I get asked this question all the time. Some CD-Rs, DVD-Rs, and DVD+Rs are gold with a green dye, and others are silver with a blue or purple dye. Everything acts the same: You're just looking at two different recipes for the dye used by different manufacturers. Most drives record on either type of disc, but in rare situations, an older drive seems to work better with one or the other color combination. Personally, I think that it has something to do with the alignment of the planets and the phase of the moon, but I must report what I hear.

On the other hand, CD-RWs and rewriteable DVDs use the same type of crystalline layer, so they're all colored the same.

The inside of your CD or DVD recorder sounds like it's getting a little crowded with all these different laser beams, but it's really not. A recorder has a beam that can be set at two levels: a lower power setting that can read a disc and a higher setting to record it. Slick, eh?

A CD-RW, which is short for *compact disc rewriteable,* is another story. (Get ready: You're going to *love* this description. It honestly sounds like something out of *Star Trek* — the original series, not any of those later failures that don't have Captain Kirk.) Here goes: Both rewriteable CDs and DVDs use a "phase change recording process" using a "crystalline layer with amorphous properties" rather than a dye layer. Didn't I tell you? It sounds like something Spock would say! You can promptly forget that stuff because nobody but an engineer cares, and no one gives a test afterward.

Anyway, although the crystalline layer starts out clear, the correct type of laser beam can change it to opaque, creating — you guessed it — a pit. When you're ready to erase the disk, that same beam of laser light resets the crystalline layer to clear again, and you're ready to record all over again. Talk about recycling!

Behind the Curtain: Inside CD-RW and DVD Drives

Before I delve into the depths of your hardware, I want to make one thing perfectly clear: *You do not have to read this section!* In fact, if raising the hood on your car and just looking at the engine gives you a headache, I encourage you to skip this section entirely. It's definitely not necessary to know what makes your drive tick.

Still here? I didn't scare you away? Good! If you're like me, and cool machinery like your recorder fascinates you, stick with me and read on! In this section, I show you the interior guts of your CD-RW or DVD recorder.

The motor

Because pits are arranged around the entire disc, something has to turn it — in this case, an efficient, high-speed electric motor. (No coal or gas here, Bucko.) The motor turns a spindle, which holds the disc by the hole in the center — yet another similarity to vinyl record albums!

The laser stuff

A CD-ROM or DVD-ROM drive has a laser read head, and a recorder has a read head that can be set to variable power levels. When you read a disc, the laser beam is focused through a lens upward toward the surface of the disc; if the beam is reflected by a land, the light travels through a prism to an optical pickup. In turn, the pickup yells to your computer (in effect) "Hey, I just passed a land back there, so add a 1 to the file."

When a drive is recording, the laser beam is switched to its higher power; the beam simply travels up to the surface of the disc and creates a pit by discoloring or melting the dye layer in one tiny spot.

How does the laser get around the entire surface of the disc? It's on a moving track that can move forward and back between the center and outside edge of the disc.

The tray

The tray is self-explanatory but still pretty doggone important: You need some method of inserting and ejecting discs. Although most drives use a tray that extends to hold the disc, some integrated CD-RW and DVD drives use a slot with a motor-loading system that draws the disc inside the drive (just like a car audio CD player). Older drives used a thin plastic box called a *caddy* — you opened the caddy and stuck the disc inside. Although you would be hard pressed to find a new CD-RW recorder that uses a caddy, some high-capacity DVD-RAM recorders now use them to help protect the disc. (More on DVD-RAM in the section titled "The rewriteable warehouse: DVD-RAM" later in this chapter.)

The controls

Your recorder is certain to have an eject button and probably also a headphone jack and volume control for listening to audio CDs. More expensive drives can go a step further with more audio CD controls, like Pause, Play, Next Track, and Previous Track.

The emergency hole

I know that it sounds weird, but every drive has an *emergency disc eject hole.* Think of it as being similar to the ejection seat in a jet fighter plane or one of those cool emergency airlock controls that crops up in every science fiction horror movie. (How many times has Sigourney Weaver blasted something nasty into space by slapping a button?) You can use this microscopic hole on the front of your drive to forcibly eject a disc whenever your drive has locked up or if a disc is caught inside. To use the emergency eject, push the end of a paper clip or a piece of stiff wire into this hole. This technique usually works even when there's no power to the drive.

Love Those Discs: CD-R, CD-R/W, DVD-R/W, DVD+R/W, and DVD-RAM

If you've been reading this chapter at a single sitting, you may have a media-induced headache by now. No, I'm not talking about the nightly TV news — I mean all those different kinds of discs I mention from time to time in this chapter. You may have read a little about CD-R and CD-RW in this chapter, but it's high time that I identify each of the five types and fill in all the details. This section does just that.

"Hey, can't I buy just one drive?"

Yes. In fact, I've installed an all-format Sony drive in my Batcomputer; the drive can handle everything in that list except DVD-RAM. (Ah, there's the rub.) If you're already the proud owner of a CD-RW drive, I can assure you that it can't be upgraded to record DVDs — on the flip side, any DVD recorder can record CD-Rs and CD-RWs. (Hence their growing popularity. Versatility is always A Good Thing.)

 You'll often see kindred write-once and rewriteable formats grouped together as a single name: For example, CD-R/W actually stands for CD-R *and* CD-RW. (Remember, a CD-RW drive can also record CD-Rs.) Likewise, DVD-R/W stands for DVD-R and DVD-RW, and — you guessed it — DVD+R/W includes both DVD+R and DVD+RW.

First on the block: CD-R

In the beginning, there was the CD-R, and it's still by far the most popular media on the market. A typical CD-R can store anywhere from 650 to 700MB (megabytes) of computer data or 74 to 80 minutes of audio. (The higher numbers are for higher-capacity, 80-minute CD-Rs.) You can also stack more stuff on a CD-R by using the overburning feature; read more on this rather nasty-sounding feature in Chapter 2. As I mention earlier in this chapter, after you've filled a CD-R to capacity, there's no turning back; the data is permanently recorded and can't be erased.

Other sizes of CDs are indeed available — for example, discs with a diameter of 8 centimeters that can hold 184MB — but they're so specialized that you and I can safely ignore them. Some higher-capacity CD-Rs that can hold more than 700MB have hit the market, too, but they're not compatible with older CD-RW drives.

Time for the first Mark's Maxim for this book:

If you need compatibility, think CD-R.™

Take heed: Any CD-ROM drive — no matter how old — can read CD-Rs, and they're the only discs that are guaranteed to play in any home or car audio CD player. In other words, use CD-R whenever

- ✔ You're recording a disc to send to someone else.
- ✔ You're recording an audio CD for playing on anything other than your recorder.
- ✔ You're not sure whether a drive reads a CD-RW.

Reusable and loving it: CD-RW

The CD-RW is the most common rewriteable media on the market right now. It can store 650MB (74 minutes) of audio. A CD-RW must be formatted before you use it, just like a floppy disk or your hard drive; most discs come preformatted from the manufacturer. You also have to reformat the disc if you want to erase its contents.

Did you read about the amorphous crystalline stuff I mention earlier in this chapter? On the positive side, that's what allows your CD-RW drive to erase the disc and use it again. On the downside, however, most read-only CD-ROM drives that are older than three or four years old can't read a CD-RW disc, and a CD-RW can't be used in older audio CD players. Use CD-RW whenever

- ✔ You're recording a disc for use on your computer, like a backup.
- ✔ You're sure that another CD-ROM drive (or audio CD player) can read a CD-RW.

How can you tell whether a CD-ROM drive can read CD-RWs? Many manufacturers add a MultiRead symbol to their faceplates; if you're still unsure, try reading a recorded CD-RW in the drive (don't worry — you won't hurt the hardware). If you can load files from the CD-RW, you have a MultiRead drive. An audio CD player that supports CD-RW is likely to announce the fact in its documentation or specifications.

Ready for stardom: DVD-R/W

Perhaps I shouldn't say "ready for stardom" — heck, in the video world, the DVD-ROM has already overtaken the traditional VHS tape. (I don't suppose that makes Betamax VCR owners feel any better, but every dog has his day.) DVD-ROM is also poised to take over the reign of CD as the media of choice for virtually every new computer on the planet. But what about recordable DVD?

Unfortunately, things are still a little tenuous in the world of recordable DVD standards. However, two format standards are now in use and are (in my opinion) destined to win any turf battles. Luckily, they correspond pretty closely to the world of recordable CDs.

The first of these standards is the DVD-R, which is short for — you guessed it — *DVD recordable*. Like your old friend the CD-R, a DVD-R can be recorded only once. However, the DVD-R can hold a whopping 4.7GB (that's gigabytes, friends and neighbors) per side of the disc, for a total of 9.4GB of data on a double-sided disc. DVD-R is the darling of the video-editing crowd because it allows you to record a disc that can be used in a standard DVD player. Naturally, the DVDs you create with a DVD-R drive can't be read on a standard CD-ROM drive (but you can burn regular CD-Rs and CD-RWs).

On the rewriteable side, the standard is called DVD-RW. (Note the dash there; it becomes pretty important in a page or two.) These discs can also store 4.7GB, and you format them very much like a CD-RW. Any DVD-ROM drive should be able to read a DVD-RW. Unfortunately, not all DVD players can read DVD-RWs, so if you're an up-and-coming Hollywood type that's interested in producing your own movie discs, you should stick with the DVD-R standard (which is compatible with all DVD players).

Oh joy, what confusion: DVD+R/W

Okay, here's where everything gets a little hairy. No, that plus sign isn't a typo: Two other completely independent DVD standards, DVD+R and DVD+RW, are available as well. These two more recent formats are being touted by an entirely different group of computer hardware manufacturers. (I suppose that they needed different names — but couldn't they have chosen something *easier* to remember? Whatever happened to the guy who chose the name *Microsoft Bob* for an operating system? By the way, I still have my copy.)

Anyway, DVD+Rs and DVD+RWs can store 4.7GB, and a DVD-ROM player can read both types of discs. Again, however, you run into the same problem — DVD+Rs are compatible with most DVD players, but DVD+RWs aren't widely supported by DVD players. Plus, DVD-R/W and DVD+R/W are incompatible. (Insert sound of my hand slapping my forehead here.)

In fact, these two disc formats are roughly equivalent — DVD+R/Ws are cheaper to manufacture, though, so they may eventually get the nod. (Of course, if you buy an all-format drive like mine, you don't really give a darn about that plus or minus. I can record both DVD-R/W and DVD+R/W, smiling quietly to myself all the while.)

If your DVD recorder is limited to one format or the other, take care when you're buying DVD media! Make *doggone* sure that you remember which type of discs your recorder can burn — you'll be deluged by the choices on store shelves, and it's easy to mistake DVD-R for DVD+R if you're not careful. (Some readers have told me they're considering a tattoo to help them keep things straight.)

The rewriteable warehouse: DVD-RAM

Finally, there's good old DVD-RAM — a rewriteable disc that can store as much as 9.4GB of data by using both sides. (Remember, a double-sided DVD doesn't have a standard label; printing can appear only around the spindle hole.)

DVD-RAM is well-established, and there's no "plus" format competing for fame and fortune. DVD-RAM is a great option for storing those huge digital video files, and because DVD-RAMs are reusable, I find them the best media for backing up my hard drives. Note, however, that most DVD-ROM players can't read a DVD-RAMs, so use one of the other DVD formats if you're recording something to distribute to others.

What's Wrong with Tapes, Disks, and Removable Media?

Nothing, really! It's just that they're antique technologies compared with rewriteable CDs and DVDs. In this section, I list the most important reasons that optical beats magnetic hands-down.

Here I go, continuing my own personal crusade against the Great Pretender: the archaic floppy disk. I strongly recommend that you *never keep any data of value stored exclusively on floppy disks!* They are the most unreliable media on the planet — they're easily demagnetized, they don't hold much, and they often can't be read by other computers.

More reliable

First (and to many folks, most important), a rewriteable CD or DVD provides permanent storage with a high degree of reliability. Unlike magnetic media — including tape cartridges, floppy disks, and even Zip disks and hard drives — a CD or DVD doesn't stretch or demagnetize. As long as you keep your discs clean, reasonably cool, and free from scratches, you should be able to read them without error for a century or more. (I don't know about you, but I don't know just how important my tax returns will be in 100 years; then again, I want my priceless family photographs to last as long as possible!) Discs have no moving parts to wear out, and they don't rust.

Higher capacity

Forget about storing 700MB of data on a floppy disk! Even the latest Zip disks are simply no match for the 9.4GB capacity of a double-sided DVD-RAM. All that room comes in handy for backing up your system's hard drive, too.

Cheaper

Have you priced a stack of 50 blank, 700MB CD-Rs these days? At the time I wrote this book, I could find that 50-pack all over the Internet at $15; a 50-pack of 650MB CD-RWs is about $30. DVD-RAM prices are hovering around $15 for a 9.4GB disc, and 4.7GB DVD-Rs are selling for about $35 for a 50-pack.

As you can imagine, the lower the cost per megabyte for a storage method, the better, and no other type of media can beat recordable CDs and DVDs. And, if the current trend continues, prices will just drop lower. Ain't life grand?

Faster and more convenient

If you've ever waited for a tape to rewind or a floppy disk to load, you've wished for a faster method of loading your stuff — CDs and DVDs feature fast access time, and there's no rewinding. To put it another way, even if something did fit in the tight space of a floppy disk, would you want to run that program from that floppy? Unlike tape drives — which must move linearly from one section of tape to another — you can jump directly from one part of a disc to another instantly. Take my word for it, this speedy delivery makes restoring files from a backup *much* faster!

Compatibility

Virtually every PC that's still running these days has a CD-ROM drive, so compatibility is a big advantage to recordable CD for folks like software developers, network administrators, and your Uncle Milton. To put it another way: Ever tried to stick a Zip disk into your car audio player? 'Nuff said.

"What Do I Need in Order to Record?"

You knew that there would be a catch, didn't you? You're probably thinking, "I bet that I have to have a $1,000 software program and a cutting-edge computer to record discs." Not true, good reader, not true! It used to be that way when I wrote my first book on CD recording (*Recordable CD Bible,* written in the ancient mid-1990s), but CD and DVD recorders are now tame and lovable creatures. They ask for only the basics — in fact, if your computer came with a CD or DVD recorder already installed, you can skip this section because you're likely to have everything you need.

What you need for Windows

Here's a list of the basic minimum requirements you need for DVD recording on a PC running Windows 2000 or Windows XP:

- **A Pentium III PC (or better):** You need at least 64MB of memory and 1GB of free hard drive space (for a CD recorder). If you're recording DVDs, you need up to 6GB free.

- **A CD or DVD recorder:** Naturally, you also need the proper connection. Internal recorders use Enhanced Integrated Drive Electronics (EIDE) or Small Computer System Interface (SCSI) connections. External recorders can use SCSI, Universal Serial Bus (USB), or FireWire connections. If you're using an external drive, it should come with the necessary cables you need.

- **Recording software:** Most recorders come bundled with some sort of software; if your computer already has a recorder, it probably also came with the programs you need to burn your discs.

- **Blank media:** Naturally.

What you need for the Macintosh

Here's a list of the basic minimum recording requirements for a Macintosh running Mac OS 9 or Mac OS X:

- ✔ **A PowerPC Mac of any speed with at least 64MB of memory and 1GB of free hard drive space:** Again, you need up to 6GB if you're recording DVDs.

- ✔ **A CD or DVD recorder:** Most Macs use external recorders with SCSI, USB, or FireWire connections.

- ✔ **Recording software:** Mac OS X allows you to burn discs from the Finder menu, and you can burn discs from within iTunes as well. Other commercial recording programs are available, like Toast from Roxio.

- ✔ **Blank media:** Gotta have it.

If all this talk of connections is making you nervous, don't worry: It's all covered in rich detail in Chapters 2 and 3, including what you need to know before you buy and install a drive.

"What Kinds of Discs Can 1 Record?"

This question is the easiest of all to answer: Everything! If you can use it on a computer, listen to it in your stereo's CD player, or watch it on your DVD player, you can record it using either a CD or DVD recorder.

Later in this book, I take you step-by-step through the creation of different types of discs; for now, this section gives you an overview.

Briefcase backup

Never heard of that term? It's my own; I always carry a *briefcase backup* when I'm traveling with my laptop. Because my computer has a CD-ROM drive (and the notoriously small hard drive found on most laptops), I record on a CD-R any files that are specific to my trip. PowerPoint presentations, Word files, contracts, digital audio and video — even an offline copy of my Web site — they all fit on a briefcase backup. Therefore, my trip-specific data doesn't take up space on my laptop's hard drive, and it's protected from damage. Plus, copying any of that data to my client's computer if necessary is a cinch: No cables, no network configuration — just pop the disc in and read files and programs directly! (My mom always said that I had potential.)

Computer files and data of all sorts

If it can be stored on your hard drive, you can store it on CD or DVD as well. This includes

- Files and programs
- Digital images
- Sound clips
- Web sites
- Backups

Digital audio

With a CD-RW drive, you can record standard audio CDs for use in any audio CD player, mixed CDs that have both audio and computer data, and MP3 discs that can be enjoyed on your computer and some audio CD players. Plus, you can extract, or *rip,* tracks from existing audio CDs and record them on a new disc in any order you choose.

Digital video

A CD-RW drive can create standard Video CDs for your Video CD player, and a DVD-R/W or DVD+R/W drive can create interactive DVDs with your own digital video.

Network storage

If you have data that is accessed often but never changed on your home or office network, record that data to a CD-R and load it in your file server's CD-ROM drive. (Getting your network administrator's help with this process is a good idea — those folks can get very nervous about such initiatives.) Now you can still access every byte of those files, but you're not using precious network hard drive space and you don't have to worry about backing up that information.

Photo discs

You can use your CD-RW or DVD recorder to create slideshow discs with images from your digital camera or with scanned photographs.

Caring for Your Optical Pets

I tell you earlier in this chapter about how CD and DVD are nearly perfect storage media — but notice the word *nearly*. You have two or three outstanding methods of ruining a disc; the trick is not to become proficient at any of them, so in this last section I cover the best ways to use, clean, and store your discs.

You gotta grip 'em by the rim!

Let me sound like your mother for a second: Take a good, close look at your hands! When was the last time you washed them? Reading data from a disc covered in fingerprints and dust is a touch-and-go process at best because the laser beam has to work harder to get through all that crud twice (especially on DVDs because the data is packed even closer together). Therefore, you must find out how to hold a disc properly.

In my travels, I've encountered two methods of comfortably holding a disc for a decent length of time. You can even jog or tap dance when using these holds — whatever floats your boat. Either hold the disc by the outside edge, as shown in Figure 1-6 or — if your fingers are small enough — create your own spindle with a convenient finger, as shown in Figure 1-7.

Figure 1-6: I call this the Wilt Chamberlain hold.

Fingers grip on outside edge

Figure 1-7:
Look, Aunt
Harriet, I'm
a spindle!

It's time for a dire Mark's Maxim:

> **Never touch the underside of a disc, and never put a disc down (label-side up) on any surface.**™

Flipping a disc over and setting it label side down for a second or two is okay, but put the disc back in its case as soon as possible.

The deadly enemies

To keep your discs safe and avoid skips or data read errors, shelter them from these archvillains:

- **Pointed objects:** Scratches are taboo, and that goes for either side of a disc.

- **Heat:** How would you like to spend a hot summer afternoon in a closed car, baking on the seat? Underneath all that high tech, a disc is basically a circle of plastic. Keep your discs cool and out of direct sunlight: A warped disc is a terrible thing to behold. (Your audio CD player may not be able to read it, either.)

- **Surface crud:** This includes liquids, dust, dirt, and peanut butter.

You may have seen one or more CD/DVD laser lens cleaners at your local computer store; they usually look something like a disc with a little hairbrush mounted on it. *Never use one of these cleaners on a CD or DVD recorder because it can damage the laser!* In fact, the laser head inside a recorder needs no maintenance.

The Disc Hotel

So where should you put all your recorded discs? Stacking them in a big pile in front of your monitor is one answer, but it's the *wrong* answer. Your discs must be protected from dust and scratches! Of course, storing discs in their jewel boxes is a good idea — that is, until you have an entire 200-disc stand filled up, and it takes up an entire corner of your room! Take a tip from me and my collection of over 1,200 audio CDs: You can save that space and still provide the protection your discs need with a disc binder, as shown in Figure 1-8. A binder has individual pockets for anywhere from 10 to 250 discs, so you can donate your jewel boxes to your friends.

Figure 1-8:
A true technotype uses a disc binder to save space.

Sometimes you've just gotta wipe

You may say, "I've seen an entire shelf full of CD cleaning stuff at my local Maze O' Wires store. Do my discs need cleaning?" If a disc is only dusty, I recommend a lint-free photographer's lens cloth, which you can pick up at any camera shop. You can also pick up a spray bottle of disc cleaning fluid for liquid disasters, like those unavoidable soda stains. Other than a cloth and some fluid, however, you can leave all the expensive James Bond gadgets on the shelf at the store.

To close this chapter on a high note, Figure 1-9 illustrates how to wipe a disc: Start at the center spindle hole and wipe straight toward the outside of the disc, making sure that you apply no more than fingertip pressure. Wiping harder — or wiping in a circular motion, as shown in Figure 1-10 — can scratch your disc and invite chaos into its ordered world of 1s and 0s (zeros).

Figure 1-9:
Wipe correctly, and the digital world is your oyster.

Wipe a CD from the center to the edge in a straight motion.

Figure 1-10:
Wipe
incorrectly,
and your
data
eventually
shows you
the door.

If you wipe a disc
like this, you're
asking for trouble.

Chapter 2

Buying Your Recording Beast

· ·

· ·

Despite the rumors you may have heard, buying a CD or DVD recorder in the modern world is no longer a dreadful experience (at least, not with this book by your side). In days past, you would be at the mercy of that fast-moving predator of the electronics store — the computer salesperson — who would either turn on the high-pressure hose and sell you the most expensive drive on the planet or stand motionless with hands in pockets, oblivious to the answers to any of your questions. I know friends who still bear the emotional and psychological scars of such an attack.

Today, however, you may never even enter a brick-and-mortar store to buy your drive. If you're on the Web, you can choose from literally hundreds of online stores. You can shop 24 hours a day, at your leisure, and you have all the time you need to compare features and prices. It's paradise for those of us who are ready to purchase online.

If your CD or DVD recorder is already installed and comfortable, you don't need this chapter (although you still may want to read it to brush up on what's available). If your computer came with a CD-RW, DVD-R/W, DVD+R/W, or DVD-RAM drive, feel free to skip to Chapter 5. If, on the other hand, you're shopping for a CD or DVD recorder, you should devour every word to come.

In this chapter, I cover everything you need to know about buying a CD or DVD drive, including the features you should covet, the differences between internal and external drives, what type of connection you need, and the formats your drive should record. Take copious notes or just circle the important stuff directly in this book — whatever floats your boat.

I also provide you with tips on online shopping, which has both its peaks and its pitfalls. Finally, I even cover a few pointers on how to face those salespeople sharks head-on at your local store and *win.* (As my favorite actor, Jack Nicholson, croons in the film *Batman,* "Wait 'til they get a load of me — ooooOOOOooooop.")

Enough talk. It's time to go shopping.

Internal or External: Thinking Outside the Box

Your first choice to make in your trip down Hardware Boulevard is a simple one, yet it has the most effect on the price and performance of a recorder. If you've never run across these terms, an *internal* drive lives inside your computer (just like your floppy drive or your existing read-only CD-ROM and DVD-ROM drives). An *external* drive (illustrated in Figure 2-1) sits outside your computer, using a power cord of its own and a connection of some sort to your computer's case.

Figure 2-1:
An external
drive is
ready to go
solo.

Stay inside with internal

Why not pick an internal drive? Most folks do, and here are the reasons why:

- ✔ **Convenient:** Your drive is built-in to your computer, without an extra power cord to mess with and some sort of connection cable to boot.

- ✔ **Fast:** Depending on the interface, most internal drives are faster than their external brethren. (Read more about this party topic in the following section.)

- ✔ **Cheap:** Also, an internal drive is usually less expensive than an external unit because it's not carrying around its home like a digital hermit crab.

Breathe the open air with external

For some computers (for example, laptops and the stylish Apple iMac), you have to pick an external drive because you have literally no room to install a second internal drive. (I don't recommend the hacksaw route.) However, a number of good reasons explain why an external recorder would appeal to even the stodgiest PC owner:

- ✔ **It saves a bay:** To explain, a *bay* is an internal space inside your PC's case where you can add devices. Most desktop PCs have several of them, but technowizards and power users can easily fill up every bay with other gadgets. Because the case has no room inside, an external drive suddenly looks sexy and attractive (at least to them).

- ✔ **It's easy to install:** Afraid to open your computer's case? Believe me — you are not alone, and you have no reason to be embarrassed. Adding an external drive means that you can leave your desktop alone, and it may even be easier than installing an internal drive. If you choose a USB or FireWire drive, for example, the process is as simple as plugging in a connector and the power cord. (Read more about USB and FireWire later in this chapter, in the section "Edna, He Says We Need an Interface.")

  If you want to conquer your fear of computer hardware and delve inside your PC's case, let me recommend another of my books, conveniently titled *Building a PC For Dummies,* 4th Edition, from Wiley Publishing, Inc. In the process of showing you how to build an entire computer (yes, the whole ball of wax), I cover the complete process of adding all sorts of internal hardware, including an internal CD or DVD recorder.

- ✔ **It's portable:** Everyone in the building can share your recorder, perhaps as a backup device or to carry along with laptops. (By the way, you can also lock up an external drive to keep it from being carried away, if you get my drift.)

Here's the bottom line: Unless your computer simply doesn't have room or you don't want to open it, I recommend saving money and sticking with an internal recorder.

"Edna, He Says We Need an Interface"

Geez, what a word. It sounds like something you would hear from an engineer — ack! — but the word *interface* really has a simple and straightforward meaning: It's the type of connection that you use to unite your computer and your recorder in everlasting friendship (at least until you unplug them).

In this section, I help you determine which of these exotic connections is for you.

EIDE

The first connection I cover is the most popular for PC and Mac owners all over the world — which, naturally, is why I want to begin with EIDE. Because it's not a freedom-loving English word, it must therefore be one of those doggone acronyms; in this case, EIDE stands for *Enhanced Integrated Drive Electronics.* Unfortunately, EIDE drives don't come in external form, so if you need an external drive, you can skip to the next interface.

Virtually all desktop PCs built today use EIDE hard drives and read-only CD-ROM and DVD-ROM drives. To handle the workload, your PC likely has both a primary and secondary EIDE connector; each of these connectors supports two EIDE devices, so you have the capacity for a total of four EIDE drives. If you already have one hard drive and one read-only CD-ROM or DVD-ROM drive in your computer, you're using only two of those four connections.

EIDE drives are simpler and cheaper to install than SCSI and are a good pick for most home PCs.

SCSI

This time, the evil acronym, SCSI, is short for *Small Computer System Interface.* SCSI is significantly faster and more efficient than a typical EIDE drive, and a single SCSI card can connect anywhere from 8 to 14 different devices — which is great if you plan to expand your computer to help NASA with the latest Mars probe. (Seriously, a real power user can add things like scanners and tape drives to a SCSI connection.) SCSI drives are available in both internal and external form. If you have an older Macintosh computer, it likely has an external SCSI port.

Unfortunately, SCSI is harder to configure than EIDE because a number of settings have to be made correctly for anything to work. Also, a SCSI recorder is usually significantly more expensive than its EIDE counterpart.

SCSI drives are a good choice for the experienced PC or Mac owner who's willing to spend a little more for better performance and all those extra connections — but be prepared to spend more time configuring and fine-tuning.

USB

At least USB is only three letters long. It stands for *Universal Serial Bus,* a connection type that's used exclusively for external drives. Let me be honest with you: USB is the best thing to happen to PC and Mac owners since the invention of canned air. Yes, believe it or not, the same USB drive can be used by both types of computers, and Figure 2-2 shows how simple it is to connect.

USB cable

USB ports

Figure 2-2:
Yes, that
USB cable
fits only
one way.
Sheer bliss.

USB is *Plug and Play,* which means that you don't have to reboot your computer when you connect a USB recorder. Plus, your computer automatically recognizes that USB drive, so you have nothing to fiddle with or set. Many USB drives don't even need a separate power supply.

On the downside, a USB 1.1 connection is much slower than an EIDE or SCSI connection, so today's fastest CD and DVD recorders can't use it. You can't burn a DVD at all using a USB 1.1 connection, and CD burning is limited to 4X or less. USB drives tend to be somewhat more expensive because USB is external only. Finally, most older computers have only two USB ports, so if you're already using USB devices, you may need a USB *hub;* this little black box converts one of your USB ports into four ports. Cool!

Although USB 1.1 is too slow for today's recording hardware, I do have some good news: Luckily, those engineers haven't been loafing and resting on their laurels, because the recently-introduced USB 2.0 is now quickly becoming standard equipment on today's PCs and Macs. USB 2.0 connections are so speedy that they can easily handle the fastest external CD and DVD recorders available today. Naturally, your computer needs USB 2.0 ports to use a USB 2.0 drive. As the Mark's Maxim goes:

> **Demand USB 2.0 for your external drive . . . and install new ports if necessary!™**

I heartily recommend USB 2.0 for anyone who wants a typical external CD or DVD recorder.

FireWire

Imagine a — hey, wait a second, FireWire's not an acronym. Anyway, FireWire is also fast enough for today's high-speed drives, and it's been around longer than USB 2.0. (Technoheads also call it the IEEE-1394, and you may see it advertised as such when shopping for digital camcorders.)

FireWire (developed by Apple) has all the advantages of USB, and it also comes in two flavors: FireWire 400, the original standard, and the new FireWire 800 (which is twice as fast, and currently available only in the Mac world). Both types of FireWire connections work great for external CD and DVD recorders. As an additional bonus, you can use a FireWire 400 port for connecting many digital cameras, DV camcorders, scanners, and the like.

What's the catch? Only external drives need apply, and FireWire drives are typically a little more expensive than a USB 2.0 drive. All current Macintosh computers now have FireWire built-in (naturally), and PC owners can add FireWire ports by installing an adapter card.

FireWire 400 is the best all-around choice for high-performance external recorders, because it connects far more devices to your computer.

Avoid those ancient parallel port drives!

If you're using an older laptop without USB ports, you might hear about parallel port drives, which use the existing parallel printer port found on virtually every PC on the planet. (Macintosh computers have no parallel port, so this is not an option for them.)

Visualize a huge, flashing STOP sign: *Stay away from parallel port CD recorders!* These ancient relics are ridiculously slow — think 2X or slower — and more prone to errors, and they often don't work if you're already using a printer or another external device, like a Zip drive or a scanner, on your printer port.

These days, a parallel port CD recorder isn't even worth scavenging as a doorstop, so avoid such drives like the zombies they are. Instead, see whether your PC can use an adapter to provide a minimum of USB 1.1 connectivity, with USB 2.0 or FireWire 400 preferred.

The X Factor Explained

Of all the gobbledygook associated with buying a CD or DVD recorder, nothing is as foreign to a normal human being — or affects the price of a drive as much — as the *X factor.* You encounter these X numbers in every description of every drive you see, so I cover the X factor thing like a wet blanket (or a new coat of paint).

In plain English, the *X factor* is the speed at which a drive can read and record data. For CD recorders, these speeds are typically expressed as three numbers, like 40X/12X/48X. The order is always important:

- ✔ The first number indicates the CD-R recording speed.
- ✔ The second number is the CD-RW recording speed.
- ✔ The last number provides the read-only speed.

Therefore, whenever you apply these conventions to the example, you're looking at a drive that can record a CD-R at 40X and a CD-RW at 12X, and can read a CD-ROM at 48X. Naturally, higher numbers are better, so follow this general Mark's Maxim (I really like those):

The faster the X factor, the faster the drive performs at either recording or reading data.™

On the DVD side, you typically only see one X number — that's the recording speed for the drive. (Of course, because a DVD recorder can also burn CD-Rs and CD-RWs, you can see the familiar three-number X factor combination in the specs as well.)

Most internal CD drives on the market these days do at least 24X CD-R recording, and most external CD drives record at a minimum of 16X.

If you're considering a drive that's slower than 8X, promise me that you won't pay much (if anything) when you buy it. A 2X or 4X recorder is an antique now — of course, it works fine if your Uncle Milton gives it to you for free. Scavengers forever!

For those who care about such arcane measurements, the CD recording X factor is technically a multiplier of the original read-only speed for the first drives that appeared in the early 1980s. (You can call them 1X drives.) These 1X drives could send data to a computer at 150K per second. Therefore, a 2X CD-ROM drive can send data to a computer at 300K per second. Read-only drives can now reach blinding transfer rates of 52X, or 7800K per second. The same holds true for the DVD recording X factor, which is based on the original 1X DVD recording speed.

The X Factor General Maxim (or, in the acronym-happy world of computers, the XFGM) that I state earlier in this section seems to recommend that you shell out every possible penny for the fastest drive around. If you were Bill Gates, you would be right. However, common folk like you and me have things called *budgets,* so buying the fastest sports car of a recorder may not always be the best road to take. For example:

✔ If your computer already has a 40X or 48X read-only CD-ROM drive — in the DVD-ROM world, a 16X read-only drive — you don't need to spend anything extra for faster read-only speeds. Play your games and video in the read-only drive, and use the recorder just for burning discs.

✔ If you plan to use your new drive exclusively for recording audio CDs, why pay extra for a drive that records CD-RWs, DVD-R/Ws, or DVD+R/Ws faster? A faster rewriteable speed is better suited for you if you plan to use it to back up your computer's hard drive.

✔ If you plan to record once or twice a week and you can wait the extra four or five minutes per disc, an 8X CD-RW drive works just as well as a 40X drive that may cost twice as much.

In the end, the drive performance you should choose depends on the number of discs that you record, how fast you want them, and the difference in price for a faster drive.

Features on Parade

The earlier sections of this chapter cover the three big features: internal versus external, drive connections, and raw speed figures. Now consider individual features that add convenience, performance, and (coincidentally) cost to a drive. The more of these that you can pack into your purchase, the happier you will be. Note that I also mention which features are especially important for certain recording tasks. Believe me — it's better to discover that a drive has a tiny recording buffer *before* you buy it.

Make use of every pit: Overburning

Sounds like you're making digital toast, doesn't it? *Overburning* is a fairly recent phenomenon in the world of CD recording; it refers to a drive that can record more than the manufacturer's stated maximum capacity of a CD-R. For example, a drive that can overburn to 76 minutes can record 76 minutes of music on a standard 74-minute CD-R, or you could use the same drive to store 685MB of data rather than 650MB. The amount that you can overburn depends on your recorder and the specific brand and storage capacity of the discs that you're using. For example, 82-minute discs with more than 700MB of space are now available (but, as you might expect, these new discs aren't compatible with most drives older than three or four years).

Overburning is mucho grande, but you must remember two caveats:

- ✔ Most CD-ROM drives made in the past two or three years have no trouble with overburned discs, although some older drives spit them back out as unreadable. Therefore, if you distribute your discs, I recommend that you don't overburn them.

- ✔ Media manufacturers don't guarantee their discs past the 74- or 80-minute rating, so you overburn at your own risk.

How does a drive overburn? It uses the lead-out portion of the disc, which was not originally intended to store data; in fact, the lead-out area is *supposed* to indicate to your drive that it has reached the end of the disc. When you overburn, you're burning past that point. If your read-only CD-ROM drive doesn't care and can read an overburned CD-ROM, you're, in effect, storing more in the same space. Real 8-bit old-timers like myself who used the early Atari and Commodore computers remember something similar: We used to flip over a 5¼-inch single-density disk and use the other side, which you weren't supposed to do. Shameful, really.

Important: Any CD recorder can use an 80-minute CD-R — you're not overburning when you put 80 minutes of music or 700MB of data on this kind of media. Again, however, not every recorder can use these larger-capacity discs; check the specifications of any recorder that you're considering buying to see whether it can use 80-minute/700MB discs.

Three words: Buffer, buffer, buffer

For today's faster drives, a large *data buffer* (also known as an internal RAM or RAM cache) is indeed an important feature. All recorders have at least some buffer RAM. This memory stores data that your computer has retrieved from your hard drive until your recorder is ready for it. Figure 2-3 tells the tale. The larger the buffer, the more efficient this process becomes, and the less likely your drive is to return an error and ruin a disc because it ran out of data to write.

Figure 2-3:
Think of a buffer as a holding tank for all those 1s and 0s (zeros).

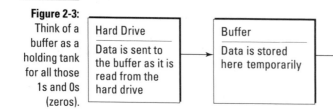

Hard Drive	Buffer	Recorder Write Head
Data is sent to the buffer as it is read from the hard drive	Data is stored here temporarily	Data is retrieved from the hardware buffer when needed

Most drives made these days have at least 4MB of buffer memory, and more expensive drives can have 8MB or even 16MB. When comparing drives, always try to pick a model with a larger buffer.

The ultimate safety net: Burnproof recording

Consider now the hottest-burning feature (horrible pun intended) to come along in several years. Burnproof recorders effectively end any problems that folks generally had when they were

- Recording on slower PCs
- Recording in the background under Windows or the Mac operating system (for example, using Word or Internet Explorer while recording)
- Recording at high speeds (12X or faster)

Before the arrival of burnproof drives two or three years ago, engaging in one of these activities was risky business indeed. As you may have read in earlier sections in this chapter, a recorder had to have a constant flow of data to prevent Buffer Underrun errors. Any interruption or hiccup in the transfer of data from the computer's hard drive to the recorder was usually disastrous. A larger buffer helped, but that still didn't solve the problem entirely, and your recorder certainly couldn't stop in the middle of a disc — it was now or never.

If your CD-RW drive doesn't support burnproof recording, you should be happy to know that I devote Chapter 6 to helping you optimize your computer and recorder to prevent Buffer Underrun errors. Virtually all DVD recorders support burnproof recording, so fear not.

Burnproof recording eliminates the potential for data errors by interrupting the recording process. The drive monitors the buffer, and when things look dangerous (for example, if you've run Adobe Photoshop, which is a notorious disk and memory hog), the recorder takes note of the position of the laser and stops recording. After the buffer has been refilled (which can take a few seconds), the laser write head is automatically repositioned at the point where the recording was interrupted and the recording process continues.

I can't stress just how revolutionary burnproof recording really is. If you can afford this feature (which is now available on virtually all CD-RW drives), by all means, get it.

Disc-at-Once: Funny name, important feature

Here's one feature I always recommend: I wouldn't buy a drive that doesn't offer *Disc-at-Once* recording. (Is that a definite enough recommendation?) Rather than record digital audio or computer data as individual tracks, Disc-at-Once records the entire disc at one time (you find out all about this subject in Chapter 7). Suffice it to say that the audio CDs that you record sound better on some audio CD players, and you can get more music on a single disc if you use Disc-at-Once. Again, check a drive's specifications to see whether it offers Disc-at-Once recording.

Sorry, but It's Time to Talk CD and DVD Formats

Formats are tricky things. Any CD-RW drive can create a simple audio CD (which by definition conforms to an international set of format standards called the Red Book) or a simple data CD-ROM with files on it (which uses the Yellow and Orange Book standards). You don't have to worry about these basic functions; for a CD or DVD recorder, they're like walking and chewing gum.

However, there's no telling when you may suddenly find yourself needing a Video CD or a CD Extra disc, and if your drive doesn't support them, it can never record those discs. You can't add formats to your drive after you've bought it.

Therefore, this section has two goals: First, I introduce you to each format, and then I help you determine which of them you're likely to need later. Here's another Mark's Maxim to chew on:

> **Cast your purchasing eye on the drive that can write the largest number of formats.™**

UDF/Packet writing

If you skipped it my discussion of burnproof recording earlier in this chapter, you should flip back to the section "The ultimate safety net: Burnproof recording" and read it. I'll wait for you here.

Anyway, *packet writing* (or, as the format is officially named, UDF) is almost as cool as burnproof recording: It allows you to write files to a CD or DVD just as you would write files to your hard drive, using Windows Explorer, the Mac OS Finder, or any of your other applications. You can add files one at a time or in groups, without having to record the entire disc at one sitting. In effect, packet writing turns your drive into a gigantic, superfast floppy that can store more than 600MB (or a whopping 4.6GB).

You can also "erase" data from a disc. Yes, I tell you in Chapter 1 that you can't erase data from a CD-R, DVD-R, or DVD+R, but I'm stretching the truth a bit. Rather than be physically removed from the disc, the data you're erasing becomes unreadable, so it can't be retrieved. The data is still there — you just can't access it.

Again, it's time to be blunt: Virtually all CD and DVD drives now available support the UDF format, and I wouldn't buy one if it didn't.

Video CD

Although DVD-R and DVD+R are the unequivocal kings of digital video recording, those of you with lowly CD-RW drives can produce your own brand of visual magic: A drive that records in Video CD format can create discs for a Video CD player (and most DVD players can read them, too). Most CD-ROMs and DVD-ROM drives can now also read Video CDs — all you need is the right software. I use Windows Media Player.

With a Video CD, you have many of the same features that you would find on a DVD player, including an interactive menu for selecting video clips and freeze-frame or slow-motion effects.

CD Extra

Another format that has recently come into its own, CD Extra allows you to record a disc with a mixture of audio and data tracks. Why create a mutant disc like this? Most computers these days have high-fidelity audio systems, so many musicians are using CD Extra to add a music video, song lyrics, and other multimedia material to their audio CDs. (Remember that the disc can also be played on your computer's CD-ROM or DVD-ROM drive.) For example, two of my favorite bands — the Squirrel Nut Zippers and the Rolling Stones — have turned out CD Extra discs in the past.

A CD Extra disc doesn't overlook the folks who just want to listen to the disc in an audio CD player. The audio track on a CD Extra disc is recorded first, so it's compatible with any audio CD player — in fact, the player doesn't know the difference. The only restriction, naturally, is the amount of audio that you can record on a CD Extra disc: Because you're adding data as well, you don't get a full 74 or 80 minutes of audio elbowroom.

Multisession/CD-ROM XA

I can't discuss CD-ROM XA format without introducing you to the idea of a *session,* so here goes: A session is, in effect, a self-contained dataset recorded on a disc. In English, think of it as a single track on an audio CD. You can store multiple tracks on one disc and access each of them individually as you like. As an example, think of one year's tax returns recorded in one session, followed by the next year's returns in the next session; it's a way to update the existing data on a CD without losing the old data. Each of the sessions on a multisession mode CD-ROM XA disc can be read, but only one at a time. (I get into this subject more in Chapter 8.)

CD-ROM XA isn't anywhere as popular as it once was because of three gotchas:

- ✔ **Not all CD-ROM drives can read CD-ROM XA:** Truly antique read-only CD-ROM drives may be able to read only the last session recorded or may not even be able to read the disc.

- ✔ **Software is required in order to change sessions:** Some sort of session-selection program or function is necessary; it comes with most CD recording programs, but if you're sending a disc to someone else and that person doesn't have the session-changing software (or a CD or DVD recorder), she's out of luck.

Digging deep for specifications

I admit that I'm letting loose a landslide of features and formats in this chapter, but I have a reason: I don't know how you will use your drive, so I can't tell you what features and formats are most important for *you*. Instead, I explain all the relevant stuff, and you can pick and choose what's necessary for your Dream Drive.

Unfortunately, the Feature Fairy doesn't drop in to tell you what formats and features are supported by a drive, or what software ships with it. To buy the best drive for you, you have to roll up your sleeves and do the research. First, visit the manufacturer's Web site and look for that all-important specification sheet. (This is also a good time to check on the quality of the manufacturer's support, like updated drivers, firmware upgrades, and FAQ files.) In many cases, the specification list should tell you everything you need to know.

Next, try visiting www.buy.com or www.pricewatch.com, where product features can be compared side-by-side among different drives. These sites are great for asking questions like "Which 12X CD-RW drives are under $300 and have burnproof recording?"

If you have an Internet connection and you're familiar with newsgroups, I recommend comp.publish.cdrom.hardware and alt.comp.hardware. Someone in one of these groups may know the features of a particular drive (although you may get opinions mixed in liberally with your answers).

Most computer magazines have online Web editions, and they often cover CD and DVD recorders with hardware comparisons and performance evaluations. Finally, use a search engine, such as www.google.com, to locate information about a specific make and model of drive; you may be surprised at what turns up.

✔ **Packet writing is better:** The availability of the UDF format on most drives has made multisession recording as outmoded as the Model T. Packet writing is far easier than recording multiple sessions.

Software You Just Gotta Have

I really shouldn't say that: Of course, the software you receive with your recorder isn't as important as the hardware itself. After all, you can always add software later or upgrade what you have. Hardware is, well, *hard*. Other than a firmware upgrade, your drive's features and performance are fixed, so the software should take a back seat (not too far back, though).

Often, one drive you're considering has a much better selection of software than another. If their prices, features, and speeds are similar, a superior software selection can tip the scales. However, every CD recorder that you consider should ship with basic recording software that

✔ Allows you to burn discs in all supported formats

✔ Erases and formats CD-RWs

✔ Tests for proper installation and configuration of your drive

My favorite recording software is Easy CD & DVD Creator, from Roxio, and I use it throughout much of this book. I'm also fond of Nero Burning ROM, though, from Ahead Software at www.nero.com (see Figure 2-4), and the great shareware program CDRWIN, from Golden Hawk Software at www.goldenhawk.com (see Figure 2-5). On the Macintosh, my recording program of choice is Roxio Toast (www.roxio.com), which I also use later in this book, in Chapter 9.

After you've taken care of the basics, however, you find that some drives offer additional software that can save you money and — as the marketing types would say — "enhances your recording experience." (In other words, the more of this nifty software you get, the better off you are.) I cover this extra stuff you want in the following three sections.

Figure 2-4:
Nero
Burning
ROM —
great
recording
program,
funny name.

A sharp-dressed disc

Can you imagine Fred Astaire in a leisure suit? No way! The tuxedo was practically made for him. Many people feel the same way about the discs they record: They want those discs to look as professional as possible. One way to do this is to spend a couple of thousand dollars on a disc label screen printer. If you would rather save the cash and put your inkjet printer to work, these programs can spruce up the appearance of a CD-ROM or DVD-ROM:

- ✔ **Label-printing software:** Print labels with everything from simple text to line art or full-color photographs. Labels are particularly nice for audio CDs.

- ✔ **Jewel box printing software:** You can print custom front and back inserts for a disc's *jewel box* (that plastic whatchamacallit that stores the disc) or DVD snap-case. I think that it completes the look of a recorded disc. Again, audio CDs benefit from track listings, and computer discs can use the space for file descriptions or installation instructions.

I cover both these bad boys in Chapter 14, including a step-by-step project that shows how to create inserts and a label.

Slick recording add-ons

As I mention earlier in this chapter, any self-respecting recording program should be able to take care of basic recording tasks all by itself, although separate add-on programs can take care of specialized recording jobs:

- ✔ **Packet writing software:** Why run that big, stodgy recording program each time you want to write a UDF disc? With this thought in mind, most software developers spin off packet writing into a separate program that can run in the background under Windows or the Mac operating system. The perfect example is Drag-to-Disc, from Roxio: It runs automatically when you start your PC and doesn't require Easy CD & DVD Creator. (Read more about this program in Chapter 10.)

- ✔ **Backup and disaster-recovery software:** Call these programs digital peace of mind — use your CD-RW to back up either part or all of your system, and you can rest easy at night. I use Retrospect, from Dantz Development (see Figure 2-6), which can even format your rewriteable media for you. I've said it before in most of my books, and I say it again: *If you value your data, back it up.*

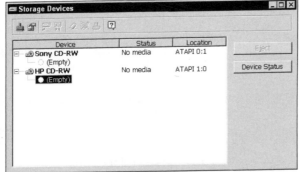

Figure 2-6:
I'm backed up. *Are you?*

Are you already using a backup program with a tape drive or Zip disks? If so, check to see whether it already supports the use of a rewriteable CD or DVD drive: If so, you can keep original backup sets, avoiding a hole in your backup schedule while you switch to the optical world.

Tools to organize and play your stuff

I go into the organization of your recording projects in complete detail in Chapter 7. For now, suffice it to say that some of the following programs make finding stuff on your finished discs easier, and other software is required to play the digital video and audio you've recorded:

- ✓ **Image- and video-editing software:** Many drives are bundled with an image editor for digital photographs and a simple video editor for chopping Uncle Milton out of this year's Christmas video. This feature makes sense because the majority of recorder owners probably burn digital images and video all the time.

- ✓ **Multimedia filing software:** Think of these programs as organizers for your audio, video, and images; the programs can help you locate and retrieve a single clip or image from thousands stored on a single disc for your next presentation or Office document. Plus, you can play or view those images from within the program to make sure that you've found the right one. My favorite multimedia filing program is Media Center Plus, from Jasc Software, as shown in Figure 2-7.

- ✓ **Audio CD/MP3/WAV player:** If you don't get an audio media player with your recorder, you will need one eventually. My favorite is Winamp (see Figure 2-8), from Nullsoft, Inc., which can handle almost anything you encounter: audio in MP3 format, audio CDs themselves, Windows WAV files, and Macintosh AIFF files. Plus, it marks you as technokeen. You can find Winamp at www.winamp.com.

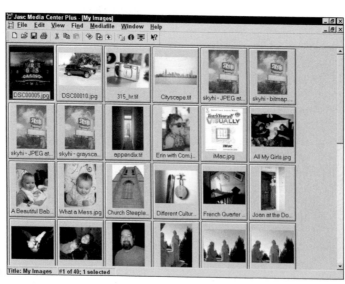

Figure 2-7: Finding a needle in a haystack (and retrieving it) is what Media Center Plus is all about.

Figure 2-8:
Winamp
can rock
the socks off
your llama.
(Don't ask —
private joke.)

✔ **Video CD/MPEG player:** The counterpart to your audio media player, a video player is a welcome addition to any recorder's software bundle. My favorite is PowerDVD, from CyberLink, which can play Video CDs on any CD-ROM drive; if you have a DVD-ROM or DVD-R drive, it can also turn your computer into your own, personal DVD theater. Figure 2-9 shows PowerDVD playing one of my collection of *Batman* episodes: Go, Adam West!

Figure 2-9:
PowerDVD
is great for
watching
my favorite
TV series of
all time on
Video CD.
Sweet!

Scavenging Fossilized CD and DVD Drives

The vulture may not be the prettiest scavenger on the planet, but it gets the job done. In the world of computer hardware, a scavenged component can often bring you and your computer a world of new possibilities for little or no cost. This is a good thing, and I'm proud to say that I've been scavenging for many years.

Fate can present a number of different ways to acquire a used recorder: You may inherit one from a family member or friend who's upgrading, or you may stumble across one at a garage sale. The most popular method of picking up a used drive, however, is probably one of the online auction centers; eBay is the prime location (www.eBay.com). If you're looking for a used drive, here's what I recommend:

- **Don't settle for less than 8X for a CD-RW drive:** Unless someone flat out gives you a 2X drive for free, ignore the deal and move on. These drives are just too slow, and any drive with such poor performance probably doesn't have features like Disc-at-Once recording or a decent-size buffer. (Any DVD recorder is still worth scavenging if it's free, no matter what the speed!)

- **Get those drivers:** Nothing is quite as frustrating as searching the world over for CD recorder device drivers, especially when the drive is five years old or more. If you're running Windows 98 or later, the process is easier because the operating system comes with a host of drivers built-in. The moral? Whenever possible, get the original software and manual for a drive, and check the manufacturer's Web site to see whether you can still find software and support.

- **Buy from recognized sellers:** The seller feedback ratings on eBay make seeing who has a good track record easy, so use them; if a seller has a feedback rating of less than five or has a number of negative feedback entries, be wary. Don't be shy about asking questions through e-mail, and keep an eye out for exorbitant handling charges. (I do lots of selling on eBay myself, and I've never charged someone for the overwhelmingly difficult act of slipping something into an envelope or packing it in a box.)

- **Consider new versus used:** Finally, consider the current prices for a new drive: At the time this book was written, I could pick up a 40X/12X/48X CD-RW drive for less than $50. Before you spend more than $25 on a used drive, make sure that you're really getting a bargain.

Buying Your Drive at the Maze o' Wires Mall

Let me set one thing straight: You should feel no shame in buying locally. In the following section, I harp away on the advantages of buying online, and I admit that I buy most of my hardware on the Web these days. However, where you buy your drive is your business, and I don't try to push you into shoving dollars through your modem.

Besides the help from a salesperson (hopefully one who really knows all the ins and outs of recording), a local store offers three things that no Web store can ever match: immediate delivery, hands-on shopping, and a fast, friendly return policy. (No matter how good Internet Explorer becomes, you can't use your mouse to open a box that's 2,000 miles away.) No waiting is involved to either receive your drive or to bring it back if you find that you're the proud owner of a lemon.

Watch out, however, for pressure tactics from a sales thug. Ask plenty of questions, request a demo, and bring along a knowledgeable friend to help you shop. Check out several stores before settling on one drive.

Considering buying returned (or refurbished) hardware? Have the salesperson connect the drive and give it a thorough check before you take it home. Also, don't forget to ask what kind of warranty you receive on your purchase.

No lock, no sale

If you're ready to buy a recorder online and the Web store doesn't offer a secure connection, tell 'em to take a hike. A secure connection is encrypted to protect your credit card number and personal information, which makes it challenging for the online criminal element to intercept your data as it's sent to the Web site.

If you're using Internet Explorer or Netscape Navigator, look for a closed padlock icon on the status bar at the bottom of the browser's screen. (For Mac owners using Safari, the lock appears at the upper-right corner of the window.) If you see the lock, the connection is secure, and you can enter your information. If you don't see a locked padlock icon (or the lock is open and not closed) and you're being asked for your personal information and card number, I would immediately move on to the next online store.

Your drive costs you more, and you pay local sales tax, but if you're nervous about buying online or you want to install that drive tonight, jump in the car and head to your local computer marketplace.

Buying Your Drive on that Web Thing

"Okay, I need to save money, and I've got a credit card — plus, it's hurricane season, I have nothing clean to wear, and my favorite episode of *My Three Sons* is starting in five minutes. Can I buy a drive online?" Indeed, you can — in fact, in a situation like that, it's sheer madness to buy locally.

It really does take only five minutes to buy your recorder on the Web (after, of course, you've done your thorough research). The Web offers the widest selection of drives at the lowest prices, and you can use sites like www. pricewatch.com to search out the best deal. Depending on the state you're in (pun not intended that time), you may be exempt from local sales taxes, too.

Why pay for next-day or second-day shipping if you're not itching for the fastest delivery? Many sites select next-day shipping as a default option, and you're stuck paying twice or three times the cost of five-day shipping. Don't fall for this old trick: Choose the shipping option that suits your pocketbook.

One final word about ordering on the Web: Most mail-order companies charge a virtual arm and a leg for restocking your drive if you decide to return it. Make sure that you're not charged if you have to return a defective recorder.

Chapter 3

DVD Is the Cat's Meow

· ·

· ·

*I*n the early 1980s, the acceptance of CD-ROM by the general public was painfully slow but perfectly understandable. For example, John T. Everyman had listened to vinyl albums all his life and had just begun to mesh with the psychology of the cassette tape. Along came the audio CD, and many folks couldn't help but ask, "Is this just a flash in the pan, like my Betamax VCR?" Because only a handful of plants manufacturing CDs existed, CD-ROMs started out prohibitively expensive, and the first year or two saw only a pitiful selection.

What was worse, recording your own CD was science fiction for more than a decade: Developing the technology took several years, and then when the first CD-R drives appeared, they were priced so high that technotypes like myself got nosebleeds just reading the advertisements. I can remember wishing that I had $6,000 — that's right; six *thousand* dollars — so that I could become an optical alchemist and burn like professional musicians and video editors. Only around 1995 or so did CD recorders descend from the heavens to less than $1,000, and it took three more years for the typical CD recorder to drop to less than $500. Recording software? You may as well have written it yourself because what was available was almost as expensive as the drive.

Thank goodness, we have all learned our lesson. Things have changed so dramatically that the introduction of DVD a few years ago was a complete mirror image of the early years of the compact disc. First, the CD-ROM has become so common that DVD was immediately accepted as "the next step in optical media." No uncertainty, wailing, or gnashing of teeth this time. We all want the storage space and convenience of DVD. A large number of well-established factories were already ready and waiting to produce DVDs, and the selection of films has mushroomed quickly. Prices on many popular DVD movies are less than $10, and the selection grows every day.

Finally, DVD recording is light-years ahead of where CD recording was at this stage of the game. Drives have reached rock-bottom prices, and software abounds to help you produce your own interactive discs. Many computers are already shipping with DVD-R/W and DVD+R/W drives, and prices continue to drop across the board for all types of recordable DVD blank media.

Many features that I cover in Chapter 2 apply in this chapter as well, such as internal versus external drives and the connections you can use. Therefore, I focus more on the important questions you need to ask before you plunk down your hard-earned greenbacks for a new DVD drive. I also include a discussion of additional hardware and software that comes in handy before you record as well as information on those pesky DVD formats.

"Do I Need DVD-R/W, DVD+ R/W, or DVD-RAM?"

Do you need a rewriteable DVD-R/W drive or a DVD-RAM model? Why not get all three? (Oh, brother.) Unless you've been hanging out with the good folks at the lottery commission, that's probably not an option. You can, however, find many drives on the market that can use both DVD-R/W and DVD+R/W, like the Sony DRU-510. (Talk about alphabet soup! For the definition of each acronym that I'm tossing around, visit Chapter 1.)

However, I still have good news: The relative strengths of all three types of recordable DVD media make it easy to decide which one you need. Check out Table 3-1 for the scoop.

Table 3-1	Will DVD-R/W, DVD+R/W, or DVD-RAM Escort You to the Ball?		
Media Type	*Can Be Read in DVD Players*	*Reusable/ Rewriteable?*	*Media Cost*
DVD-R	Almost always	No	$2 per disc (4.7GB)
DVD+R	Almost always	No	$2 per disc (4.7GB)
DVD-RW	Usually not	Yes	$4 per disc (4.7GB)
DVD+RW	Usually not	Yes	$3 per disc (4.7GB)
DVD-RAM	Usually not	Yes	$15 per disc (4.7-9.4GB)

Although I break DVD-R and DVD-RW into separate categories in the table, it's getting harder and harder to find a drive that records *only* DVD-R — and the same holds true for DVD+R/W. This trend mirrors the development of CD-RW technology. Try finding a drive that burns *only* CD-Rs these days! (I dare you.)

I should point out something else about Table 3-1: Besides being incredibly informative, it uses the words *almost* and *usually,* which don't show up in many definitive tables. Why? The answer lies not in today's recorders, but rather in yesterday's DVD-ROM players: *Four* distinct generations of DVD-ROM players have existed since their introduction in late 1997, and each succeeding generation has a better chance of reading DVD-Rs, DVD+Rs, and DVD-RAMs.

The result is a big question mark. Because of the wide disparity in manufacturers, I honestly can't tell you whether the DVD-ROM player you have now reads *any* type of burned disc. If you're using a DVD+R or DVD-RAM, you have the best chance with a DVD-ROM player manufactured since the beginning of 2001. If you're using DVD-R, you have the best chance with a DVD-ROM player made after late 1999. Thoroughly confused now? Sorry about that. This alphabet soup of different standards and rapidly evolving hardware can turn a computer book author's hair very gray very quickly.

Anyway, here are my recommendations. First, pick DVD-R/W if

- ✔ You're looking for the highest level of compatibility with all DVD-ROM drives.
- ✔ You're distributing discs to others.

Pick DVD+R/W if

- ✔ You're looking for compatibility with the latest DVD-ROM drives.
- ✔ You want to spend a little less on media.

Choose DVD-RAM if

- ✔ Compatibility with DVD-ROM drives is not an issue, such as when you're creating backups or discs that you read only on your computer.
- ✔ You want to rewrite the largest amount of data on an existing disc.

Oh, and yes, Virginia: You can read a commercially manufactured DVD-ROM movie disc in either type of recorder. At least I can guarantee you the extra bonus of adding a DVD-ROM drive to your computer when you install a DVD recorder.

"Hey — I Can't Copy 'Curse of the Mollusk People'!"

Man, of all the clunkers that Hollywood has turned out, why would you possibly want to copy a movie about mobile glowing clams that enslave the minds of simple townsfolk? (I've bought titles like *Robot Monster, Nude on the Moon,* and *Blood Feast* for my collection. Perhaps I shouldn't be too proud.)

Anyway, you can't just copy a DVD-ROM movie for good reason: Lots of smart engineers, software developers, and designers worked hard to make sure that you can't. Some discs are protected by the addition of unreadable areas on the disc during manufacture, and other protection schemes involve encrypted key codes that must be present on the disc for it to be recognized by either your player or your computer's DVD-ROM drive.

Sure, some programs on the market purport to create direct copies of DVD movies, but most DVD movies hold more than 4.7GB — in fact, many now cram a whopping 8GB onto a single disc. (After all, commercial DVDs can be mastered with more than one data layer. Turn to Chapter 1 for details.) Because current DVD technology can only burn 4.7GB on a DVD-R or DVD+R, those pirating programs have two options:

- Spread a single movie across two or more recordable discs, with a nasty pause involved (while you or your significant other is banished from the couch to change the discs).

- Compress the digital video on the disc up to 50 percent so that it can be stored on a single disc, which typically results in a noticeable loss in picture quality.

This stuff gets really technical really quickly, so I don't go into it here in any great detail. Suffice it to say that buying a DVD-R/W, DVD+R/W, or DVD-RAM drive is not a free ticket to a shelf of cheap movies.

(And no, I didn't think that you would do such a thing. Copyrights are important — ask any book author.)

Weird, Wild DVD Format Stuff

Close the windows, bar the door: You can't escape them. I have two more acronyms to discuss, and I do the best I can to make sure that we all make it out of this section in one piece.

DVD-V

If you've been perusing the DVD movie aisle at your local discount store, you may think that you were looking at DVD-ROM — and you would be right. However, I can be even more specific than that: A *DVD-V* (short for DVD-Video, of all things) is a DVD-ROM that holds broadcast-quality digital video in a special compressed format named MPEG-2. (You find out a little more about MPEG in the section "The MPEG card: Aye, Matey, 'tis indeed a tiny file" later in this chapter, and much more in Chapter 13.) You also get niceties like Dolby audio, surround sound, subtitles, and different aspect ratios with a DVD-V. You can even run programs from a DVD-V if you're playing it in a computer DVD-ROM drive.

You may ask, "Can I burn a commercial-quality DVD-V with my new DVD recorder?" Technically, yes. However, lots of work is involved in compressing digital video, creating interactive menus, and adding a quality audio track. It's nowhere near as simple as recording something on comfortable old VHS tape, but I show you how to do some of this good stuff in Chapter 13 of this book.

DVD-A

I know that this might break your heart, but even your friend the audio CD is eventually going out to pasture. The likely replacement is a format standard named *DVD-A,* or DVD-Audio. Imagine a standard audio CD that has been to the gym four nights a week for the past 10 years, and you get some idea of what DVD-A is like: either two or four hours of stereo music (depending on the type of media); interactive menus, like with the current crop of DVD-Vs; and even the ability to store video clips. Plus, DVD-As store music at a higher quality than standard audio CDs and with an even higher dynamic range . . . in other words, they sound even better than your rusty old CDs.

For me, however, the most exciting new feature of DVD-A is the addition of surround sound support. If you're enjoying a surround sound system, you know how realistic it is. If not, try out this type of system the next time you're in a stereo and video store. Although the extra data needed for surround sound cuts the capacity of a DVD-A in half, you're still talking about an hour or two of incredible music.

Additional Toys You Just May Need

Before the sun sets on this introductory discussion of DVD recording, I would be remiss if I didn't tell you that you're likely to need a little additional hardware and software. Why? To make the most of the expanded features of DVD, you need to import video, edit those clips, convert them to different formats, and design your menu system — not necessarily in that order — and there just isn't the need to do most of those things when you're recording a CD-R or CD-RW.

In this section of your palatial mansion, allow me to show you some of the extras you're likely to use.

The MPEG card: Aye, Matey, 'tis indeed a tiny file

If you're serious about creating your own DVD-Vs — or even experimenting with simple Video CDs and digital video clips — you should consider an MPEG-2 adapter card for your computer. As I mention earlier in this chapter, MPEG-2 is a compression format; it's somewhat similar to the space you save when you use Zip compression to shrink a file on your hard drive. And, boy, howdy, do you need it: High-quality digital video that's bigger than a postage stamp on your screen takes up an incredible amount of space. Without compressing (or *encoding*) the video, you're likely to run out of room on even the highest-capacity DVD media.

If you're wondering about that term *digital video* (also called DV, for short), indeed, no film or magnetism is involved. Digital video is composed of the same familiar 1s and 0s (zeros) that are written to a recordable CD or DVD. Unlike a traditional videotape (which can stretch and lose its magnetic properties), you can edit, copy, and play digital video as many times as you like without losing quality.

Most MPEG-2 cards have two functions: They can encode video to shrink it, and they can also *decode* it so that you can watch it on your computer's screen. (If you receive an MPEG-2 card with a DVD-ROM drive, however, it likely just decodes so that you can watch DVD movies.)

Both these chores can be taken care of by software programs, but I always recommend a hardware solution for folks who want to do any serious MPEG-2 video work. The advantages of the card over software include

- ✔ **Speed:** Software encoding and decoding programs are nowhere near as fast as an MPEG-2 card, so a process that can take minutes with a card can take hours with a program. The encoding speed depends on the raw power and performance of your computer's processor.

- ✔ **Efficiency:** An MPEG-2 card does all the heavy thinking about MPEG-2, so even an older PC with an original Pentium brain can keep up.

- ✔ **Convenience:** Most MPEG-2 cards offer connectors so that you can plug your TV directly into your computer and pipe your DVD movies to The Tube. These connectors are handy little beavers to possess.

The FireWire port: The real information superhighway

No ifs, ands, or buts with this one: If you work with digital video recording, you need one or two high-speed FireWire ports on your computer. Virtually every piece of machinery on the planet that works with DV uses FireWire to connect to everything else, including digital video camcorders and external DVD recorders. Many high-resolution digital cameras and scanners are now using FireWire as their connection of choice as well.

By the way, some manufacturers seem determined to call a FireWire port an i-LINK connection, for some reason. Heck, if you want to be perfectly accurate, the full international title for the original FireWire standard is IEEE-1394. You may see several of these names on the same box.

If you're using a late-model Macintosh, you're probably doing the Technological Twist right now, dancing in front of your monitor like a Druid partying around Stonehenge. That's because Apple developed FireWire, and all current Macintosh computers include built-in FireWire ports. However, if you're using a PC that didn't come graced with the Wire of Fire, be reassured that you can party just as well by installing a PCI card in your computer. PCI cards average about $100 on the Web, and they provide you with two FireWire ports and all the software and drivers. You need an open PCI slot in your PC, naturally.

A new FireWire standard — called FireWire 800 or FireWire B, depending on whom you talk to — started appearing on high-end Macintosh models in 2003. This Speed Racer delivers twice the data of the original FireWire port, but it hasn't become popular yet in the PC world. Luckily, the original FireWire 400 still does the trick and is compatible with just about everything.

The digital camcorder: Your digital muse

By law (it's written down somewhere, I know it), you can't record digital video without a *digital camcorder* (sometimes also called a DV camcorder). Note that a DV camcorder is not the same as the VHS-C or Hi-8 camcorder that you already own. Oh, no, things couldn't be that simple, right? Yesterday's typical video camcorder records an *analog* signal (which doesn't use the precise 1s and 0s (zeros) of the digital world that we love so well), so you can't use that video feed with your computer and your editing software. (The next toy I show you, however, helps you get around this problem.)

Virtually all digital camcorders download their video directly through a FireWire port to your computer, where you can have fun with it to your heart's content. DV camcorders are quite a bit more expensive than their traditional analog brethren, but they're much more versatile: You can take still photographs with most digital camcorders, and most models allow you to perform simple editing jobs onboard ("Can you *please* get the police out of our wedding video?") before you download the video to your computer. For the George Lucas in you, most digital camcorders now allow you to shoot footage in a 16:9 widescreen aspect ratio.

You now shell out anywhere from $400 to $3,000 or more for a digital camcorder (see Figure 3-1). For example, the Panasonic PV-DV401 sells for about $500 online. It looks deceptively like a typical VHS-C analog camcorder, but it sports both FireWire and USB ports and a digital camera mode for taking still photographs. You can add special effects during recording or playback, and it can even record in near darkness.

Figure 3-1:
A digital camcorder can turn you into a walking film crew.

The A-D converter: A bridge to the past

If you're shaking your head and mumbling, "I can't possibly afford that kind of cash right now for a digital camcorder," I've got a card up my sleeve that may well set things straight. This joker is called an *analog-to-digital converter* — usually called an A-D converter by those who dislike $5 words. The A-D converter freshens up the signal from a prehistoric analog TV, VCR, or camcorder, and — voilà! — you've turned that analog signal into digital video.

Figure 3-2 shows one of the most popular A-D converters on the market, the Hollywood DV-Bridge, from Pinnacle Systems, Inc. (www.dazzle.com). This alchemist's magic box costs a mere $200 or so on the Web, yet it can

- Connect your computer, your analog devices, and your DV devices in perfect harmony with a full set of ports (including a FireWire port)

- Convert digital video to an analog signal so that you can use your VCR to create tapes from a DV source

✔ Monitor your DV feed on a TV while it's being converted

✔ Mix both DV and analog material in one production

Figure 3-2:
The
Hollywood
DV-Bridge
just plain
rocks your
analog
world.

You also get two different types of Windows video-editing software. I highly recommend the Hollywood DV-Bridge if you're itching to try your hand at digital video, but you want to spend as little as possible and use the analog equipment you already have.

Video-editing software

Speaking of software, I end this opening gambit in the world of DVD recording by describing the typical software you use. In fact, two of these three programs ship as part of the computer's operating system. (Is DV mainstream these days or what?)

Video-editing software now offers a basic set of tools that take care of all common tasks, such as

✔ Importing and arranging video clips

✔ Removing unwanted footage

✔ Adding basic transitions between clips, like fade-ins and dissolves

✔ Adding and synchronizing audio

Figures 3-3, 3-4, and 3-5 illustrate three great examples of these DV Swiss army knives: iDVD 3, which ships with a new Macintosh computers (you may be familiar with its little brother, iMovie 3), Microsoft Movie Maker (Windows Me and XP), and the Adobe Premiere (both platforms). Any one of these programs can deliver a quality digital video production.

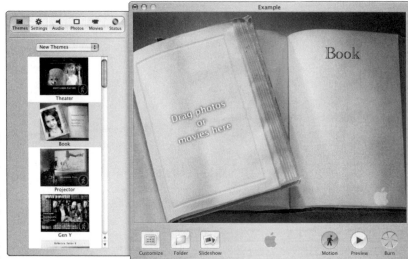

Figure 3-3: iDVD is my favorite basic DV editor for the Macintosh.

Figure 3-4: Movie Maker follows in the footsteps of iMovie.

Figure 3-5:
Adobe
Premiere
ships with
many digital
camcorders.

Granted, you can spend a heinous amount of money on high-end editing software that toots your car horn and can make doughnuts, but it typically starts at $1,000 (and that's for the cheap seats, my friend). Most programs I cover in this book are free or under $200, and even the commercial version of Adobe Premiere costs less than $500 on the Web at www.adobe.com. (Chapter 13 includes coverage of iDVD and Premiere.) Other programs, like Adobe After Effects, can add everything from a flaming hoop to a scrolling marquee underneath the video.

Because this book is devoted to CD and DVD recording, I can't get more than ankle-deep in the river of DV — however, I recommend the book *Digital Video For Dummies,* 3rd Edition, written by Keith Underdahl and published by Wiley Publishing, Inc. He can have you swimming in DV in no time.

Chapter 4

Poof! You're a Computer Technician

A certain mystique surrounds today's professional computer technicians: Most folks think that we're one part James Bond, one part Merlin the Magician, and one part Barney Fife. Armed with nothing more than a pair of taped glasses, a Phillips screwdriver, and a spare power cord, techies are supposed to be able to work hardware miracles beyond the reach of a mere computer owner. (The pocket protector is no longer required equipment; in fact, I've never used one.)

If that nerdy stereotype is still your impression of a typical computer technician, this chapter should open your eyes — because *you* can be your own tech. Sure, you can pay someone at your local computer shop to install your new recorder, but why not save that cash and apply it to something else, like your rent? Come to think of it, that $50 you would have paid someone can buy you a stack of 100 blank DVD-Rs.

This chapter focuses exclusively on the installation and troubleshooting of CD and DVD recorders — consider it the one-chapter, abridged version of my book *Building a PC For Dummies,* 4th Edition (published by Wiley Publishing, Inc.), which shows that you can assemble an entire PC from the ground up. And yes, I cover possible solutions when the worst happens, such as when your new drive sits there silently like a bump on a log.

Preparation Is the Key

Ever made a complex dish with a dozen ingredients without first reading the recipe? Or how about climbing on your roof to fix a few shingles and discover that you didn't bring your hammer? Preparation makes all the difference when you're installing computer hardware as well, and in this section I describe the things you need to cover before you get started.

Read the instructions

The steps I cover in this chapter apply to 99.9 percent of the computers and recorders on the planet — but guess who may have bought the drive specifically designed for the other .1 percent of the population? That's right: The Fates may have chosen you as the person who has to cut the blue wire, not the red wire. Certain software may need to be loaded first, or you may need to flip switches to configure your drive correctly, which I don't cover in these generic procedures.

Here's a Mark's Maxim that actually applies to all computer hardware:

> **You must read the installation instructions for your recorder!™**

(And yes, that includes external recorders.) If the installation process described by the manufacturer is significantly different, follow the general steps I provide in this chapter, and then jump ship to follow the manufacturer's steps instead.

Collect what you need

No surgeon (or car mechanic) wants to operate without tools at hand, and you should follow their lead:

- **Gather the stuff you need.** Most installations require just a screwdriver, but bring your drive's installation instructions and any extra parts.

- **Prepare your work surface.** If you're installing an internal drive, prepare a flat, soft, well-lighted surface — several sheets of newspaper on a table work fine, or you can use an anti-static mat.

- **Take your time.** No one's looking over your shoulder with a stopwatch, so relax and follow the steps the right way the first time.

✔ **Keep those parts.** You're likely to remove small parts, like screws and a bay cover, when installing an internal recorder; keep a bowl handy that can hold everything you remove. You need some of the parts when you reassemble your computer, and anything left over should be saved as spare parts for future upgrades and repairs.

Ask for help

Do you have a friend, loved one — in fact, *anyone* other than your mortal enemy — who has installed a recorder already or who is experienced with computer hardware? If so, buy that person a meal and ask for assistance while you're installing your drive. If this is your first time working on the innards of your computer, you can probably benefit from the moral support, too.

By the way, as soon as you've successfully installed an internal drive, don't be surprised if someone you know asks for *your* help with a computer.

Choose a spot to be external

If you're adding an external recorder to your computer, take a few moments beforehand to select the right space for your new drive. The best spot should be

✔ **A minimum of six inches away from your computer:** This space helps minimize interference from your computer's power supply and monitor.

✔ **Well ventilated:** An external drive can give off a significant amount of heat, so make sure that your recorder has room on all four sides.

✔ **Free of vibration:** For example, don't park your recorder next to your computer's subwoofer (that big speaker box that delivers the deep bass for your computer's sound system). Vibration can ruin a recording and eventually damage your drive.

Installing an EIDE Drive

As you may have read in Chapter 2, Enhanced Integrated Drive Electronics (EIDE) drives are internal, inexpensive, and fast — no wonder they're the drive of choice for most PC owners. If you've bought an EIDE CD or DVD recorder, now is the time to get down to business and get your new toy installed.

What you need

First, make sure that your PC has these items:

- ✔ **An unoccupied drive bay:** Your drive needs a 5¼-inch drive bay that can be opened to the front of your case. Most PC cases have at least two or three of these bays (although a hard drive may be hogging one, even though it doesn't need an opening to the outside world).

- ✔ **An unused EIDE connector with a cable:** As I mention in Chapter 3, most PCs made in the past two or three years have four available EIDE device connectors (a primary master and slave and a secondary master and slave). You need at least one unused connector for your new recorder. You may also need to buy a cable if you're using your secondary EIDE connector because many PC manufacturers don't provide a cable if the connector isn't being used.

- ✔ **An unused power connector:** No recorder works for long without a power supply. An internal drive uses a connector like the one shown in Figure 4-1. You can also buy a power splitter (or a Y connector) that can convert one power cable into two.

Figure 4-1:
Your internal drive needs a connector to supply the juice.

Cable from
power supply

Connector on a
component

The EIDE dance, step-by-step

This section covers the installation process for an EIDE drive. Follow the steps in this section (and yes, you have to follow them in the order I show here).

Static electricity isn't fun, it's not amusing, and it's *not* your friend: It's the sworn enemy of everyone who's ever installed computer hardware. Static can damage any electronic component in the blink of an eye, and it may not even be easy to spot the damage until you discover that you have a dead drive on your hands. Therefore, you *must* discharge any static electricity on your body before you touch the drive, your PC's motherboard, or any of its internal parts. Touch a metal surface before you open your computer's case — usually, you can just touch the case itself — and touch the internal *chassis* (that's the metal framework) often during the installation process.

1. **Turn off your computer and unplug it from the AC outlet.**

2. **Remove the screws holding your computer's cover in place and set it aside.**

   Don't forget to put those screws in that high-tech bowl I mention earlier in this chapter.

3. **Set the EIDE drive configuration.**

   Every EIDE drive uses a specific configuration that allows your new recorder to cohabitate peacefully with your existing EIDE hard drive(s) or read-only CD-ROM or DVD-ROM drive.

   Setting up your recorder is not an overwhelming task, although the exact settings for your jumpers vary between brands and models. (If you've never handled a *jumper,* it's the workhorse of the computer hardware world — a tiny, metal-and-plastic crossover that allows you to make connections on the drive's circuit board.) Check your drive's manual for the correct set of pins, and use a pair of tweezers to add or remove jumpers to match that pattern. If you're working with a scavenged drive or you don't have the manual, check the manufacturer's Web site or call its technical support number.

   - **One hard drive:** Configure the jumper on the hard drive as "multiple drive, master unit" and configure the jumper on your recorder as "multiple drive, slave unit."

   - **One hard drive and one CD-ROM drive on the same cable:** Set the jumper on your recorder as "single drive, master unit" and connect it to the secondary EIDE cable. Leave the existing drives alone.

   - **One hard drive and one CD-ROM drive on different cables:** Configure the jumper on your recorder as "multiple drive, slave unit" and connect it to the EIDE cable that the hard drive is using, and then set the jumper on the hard drive to "multiple drive, master unit." Leave your existing read-only CD-ROM or DVD-ROM drive settings alone.

   You may have to change the jumper settings on your existing EIDE devices to get things working. For example, if you're adding a DVD recorder on your primary EIDE connector and you already have an EIDE hard drive on that cable, you have to switch the hard drive from "single drive, master unit" to "multiple drive, master unit." In this situation, your new DVD recorder is set to "multiple drive, slave unit."

4. **Check the bay that will hold your recorder.**

   If a plastic insert is covering the bay, you should be able to remove the insert by removing the screws holding it or by carefully prying it off with a screwdriver.

5. **Align the drive into the bay and slide it into the front of the case, with the rear of the drive (the end with the plugs and connectors) going in first.**

   The faceplate and buttons should be visible from the front of the case, as shown in Figure 4-2.

   Naturally, the printing and logo on the front should be facing right side up.

Figure 4-2:
Showing
your
recorder its
new home.

6. **Move the drive forward and backward until the screw holes are aligned with the screw holes on the side of the case, and then attach the recorder.**

7. **Connect a power cable to the drive and make sure that you press it in firmly.**

   Notice that it goes on only one way, so don't try to force it on backward.

8. **Connect the ribbon cable coming from the EIDE connector on the motherboard to the EIDE connector on the back of the recorder.**

   No need to worry about this connector either because it's notched to fit in only one way. Press it on firmly after it's correctly aligned.

9. **Because pulling and tugging on things inside your computer can result in an unplugged cable, take a moment to check all your connections — even the ones that don't lead to your recorder.**

10. **Replace the cover on your PC with the original screws.**

    Did you read about that parts bowl earlier in this chapter?

11. **Plug in the PC's power cable.**

12. **Turn on your PC and allow it to boot up normally.**

    I love that phrase — like your computer will suddenly grow wings and a tail, leap off your desk, and fly around the room like a dragon. I would say that that would be an abnormal boot — wouldn't you?

13. **Uh-oh. I hope that you're not superstitious and that you don't mind my ending on Step 13. Anyway, install the software that accompanied your recorder.**

To verify that the installation was successful, jump to Chapter 8 and try your first recording. If things don't fly, read the troubleshooting section at the end of this chapter.

Plugging and Playing with a USB Drive

Made the Universal Serial Bus (USB) external choice, did you? (Hopefully, you settled on a USB 2.0 drive, but older USB 1.1 drives are installed the same way.) Notice that this step-by-step section is much shorter than the internal EIDE installation in the preceding section; that's part of the beauty (and the popularity) of USB:

1. **Plug the power cord from your new drive into the AC wall socket.**

   Note that some USB drives are powered through the USB connection itself, so they don't require an external power supply.

2. **Connect the USB cable to the drive (don't connect the cable to the computer's port yet) and turn it on.**

3. **Turn on your computer and allow it to boot up normally.**

4. **Plug the USB cable from your drive into the USB port on your computer, as shown in Figure 4-3.**

   Your next step depends on the software and the operating system you're using: You may see a dialog box prompting you to insert the driver disc that came with your drive, or you may have to install the drive's software separately.

5. **Check your drive's installation instructions to see which path you take.**

USB cable

USB ports

Figure 4-3:
Living the
carefree life
of a USB
connection.

That's it. Follow the steps in Chapter 8 to record your first disc and make sure that everything's working well. If your drive isn't working, visit the troubleshooting section at the end of this chapter.

Running the SCSI Gauntlet

Decided on an internal or external Small Computer System Interface (SCSI) recorder? Memorize these two important commandments (add them to the original ten):

- ✔ Thou shalt assign no two devices the same SCSI ID number.
- ✔ Thou shalt terminate the ends of your SCSI device chain.

In this section, I explain exactly what I just said — in modern English, without technobabble — and you install your drive.

IDs 'R' Us

Think of a SCSI *device chain* as a neighborhood on a cable — to be precise, a chain is at least one SCSI adapter (which may be built-in on your computer's motherboard) and at least one device, which could be your recorder. For your computer to transfer data to or from your drive, it has to know the "address" of your recorder in the SCSI neighborhood. In other words, every SCSI device in your computer needs a unique *SCSI ID number* to identify it, as you can see in Figure 4-4. This sample SCSI device chain has a SCSI card and three devices.

Figure 4-4:
Everyone got their own unique ID number? Good!

| SCSI card | CDRW drive | SCSI hard drive |
| SCSI ID: 7 | SCSI ID: 4 | SCSI ID: 3 |

Typical SCSI devices can use a range of ID numbers from 0 to 7, with ID number 7 usually the default for your SCSI adapter. (Your SCSI card manual tells you which number the card uses.) Manufacturers of SCSI hardware use different methods of configuring the ID number; most drives use a jumper, which you can set on the correct pins with a pair of tweezers. Again, your drive's manual shows you which jumpers to move when setting the ID number. Some drives also use a thumbwheel you can turn to choose the number.

By the way, there's no reason to assign SCSI ID numbers in sequence; as long as all the device IDs are unique, it doesn't matter what order they're in.

If your SCSI adapter and your SCSI devices are all SCAM ready (man, what an acronym!), you can forget about assigning numbers manually. That's because SCAM stands for *SCSI Configured Automatically.* Enabling this feature on your SCSI adapter allows it to automatically set SCSI ID numbers each time you boot your PC.

Coming to grips with termination

No, I'm not talking about the Flintstones kind of termination, where Fred ends up without a job (again). In the SCSI world, a chain must be correctly *terminated* on each end to tell your SCSI adapter where the chain ends. Without termination, your poor SCSI adapter continues to scan the horizon in vain, looking for straggling SCSI devices that aren't there — and your computer either locks up or fails to recognize the last device on the chain. If the termination is set on a device that *isn't* on the end of the chain, it becomes the end anyway, which again leaves at least one SCSI device out in the cold; it either refuses to work or locks your computer. In short, without proper termination, you never get your SCSI devices to work.

Consider the simplest installation of a CD or DVD recorder on a SCSI chain. As you can see in Figure 4-5, this is just the SCSI adapter and the drive, and the drive could be internal or external. Both these devices naturally indicate the ends of the SCSI chain, so both need to be terminated. When your SCSI adapter looks for terminators, it finds that one device is on one end and the card itself is terminated on the other.

Figure 4-5:
May all your
SCSI chains
be this
simple.

However, what if you want to install an internal recorder into an existing SCSI chain that already has a hard drive? If no changes are made and you just added your spiffy new CD-RW drive to the end of the cable, you would invite the disaster shown in Figure 4-6. Because the hard drive is still terminated, your new toy is useless, and it can't even be recognized within Windows or the Mac operating system.

Figure 4-6:
With
improper
termination,
your
recorder is
out to lunch.

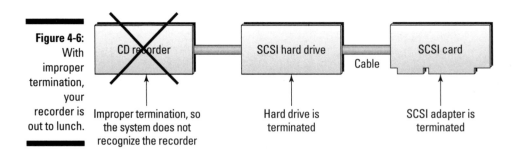

For this reason, heed this Mark's Maxim carefully:

> **Always review all your termination settings when installing SCSI or adding a new device to an existing chain.™**

Figure 4-7 shows how the same chain *should* be terminated. Now the SCSI adapter can "see" and communicate with the recorder, and all is well.

Figure 4-7:
Setting the
termination
correctly
solves the
problem.

CD recorder   SCSI hard drive   SCSI card

Cable

Terminated   Hard drive is   Terminated
not terminated

Depending on the manufacturer, setting the SCSI termination usually involves your old friends the Jumper family. You may also encounter a *resistor pack,* which you plug in to add termination and remove to drop termination. Finally, you may set termination by flipping the tiny plastic switches on a *DIP switch* (a tiny switchbox that's wired as part of the circuit board) — use a pencil to set the correct pattern of switches to either On or Off. Again, all these interesting settings appear in your recorder's manual, so keep it handy during the installation process.

What you need

If you're installing an internal SCSI recorder, you need these items:

- ✔ **An open drive bay:** Look for a 5¼-inch drive bay that's accessible from the front of your case.

- ✔ **A SCSI connector:** Your SCSI adapter should come with a cable, and you should use the first open connector that's closest to the SCSI adapter. If you're adding a drive to an existing chain, select the next open connector on the cable after the last existing device.

I've always recommended this technique of adding devices to the end of the cable (instead of trying to stick them in the middle of a SCSI chain). Why? You have less to worry about come termination time; you simply remove the termination on the last existing device on the cable and make sure that your new device is terminated. Because it's now the last device on the cable, you always know that it marks the end of the chain. Sometimes, this process isn't possible (for example, if you have only one open drive bay and the end of the SCSI cable doesn't reach it), but whenever you can, adding devices at the end of the cable is a good idea.

- ✔ **An open power connector:** Most PCs come with a veritable forest of available power connectors. If you've used them all, buy a Y connector that splits one power cable into two. 'Nuff said.

Your step-by-step guide to internal SCSI happiness

Ready to dive in? Follow these steps:

1. **Turn off your computer and unplug it from the AC outlet.**

2. **Touch a metal surface to dissipate any static electricity that may be stowed away on your person.**

   Usually, your PC's case suffices just fine.

3. **Remove the screws holding your computer's cover and place it out of harm's way.**

   Put the removed screws in your parts bowl.

4. **Set the SCSI device ID on your drive to a unique number.**

   Refer to the drive's manual to determine where the ID control is located, and then configure it with a unique number that's not used on any other SCSI device in your system.

5. **Determine the correct termination — don't forget that the correct termination includes *all* existing SCSI devices on the chain.**

   Check the position of the SCSI connector you want to use. If the recorder is on the end of your SCSI cable, make sure that the device is terminated (and all intervening devices have had their termination removed).

6. **If necessary, remove the plastic insert covering the drive bay.**

   If the cover is the snap-on type, you can carefully pry it off with a screwdriver.

7. **Slide the drive into the front of the case, with the rear of the drive (the end with the plugs and connectors) going in first.**

   The tray and buttons should be facing the front of the case, as shown in Figure 4-2, and any printing or logos on the front should be facing right side up.

8. **Move the drive forward and backward to align the screw holes on the side of the drive and the case, and then attach the recorder with the manufacturer's screws.**

9. **Connect a power cable to the drive and make sure that you press it in firmly.**

10. **Connect the SCSI ribbon cable to the SCSI connector on the back of the recorder.**

    Note that it's notched to fit only one way. Press it on firmly after it's correctly aligned.

11. **Take a moment to check all your power and cable connections — even the ones that don't lead to your recorder.**

12. **Replace the cover on your PC with the original screws.**

13. **Plug in the PC's power cable.**

14. **Turn on your PC and allow it to boot up normally.**

    You should see the SCSI adapter verifying each of the devices on the chain, including your new recorder.

15. **Install the software that accompanied your recorder.**

Sweet! It's time to test things out by taking a quick detour to Chapter 8. If you can't record, remain calm and turn to the troubleshooting section at the end of this chapter.

External SCSI stuff

Like USB and FireWire external drives, an external SCSI recorder carries its house along with it — however, you still have to select a unique SCSI ID and correctly terminate that external recorder before everything starts humming. Use your SCSI adapter's external SCSI port to connect your recorder. A number of different SCSI port configurations are possible, so if your card didn't come with a cable, make sure that you're buying the right type with the right connections.

All external SCSI devices come with two connectors, so you can add more than one external device with additional cables — a classic example is a SCSI system with an external SCSI recorder and a SCSI scanner. The same termination rules you followed for internal drives apply when you're installing multiple external SCSI devices. As shown in Figure 4-8, make sure to terminate the last external device in the chain.

Figure 4-8:
Feel free to
hang more
than one
SCSI device
outside your
computer.

Remember that your SCSI adapter should never be terminated if you've connected both internal and external SCSI devices (in fact, it's now at the *center* of your chain).

Installing a FireWire Drive

Like USB, the data superhighway that is FireWire makes the installation of your external recorder an easy process. Granted, producing microwave popcorn is easier, but everyone can do that, and it doesn't sound nearly as impressive for the uninitiated. (Remember, let others *think* this stuff is complex . . . techno-types have been doing it for decades now.)

Anyway, follow these steps to install your FireWire drive:

1. **Plug the power cord from your recorder into the AC wall socket.**

2. **Connect the FireWire cable to the drive and turn it on.**

3. **Plug the cable from your drive into the FireWire port on your computer.**

4. **Turn on your computer and allow it to boot up normally.**

   Your next step depends on the software and the operating system you're using. You may see a dialog box prompting you to insert the driver disc that came with your drive, or you may have to install the drive's software separately.

5. **Check your drive's installation instructions to see which path you take.**

To double-check your work, rush to Chapter 8 and try burning your first disc. If your drive appears to be suffering from rigor mortis, jump to the following troubleshooting section.

"Um, It's Just Sitting There"

I *really* hope that you're not reading this — I hope that your recorder went in as smooth as butter, lit up like a Christmas tree when you turned things on, and perfectly burned that first disc of Liberace tunes. Therefore, I assume that you're skipping this section completely. Or, perhaps you've reached this section and you're just curious about what *could* have happened, or you're generally interested in *troubleshooting* (the art of figuring out what's wrong with your computer and how you can fix it).

On the other hand, you may have reached this section with a hunk of hardware that's just sitting there like a dead weight. If so, these sentences are pure gold because they can help you diagnose the problem with your recorder installation and solve it quickly.

EIDE troubleshooting

If you've installed an EIDE drive and it appears to be acting persnickety, here are the problems that folks often encounter and how to solve them.

The drive doesn't eject the tray, and the power light doesn't turn on.

This problem is usually caused by an unplugged, loose, or broken power connector. Unfortunately, this means that it's time to crack open your PC's case and check your connections.

I tried to play an audio CD with my recorder, and I can't hear any music.

This problem is common and easy to fix: You forgot to connect the Audio Out cable from the recorder to your PC's sound card. The manufacturer of your drive should provide this cable (and it's often also supplied along with a sound card). Consult the manual for your sound card to determine where you should plug in the Audio Out cable from your new drive.

My drive ejects the tray, but I can't find the drive symbol in Windows, and my software says that it can't recognize the recorder.

The simplest explanation for this problem is an unplugged data cable. Check to make sure that you've plugged firmly into the drive the flat ribbon cable from the EIDE connector. Next, you may have the master and slave jumpers on your recorder configured incorrectly, so check them against the configurations listed in the recorder's manual. Finally — and this is the tricky one — you may have set the jumpers on the recorder correctly, but forgotten to configure the new multiple drive setting on the drive that's already on that EIDE cable.

SCSI troubleshooting

I think that even Scotty on the original *Star Trek* TV series would have thought twice before sticking one of those silver penlights into a recalcitrant SCSI setup. Just kidding. Although you have more to troubleshoot with a SCSI installation, all it takes to solve a problem is time and patience.

My computer locks up every time I boot after the installation, and I have to turn it off manually.

I bet that you already suspect that your SCSI termination or ID numbers are configured wrong — and if so, you're right. Double check all your termination settings and make sure that they're correct, and then verify that each SCSI device on your chain has a unique SCSI ID number.

I can't get my SCSI drive to eject the tray, and the power light doesn't turn on.

On an internal drive, check your power cable — if you've added an external SCSI drive, the external power supply is the likely culprit.

The drive ejects the tray, but my computer acts like the recorder isn't there. (Alternatively, the recorder works, but my existing SCSI scanner is now broken.)

Poke your drive with a finger to make sure that it's there. (Sorry, I couldn't resist that one.) The real problem is likely your old friends: two or more devices trying to share the same SCSI ID number, or termination that's incorrectly configured for your new drive. Also, make sure that all other SCSI devices on the chain are powered up and connected, and wiggle your data cable to make sure that it's firmly connected.

If your SCSI adapter card came with any SCSI diagnostics programs, run them now and see what error messages the programs display. Also, check your SCSI adapter manual to see whether you can run a self-test mode.

USB and FireWire troubleshooting

Although both USB and FireWire are Plug and Play (meaning that you can simply connect and disconnect them without rebooting your computer), that doesn't mean that they're trouble-free. If your external recorder isn't working, check these possible solutions:

My computer complains that it doesn't have a "USB (or FireWire) device driver" when I plug in my recorder.

This message is a clear cry for help from your computer: You either need to install the manufacturer's driver from the disc or the driver you installed has been corrupted. To fix this problem, reinstall the recorder's software. Checking the manufacturer's Web site to see whether an updated USB driver is available is a good idea. If you're using a Macintosh computer under Mac OS 9.2 and a FireWire recorder, you should check your Extensions list for the device's

FireWire extension. To check your Extensions list, click the Apple icon in the Finder menu, and select the Extensions Manager from the Control Panel list. (Mac owners running Mac OS X don't have to worry about extensions.)

My recorder has no power; the tray doesn't eject and, and no power light turns on.

Your first thought is probably the drive's power supply, and if it does have an external power supply, you're likely right. If you bought your drive locally, take it to the salesperson and ask that person to check it out with another supply. However, if your USB drive is designed to be powered from the computer's USB port, it doesn't have a separate power supply. In this case, the port is probably not providing enough power to meet the USB standard. (This problem happens frequently with USB hubs and keyboard and/or auxiliary USB ports.) Plug your recorder into another computer's USB port and see whether it jumps into action.

My drive has power, but my computer doesn't recognize it.

If the recorder's software installation ran without a hitch and the driver is present, this problem is usually caused by a faulty cable, a faulty USB or FireWire hub, or a USB cable that's too long (it shouldn't be more than 10 feet). Try connecting your drive to your computer with a different standard cable and without an intervening hub. Most USB and FireWire devices don't pass a signal when they're turned off, either — this can cause any daisy-chained peripherals that may be connected to suddenly go silent as well. Make sure that all the external devices that connect your recorder to your computer are turned on.

Part II
It's All in the Preparation

The 5th Wave   By Rich Tennant

"Before we could record any of their ceremonies, they'd like to perform the ritual of the copyright release for us."

In this part . . .

Here I get to discuss the preparations that you should take before you burn your first disc. (Put that match down and read this part before you do anything hasty.) I show you how to optimize your computer's performance to help ensure an error-free disc, and how to select the right recording software for the job. I also help you select the right configuration settings for the type of disc that you want to record (settings like the format, the organization, and the file system). Fear not the technospeak, for all is made clear in this part.

Chapter 5

Letting Loose the Software Elves

*H*ardware. Are you up to your gills in it? I devote the entire first portion of this book to describing your CD or DVD recorder, buying it, and installing it. Sure, I admit that your drive is the most important part of your computer-based Optical Recording Studio (or ORS), but does it run itself? Can it do anything by itself besides blink a light or two and stick out its tray?

The answer, of course, is a big, fat *No*. You need software to tame your recording beast. It's like Santa at the North Pole: The old guy gets all the credit, and his elves are constantly toiling behind the scenes all year-round while he's watching marathon reruns of *The Andy Griffith Show* and eating leftover popcorn balls. Without the elves, who would load the sleigh, make the toys, and feed the reindeer? Not to mention the work that Mrs. Claus must be doing to keep everyone fed and clothed. (Sorry, I tend to get a little carried away — I have three kids.)

In this chapter, doggone it, I change all that. I cover the highlights and special talents of each elf — whoops, I mean *program* — that I use in this book. This information comes in handy if you're considering a shareware or commercial recording package to replace the lame program that came with your recorder. If you decide to buy a different program from the favorites I recommend in this chapter (insert look of shock and chagrin here), make sure that the program you're buying has at least most of these primo features.

The Windows Tool of Choice: Roxio's Easy CD & DVD Creator 6

For PC owners running Windows, the choice is clear: Easy CD & DVD Creator 6 (which I call Creator 6, for short) from Roxio (www.roxio.com). This showpiece has been the solid, reliable Swiss army knife of CD and DVD burning for many years. It has the widest range of features of any recording software I've ever used in my travels, it can burn a host of different formats and disc types, and it's simple enough for a novice to use. (See Figure 5-1.)

Formats and disc types out the wazoo

If you're likely to need just about any specific type of disc on planet Earth, this program can do it. Of course, Creator 6 can burn simple data discs and audio CDs using Track-at-Once or Disc-at-Once without even lifting an eyebrow, but it can also pump out

- CD-ROM XA (multisession) discs
- DVD-Video discs
- Video CDs
- Mixed-mode discs
- CD Extra discs
- Photo slideshow discs

This lineup also includes two types of discs that both deserve special attention: the *bootable* CD-ROM and the *MP3 music* disc. As you may have already guessed, you can boot most PCs by using a bootable CD-ROM, so you can even run your PC without a hard drive — after a fashion, anyway. A bootable disc can also carry other programs and data besides a basic operating system. A Microsoft Windows XP CD-ROM is a good example of a bootable CD: It uses DOS as a basic operating system to display simple prompts, but after your computer is up and running, you can install Windows from it and *really* screw up your system. (Sorry, Mr. Gates, I didn't mean that. Please don't pull the plug.)

An MP3 music disc, on the other hand, is a specialized data CD-ROM. Although it carries music in MP3 (MPEG Audio Layer 3) format, its songs are not recorded in the Red Book digital audio format (refer to Chapter 2), so you can't play the disc in an older audio CD player. MP3 discs are meant to be played exclusively on either your computer, using a program like Winamp, or on specially designed MP3 CD players. (Many of the current crop of audio CD players now support MP3 music discs; check your player's manual to see whether your model can use them.) You find more on MP3 music discs in Chapter 7 — these CDs are called *MP3 player discs* in Creator 6.

Figure 5-1:
Creator 6
is the
recording
software of
choice for
most PC
owners.

Wolfgang woulda loved this

Interested in burning hot music on a compact disc? Whether those songs are in MP3 format or stored on older cassettes and vinyl albums or you're collecting tracks from a number of existing audio CDs, Creator 6 can do it in style. Although I've tried many different programs that record audio CDs, Creator Classic (the primary recording application included with Easy CD & DVD Creator 6) continues to be my favorite: It's the easiest to understand and the fastest to use. On the audio side, the program can

- ✔ Automatically convert songs in MP3 and WMA (Windows Media Audio) formats and prepare them for recording
- ✔ Extract tracks from existing audio CDs and save them as MP3 files on your hard drive
- ✔ Store CD text for display on many CD players with digital readouts
- ✔ Add transition effects, like fade in, fade out, and cross fading
- ✔ Preview WAV and MP3 songs before you record them

I especially like how Creator Classic can venture onto the Internet — it can check online music databases and download all the track names for CDs it finds. This feature can save you both time and sore fingers because you avoid typing all those track names by hand.

Extra stuff they give you (without even asking)

If the Creator 6 feature list ended in the preceding section, most folks would be satisfied. But, wait — what if I told you that you also get these great stand-alone (separate) programs to boot?

CD Copier

CD Copier makes it easy to produce a duplicate of an existing data CD, data DVD, or audio CD (without requiring you to start Creator 6 and produce a disc image, which is a much longer process that accomplishes the same thing). Folks who date back to the glory days of floppies should remember programs that allowed you to copy a disk read from one drive to another. If you have both a read-only CD-ROM or DVD-ROM drive and a recorder in the same PC, you can use the read-only drive as the source (as I'm doing in Figure 5-2). No swapping required. If you have only a recorder, however, you can still use CD Copier — you just have to eject the original disc and load a blank.

Figure 5-2: Copying an audio disc is child's play with CD Copier.

I show you how to use CD Copier in Chapter 8.

Roxio Retrieve

How many times in this book do I harp about backing up your hard drive? Would you mind losing every file you've ever known if your hard drive crashes? If you don't have a current backup, I'll nag you like your mother until you make one. (There's a scary thought, eh?)

With the combination of Creator Classic and Roxio Retrieve (see Figure 5-3), you no longer have any excuse. It can back up a drive to multiple CD-RWs as fast as your drive can shovel 1s and 0s (zeros).

Figure 5-3:
Use Roxio
Retrieve!
Back up!
Do it!

Chapter 8 includes the steps for a typical hard drive backup.

AudioCentral

AudioCentral is an exciting program for anyone interested in recording music: You can copy your favorite old cassettes and albums to audio CDs. Those of us with extensive piles of vinyl and tape still occupying the corners of a room know the heartbreak of losing an old favorite that hasn't been released in compact disc format. Scratches and stretched tape can ruin your treasures, but after you use AudioCentral to transfer them to CD, you can keep them for their cover art. The program can also play your digital audio files and includes an editor that can modify tracks before you burn them to disc. (See Figure 5-4.)

I show you in Chapter 11 how to transfer that "H.R. Puffinstuff" soundtrack album to CD.

Figure 5-4:
Audio-
Central is
a complete
analog-to-
digital music
solution.

Label Creator

Let me be honest: I like a labeled disc, but I don't label everything I burn. For example, if I'm going on a business trip and I've just recorded a disc of material for a book I'm writing, I don't go to the trouble of printing a label — I just use my trusty CD/DVD-marking pen and write a short title right on the disc.

On the other hand, Label Creator (shown in Figure 5-5) is the program you want to use when a disc needs to look its best — if you're giving it to someone else or you're particularly proud of that DVD-Video disc you made at your cousin's wedding. The program can also produce front and back jewel box inserts and DVD box inserts, with classy clip art, photographs, and different fonts. You can even choose one of the themes that's already set up in the program, which can produce a matching set with a label and a complete set of inserts. Neat!

Figure 5-5:
Puttin' on
the Ritz with
CD Label
Creator.

Chapter 14 includes a step-by-step example using Label Creator.

Burning Up Your Macintosh with Roxio's Toast 6 Titanium

As you can see from Figure 5-6, those Mac folks look different again: This time, it's Toast 6 Titanium, from Roxio, the king of recording programs on the Macintosh. (Don't ask how the program got its name — I'm sure that a funny story is in there, but I don't know it.)

Besides the standard formats — audio, data, mixed-mode, Video CD, and CD Extra — that we all expect, Toast 6 can produce a couple of nifty extras:

Figure 5-6:
No butter,
no jelly —
just Toast.

✓ **Hybrid discs:** These strange beasts can be read under both Windows and the Mac operating system — they're often used for cross-platform applications that have both a Mac and Windows version. Games are often shipped on hybrid discs for the same reason.

✓ **Super Video CD:** Also called SVCDs for short, Super Video CDs can store digital video files just like standard Video CDs. As the name suggests, however, Super Video CDs provide significantly better video quality (at the expense of disc space, so SVCDs typically hold only about 45 minutes of video). Standard Video CDs can usually store up to 60 minutes of digital video.

✓ **MP3 music discs:** As I discuss in earlier chapters, these discs store music files in MP3 format.

✓ **DVDs:** Toast can burn both DVD data and DVD-Video discs on supported drives.

If you're burning discs for older Mac operating systems, you can use the Mac standard format. However, if your disc is used on a newer machine running Mac OS 9.0 or later, you should use the enhanced Mac OS Extended mode.

As any Mac technotype can tell you, the Mac operating system can mount a disk image as a virtual drive on your desktop. Toast can both create and mount these images for you, so you can store multiple images on a single CD or DVD and use them rather than hunt for a physical disc. (I leap headlong into the subject of disc images in Chapter 8.) I also like the Compare feature in Toast, where you can compare two folders or files and view the differences — usually one folder or file on your hard drive and another on a CD or DVD disc.

Chapter 9 is devoted to burning with Toast. (I'm sorry — that one just slipped in subconsciously.)

Packet Writing Made Easy with Drag-to-Disc

Packet writing is *almost* as foolproof as a burnproof recording: You simply format the disc, write to it just like it's a huge floppy or Zip disk, and then finalize it for reading just like an ordinary CD-ROM or DVD-ROM. Teamed with a CD-RW or DVD rewriteable drive, packet writing software can produce the nearly perfect, reusable, low-cost storage solution that everyone has been chasing since the first 1GB hard drive appeared way back when. Figure 5-7 illustrates the Roxio Drag-to-Disc hard at work.

Figure 5-7: Drag-to-Disc is the key to oneness with your CD or DVD recorder.

You can find a complete rundown on Drag-to-Disc in Chapter 10.

Introducing the Editors: iMovie 3, iDVD, and Premiere

Not one of these three programs counts as true disc-recording software: Instead, they're programs for digital video editing, disc design, and the creation of special effects that just happen to have recording features built-in. (As you can tell, these programs cross a number of boundaries when it comes to genre.) Because I use them later in this book, however, I thought that I would introduce at least a little something about each one here.

iMovie 3, as shown in Figure 5-8, was a groundbreaking arrival for both Apple and the world of digital video. iMovie marked a revolution where practically anyone who could connect a FireWire cable, drag and drop video clips, and select a transition or two could develop their own professional-looking movies. For the first time, you didn't need several hundred dollars to spend just on editing software. The software has been shipping free with iMacs since the program was first introduced. iMovie was simple enough to appeal to novices, who definitely didn't want to spend hours understanding the basics of a more powerful, traditional editor. Unfortunately for Windows folks, iMovie 3 runs on only Mac OS X. However, Windows Movie Maker is *very* much like it.

iDVD 3 is the recently released big brother to iMovie 3: At the time I wrote this book, it was available only on Macintosh computers that offer the CD-RW/DVD-R SuperDrive. With iDVD, you can master your own DVD-ROM titles, complete with basic menu and submenu interaction. For example, viewers can select a video clip to watch or view a slideshow of digital photographs. While designing your disc, you can use a prepared theme to automatically set the appearance of your buttons and background, or you can add your own. Finally, iDVD allows you to preview your work and burn the DVD within the program itself. Figure 5-9 shows iDVD in action. (For more detail on iDVD, check out Chapter 13.)

Figure 5-8:
If you buy a Macintosh these days, you pick up iMovie 3 for free.

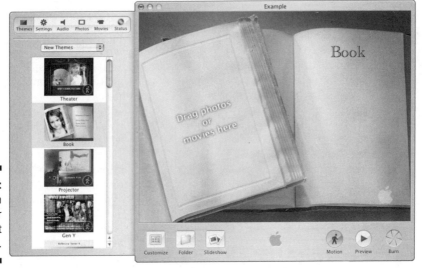

Figure 5-9:
Deciding on
a theme for
my newest
hit DVD title.

The excellent Adobe digital video editor Premiere Pro (as shown in Figure
5-10) is available for Windows. Premiere is much more powerful than either
iMovie 3 or iDVD 3, offering professional special effects, better control over
audio and timing, output as streaming Web video, storyboarding, and the
ability to handle more formats of digital video. However, it's not anywhere
near as simple to use as iMovie 3 or iDVD 3. Because it's a commercial program, you're likely to spend around $500 or so for a copy. Premiere is the
right choice for those folks who know that they're in digital video to stay,
want to grow into a professional package, and want its tight integration with
other Adobe products, like After Effects.

Figure 5-10:
You pay for
it, but Adobe
Premiere is
the classic
digital video
editor.

Chapter 6

Fine-Tuning Can Be Fun

. . . .

. . . .

*I*n the beginning, there were Windows 3.1 and the 486 processor, and many did try to record their first CD-ROMs and fell by the wayside. For Buffer Underruns roamed the land, ruining those early discs because the computer could not keep up with the recorder. And many threw up their hands in anger and frustration, and they knew then that they must optimize their systems."

Such tales are few and far between these days because you're likely using a PC or Macintosh that performs much better than the 486-based computers of old. The latest hard drives can deliver data much faster than a recorder can burn it, and today's burnproof recorders no longer fear multitasking and disk-intensive applications. So why do I dedicate a chapter to optimization and fine-tuning? I have two important reasons (besides the fact that I needed a topic for Chapter 6).

First, you may not be lucky enough to own only the cutting edge in hardware. I own and use seven computers, and only one of them is state-of-the-art (meaning that it's less than a year old). If both your computer and your drive have been hanging around for three years or more, optimization is just as important as ever.

Second, optimization helps your entire system run like the Six Million Dollar Man: better, faster, and farther. I recommend many of these steps even if your computer doesn't sport a CD or DVD recorder right now — you'll thank me the next time you open Microsoft Word or Adobe Photoshop.

Therefore, this chapter is designed to help you tinker and tune. Just hand me a wrench and the proper screwdriver from time to time, and your computer will soon be running at its best.

Creating Elbowroom

No matter how you cut it, 700MB of data takes up a fair chunk of hard drive territory — and that's just what you store on a CD-R or CD-RW. As you may have read in earlier chapters, a DVD-R or DVD+R can hold 4.7GB, and a double-sided DVD-RAM can store as much as 9.4GB! You can see how hard drive space can become important very quickly, and there never seems to be enough. You find that your data expands to fill your drive, whatever the size (rather like The Blob). In this section, I cover a number of tips and tricks that can help you clear space for your next burning session.

'Course, you could just buy a bigger hard drive

Although a bigger hard drive is the likely option for the fine folks living in the Gates mansion, I bet that you would rather conserve space, reduce clutter, and just keep your current drive. Besides the space you need in order to temporarily store the data or audio you want to record, two other important temporary files take up space behind the scenes:

- **Temp files used by your recording software:** If you're recording in Disc-at-Once mode, for example, your software is likely to create a temporary image file of the entire disc — this process typically takes as much space as the data itself!

- **Virtual memory:** All versions of Windows (as well as Mac OS 9.2 and Mac OS X) use territory on your hard drive as *virtual memory,* which is storage space for all those 1s and 0s (zeros) that don't fit into the physical RAM installed in your system. (Ever wonder how a computer with 64MB of RAM can run a 10MB program that opens 256MB files? That's virtual memory at work.) Figure 6-1 shows how limited your system becomes if virtual memory is disabled. I talk more about virtual memory throughout the rest of this chapter.

As you may have guessed from the word *temporary,* these files are deleted after the recording has finished or the additional virtual memory space is no longer needed. (Insert ominous chord here.) However, good people, not all programs are as tidy in cleaning up behind themselves. Shame!

Without virtual memory
64MB of RAM
= 64MB system RAM

Figure 6-1:
Need more
RAM for
your
programs?
Virtual
memory is
the ticket to
wide-open
spaces.

With virtual memory
64MB of RAM
+
64MB of hard drive space
= 128MB system RAM

Locate unnecessary stuff

If you've ever deleted programs and data files manually from your computer, you know that you're waltzing in a potential minefield, and you're a prime candidate for this important Mark's Maxim:

> **Never, *never* — *never* — delete files willy-nilly!**™

(By the way, "willy-nilly" is a non-technical term for opening Windows Explorer and simply deleting an entire folder.) Luckily, programs that are both built into your operating system and available separately at your neighborhood computer store can help you remove accumulated hard drive crud safely.

First, though, here's a rundown of which files you can likely kiss goodbye without sending your computer into a coma:

✔ **Demos, samples, and Aunt Harriet's fruitcake recipe:** First things first: Get rid of those 10-year-old game demos and one-shot software installations that you'll never need again! Naturally, you should drag whatever unnecessary documents you have created to the Recycle Bin or Trash — I mean, how many Top Ten joke listings should you save? Anyway, after you decide what to trash, choose Start⇨Settings⇨Control Panel⇨Add/ Remove Programs to display the dialog box shown in Figure 6-2. (You should always use this method to delete an entire program under Windows!) Click the program you want to delete from the list and select Remove to start things moving.

Figure 6-2:
Deleting a
program
(the right
way).

✔ **The contents of your Trash or Recycle Bin:** Hey, you didn't want these files anyway, and they already have one foot in the Great Beyond! To clear the space under Windows, right-click the Recycle Bin icon and select Empty Recycle Bin. Under Mac OS 9.2, click the Special menu and choose Empty Trash; under Mac OS X, click Finder and choose Empty Trash.

✔ **TBR:** That's an acronym of my own — I guess I just snapped from all these silly technobabble terms. It stands for *t*ypical *b*rowser *r*efuse: the images, Web pages, and sound files your browser stores in its cache to speed things up when you reload a page. Luckily, shoveling this stuff out the door is easy because both Internet Explorer and Netscape Navigator allow you to purge their cache directories. (In Internet Explorer, choose Tools⇨Internet Options, click the Delete Files button, and click OK to confirm that you want to sweep up the place.) If you're a big-time Web walker, you may be surprised at the sheer amount of space you can reclaim!

Let the wizard do it!

Fans of J.R.R. Tolkien's classic *The Hobbit* will agree: Dwarves would much rather leave the heavy work to the burglar or the wizard! If your system is running Windows 98 or later, you can turn to the Disk Cleanup Wizard to help you automate the removal of accumulated disk gunk.

To run the Disk Cleanup Wizard under Windows XP, follow these steps:

1. **Choose Start⇨All Programs⇨Accessories⇨System Tools⇨Disk Cleanup.**

   Geez, can the friendly folks in Redmond hide useful stuff like this any further under the rug?

2. **If you have more than one hard drive on your system, select Drive C: from the drop-down list box and click OK.**

3. **Windows displays the Disk Cleanup dialog box, shown in Figure 6-3.**

   As you can see, you save quite a bit of space here! Click OK to begin the cleanup.

Figure 6-3: Not even Gandalf can clear space as fast as the Windows Disk Cleanup Wizard!

4. **Click Yes to assure Windows (which is often slightly paranoid) that you do indeed want to delete files.**

Sit back and watch while the wizard safely sweeps your system clean. Neat! (And yes, Virginia, I bet Dumbledore could do just as good a job.)

Call in the professionals

I heartily recommend two commercial programs that can help you clean up either a PC running Windows or a Macintosh running Mac OS 9.2/Mac OS X. Figure 6-4 illustrates Norton CleanSweep for the PC, from Symantec (www. symantec.com) — it offers a high level of safety. I especially like the feature that locates and deletes temporary, zero-length, and duplicate files that can nibble at your free space.

Figure 6-4:
Under
Windows,
you can use
Norton
CleanSweep
to tidy up
your drive.

On the Macintosh side, I recommend Spring Cleaning, from Aladdin Systems (www.aladdinsys.com), which does everything from uninstalling old programs to zapping browser cache files.

Checking under the Rug

Your computer may be hiding something from you: No, not a winning lottery ticket or a love affair with a coffee machine, but rather nasty errors on your hard drive that may be robbing you of both free space and performance. If you don't look for these errors, I can guarantee that they won't leap up and identify themselves (except, of course, those errors that continue to grow worse and eventually cause you to lose files and data *permanently*). Before you burn a disc — or, for that matter, once every couple of days — running your computer's disk diagnostics program takes care of anything hiding under the rug.

These errors fall into two categories:

✔ **Logical errors:** These are the most common file problems, and they're usually caused by improper shutdowns, power outages, and misbehaving programs. If you have already encountered lost clusters and cross-linked files, you have already met (and hopefully fixed) logical errors on your hard drive. Most logical errors can be solved with the right software.

✔ **Physical errors:** These errors, on the other hand, are caused by a malfunction in the hard drive itself. The classic cause of physical errors is the infamous and frightening hard drive crash, where either your entire drive croaks or the magnetic platters inside are damaged. Physical errors usually can't be corrected by the layman: If you're willing to spend a rather unbelievable amount of money, some companies can fix the innards of your hard drive, but in most cases it's simply not worth the effort. Therefore, if your drive is acting up and returning physical errors, I strongly recommend that you back up now — this second! — and buy a replacement drive.

Fixing your drive the Windows way

Checking a drive under Windows 98 and Windows Me is child's play, thanks to a program named ScanDisk; using it at least once a day to fix any logical errors that may appear on your drive is a good idea. Follow these steps to put ScanDisk through its paces:

1. **Choose Start⇨Programs⇨Accessories⇨System Tools⇨ScanDisk.**

2. **Use the drop-down list box to select the hard drive you want to scan.**

3. **Select the Standard radio button to check for logical errors, or select the Thorough radio button to check for both logical and physical errors.**

   Be prepared for a long haul if you choose Thorough, especially on today's huge hard drives.

4. **Click Start to begin the scanning process.**

5. **After the disk has been checked and any logical errors squashed, ScanDisk displays the results.**

6. **Click Close to return to Windows and your work.**

Under Windows 2000 and Windows XP, ScanDisk has been integrated into the operating system, so you can check a disk for errors from the drive's Properties dialog box. Follow these steps:

1. **Double-click the My Computer icon on your desktop.**

2. **Right-click the icon for the hard drive that you want to scan and choose Properties from the pop-up menu that appears.**

3. **Click the Tools tab to display the panel shown in Figure 6-5.**

4. **Click the Check Now button to display the Check dialog box.**

5. **Enable the Automatically Fix File System Errors check box.**

6. **For a full scan, select the Scan For and Attempt Recovery of Bad Sectors check box to check for both logical and physical errors.**

   Because a full scan takes so much longer, I only perform bad sector testing every six months or so. Otherwise, I leave the Scan For and Attempt Recovery of Bad Sectors check box disabled.

7. **Click Start to begin the scanning process.**

8. **After the disk has been checked, ScanDisk displays the results.**

9. **Click Close to return to Windows.**

Figure 6-5:
Scanning
for pesky
errors in
Windows
XP.

Fixing things with Mac OS 9.2

In the Macintosh world, with Mac OS 9.2, Apple includes a drive checkup program named Disk First Aid. Follow these steps to use it:

1. **From the Mac OS 9.2 desktop, double-click your hard drive and then choose Applications (Mac OS 9)⊏⟩Utilities⊏⟩Disk First Aid to launch the application (see Figure 6-6).**

2. **Click the icon for the hard drive that you want to scan.**

3. **Click the Repair button.**

   Disk First Aid automatically checks the selected drive and repairs any errors.

   To repair some errors on your startup disk, you may have to boot your Macintosh by using your Mac OS 9.2 CD-ROM. To do this, insert the CD-ROM, restart your Mac, and hold down the C key throughout the boot process.

4. **Done? Choose File⊏⟩Quit to return to the Mac OS desktop.**

Figure 6-6:
Should I
call this
*iPreventive
iDisk
iMainte-
nance?*

Fixing things under Mac OS X

If you're running Apple's Mac OS X 10.3 — or *Panther* to the In Crowd — don't
feel left out! You have an application called Disk Utility that can repair drive
problems. To use Disk Utility, follow these steps:

1. **From the desktop, double-click your hard drive and then choose
   Applications⇨Utilities⇨Disk Utility to launch the application, as
   shown in Figure 6-7.**

Figure 6-7:
Preparing to
pulverize
disk
problems
under
Panther.

2. **Select the hard drive that you want to scan.**

3. **Click the Repair Disk button.**

   Disk First Aid automatically checks the selected drive and repairs any errors.

   If the Repair Disk button is disabled, you have to reboot your Macintosh by using your Mac OS X Installation CD-ROM. To do this, insert the CD-ROM, restart your Mac, and hold down the C key throughout the boot process. After the first Installation screen appears, click Installer and click Open Disk Utility, and you should be able to repair your hard drive.

4. **Done? Choose File⇨Quit to return to the Mac OS X desktop.**

Most commercial disk utility programs can also check your drive. One example is Disk Doctor, which comes with Symantec Norton Utilities for both Windows and the Macintosh.

Avoiding Fragments

It's time to cover another insidious problem that can rob your computer of the performance you need for recording: *hard drive fragmentation*. Geez, more buzzwords.

I could get into a convoluted description of sectors, files, and your computer's operating system — but this is a *For Dummies* book, so I distill all that hoorah into a sidebar. If you're interested about what you're doing and why fragmentation occurs, read a little more. Otherwise, just remember this important truth: Defragmenting your hard drive is A Good Thing to do once a month or so, and it speeds up the overall performance of your computer (including, naturally, your recording projects).

Defragmenting For Dummies

No matter how cool I think defragmenting is, I just don't have enough material to write a *For Dummies* book about it. I know for sure because I pitched that book proposal to the publisher before I wrote this book. So, consider this sidebar your personal copy of *Defragmenting For Dummies* (definitely the shortest book in the famous series). It has no table of contents, no Part of Tens, no index, and not a single figure or

table — but I *do* tell you what's happening behind the curtain.

Why do files fragment? Well, when you delete and move files from your computer, you open areas on your hard drive for new files. However, these open areas aren't always big enough to hold a new file in one piece, so your computer and hard drive work together to save files in pieces called *segments*. For example, if you're copying a 200MB video clip to your hard drive so that you can record it later, your drive may not have 200MB worth of contiguous, unbroken open space on it — that's when the file is broken up into segments. Perhaps 20MB can fit in one place on your disk, and 100MB can fit in another, and so on. When the time comes to read the file, Windows or Mac OS X automatically and invisibly reassembles it and sends it to the proper place. All is well, right?

It is until your drive becomes badly fragmented and little chunks of thousands of different files are spread across the surface of your hard drive! If a file is saved as a contiguous whole, your drive can read it efficiently and quickly. On the other hand, it takes a significantly longer time for Windows or the Mac operating system to rebuild a file that's made up of dozens of segments in several different locations. We humans

see this lag time in the form of decreased performance and a delay of a second or two. When you're burning a disc, however (especially on an older computer with a fast CD or DVD recorder), that drop in performance can result in a coaster. Scratch another disc unless you're using a burnproof drive.

You can solve this problem by running your defragmenting program. This slick piece of software reads each file on your disk, combines the segments to form a contiguous file, and then saves the reassembled file back to disk in one piece. Plus, most defragmenting programs can also rearrange the locations of your files so that the programs and data you use most often load the fastest. When the program is finished, your hard drive is a smooth, efficient vista — a storage wonderland. (I think perhaps I need to stop now before I wax too enthusiastic.)

Windows 98/Me, Windows 2000, and Windows XP all come with a defragmenting program named (strangely enough) Disk Defragmenter, but Mac OS 9.2 and Mac OS X don't have a defragmenting program. Mac owners, I feel your pain, and I recommend using a commercial program like Speed Disk (another part of Norton Utilities, from Symantec), which works under both Mac OS 9.2 and Mac OS X.

Therefore, here are the steps for defragmenting your drive under Windows XP:

1. **Choose Start⇨All Programs⇨Accessories⇨System Tools⇨Disk Defragmenter.**

2. **Disk Defragmenter displays the window shown in Figure 6-8. Click the target drive in the list to select it.**

   Do you have more than one hard drive? If so, defragmenting all of them is a good idea (especially if you want to record files from multiple locations). If you're pressed for time, however, always pick Drive C because it usually holds both Windows and your virtual memory swap file.

3. **Click Defragment to begin the defragmentation process.**

   You can continue to work on other things, but defragmenting takes much less time if you can leave your PC to its own devices. (For this reason, I always defragment during the night, when I'm generally not using my computers.)

Figure 6-8:
Defragment
is an ugly
word, but it
can really
speed
up your
computer.

Avoiding the Unexpected

"Okay, Mark, how am I supposed to predict the unpredictable?" Good point —
I don't mean the *really* unexpected things in life, like a hard drive crash or an
honest politician. Instead, I'm talking about that doggone screen saver that
pops up while you're burning or that silly guy in the next office who bothers
you with constant network messages. Things like these are also unexpected,
and they can easily trash a disc.

In this section, I talk about a number of automatic features and functions of
Windows, Mac OS 9.2, and Mac OS X that you can disable before you start
recording, which can help you avoid these irritating interruptions.

Scheduled events and scripts

Windows allows you to set up scheduled events that run automatically at a
certain time or periodically during the day. Although this feature can be a
great convenience, I recommend that you disable any scripted or scheduled
tasks if you're set to record.

Windows 98/Me, Windows 2000, and Windows XP all allow you to temporarily pause scheduled tasks by pausing the Task Scheduler. Under XP, choose Start⇨ All Programs⇨Accessories⇨System Tools⇨Scheduled Tasks to display the Task Scheduler, shown in Figure 6-9. Choose Advanced⇨Pause Task Scheduler. After you have finished recording, you can display the Task Scheduler again and restart the schedule: Choose Advanced⇨Continue Task Scheduler, and click the Close button in the upper-right corner to banish the Scheduler from your screen.

Figure 6-9: Pause any scheduled tasks that may interrupt a recording.

Although the Mac operating systems don't have a built-in task scheduler, you should disable any scheduling software you may have added before you record; check the program's documentation to determine how to disable or pause automatic events.

Network access

Planning on using your recorder on your office or home network? All that network hard drive space makes this idea appealing, but I don't recommend recording a CD or DVD from a network source unless you have no other choice. Depending on the traffic your network carries, your file transfer rate may slow to a crawl, and your recording may be interrupted by network messages from your administrator and other users. Someone halfway across the building may decide to copy that unabridged electronic text of *Beowulf* that you have stored on your hard drive.

Worst of all, you may hit a number of hidden snags: restricted or password-protected file access, network drives that suddenly disappear because they were brought down, and so forth. When the network suddenly displays a "dropped connection" dialog box in the middle of your recording session, you have (to put it delicately) hosed a disc.

I can anchor this warning with a Mark's Maxim:

> **Rebooting and recording directly from your local computer's hard drive is the best idea; don't log in to your network unless you're sure of its stability.™**

However, if you *absolutely* have to use network storage for your recording (for example, if you have a diskless workstation at your desk), I have three suggestions:

- ✔ **Buy a burnproof recorder.** Burnproof technology prevents a ruined recording caused by a sluggish network and usually avoids optical tragedy even if the recording program is interrupted with a network message. (Naturally, though, it can't fix a disconnected network drive!)

- ✔ **Record by using packet writing.** I recommend Roxio Drag-to-Disc for packet writing, and I cover it in Chapter 10; even older recorders that don't offer burnproof protection can successfully burn a disc on a busy network when you use Drag-to-Disc.

- ✔ **Record early in the morning or late at night.** An empty office generally means an empty network, with far fewer delays and intrusions from other network users.

Power-saving mode and screen savers

Computers are now sophisticated pieces of equipment — they can even fall asleep or switch to standby mode if their lazy humans take a soda or coffee break. Allowing your computer to switch to these power-saving modes is normally a great idea: You save electricity without having to shut down your machine completely. When you're burning a disc, though, your computer may not recognize the activity — after all, you're not really moving your mouse — and a switch to a power-saving mode can be disastrous! I recommend that you either disable your computer's power-saving or standby mode (especially if you're recording on a laptop computer) or set it to at least 30 minutes (for CDs) or 60 minutes (for DVDs) before it kicks in.

The same is true of those cool screen savers that keep boredom at bay. They're neat, and I have more than 50 on my own machine, but whenever I use a screen saver, I set it for at least a 60-minute period of inactivity before it starts. This period allows me to complete any recording session before the light show starts and the fun begins.

In Windows XP, you can configure both your power-saving mode and your screen saver activity delay from the Control Panel. First, click the Power Options Control Panel icon to display the settings shown in Figure 6-10, and set both Turn Off Hard Disks and System Standby to Never. To change the inactivity delay for your screen saver, open the Display Control Panel and click the Screen Saver tab. Click in the Wait text box and type **30** or **60** for the number of minutes.

Figure 6-10:
You can change your power-saving settings from the Power Options Control Panel.

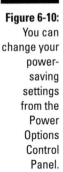

If you find yourself continually using the Power Options Control Panel, set up two power schemes you can use to switch back and forth between power-saving and recording modes.

For Macintosh owners who use Mac OS 9.2, click on the Apple menu and choose Control Panels. Then, click Energy Saver to display the dialog box shown in Figure 6-11. Move all the sliders to Never and click the Close button in the upper-left corner.

Figure 6-11:
Mac owners, saving energy while burning a disc is not a good idea!

If you're using Mac OS X, click on the Apple menu and choose System Preferences. Then, click Energy Saver to display the panel shown in Figure 6-12. Move the Put the Computer to Sleep When It Is Inactive For slider to Never and disable the Put the Hard Disk(s) to Sleep When Possible check box. Click the Close button in the upper-left corner.

Figure 6-12:
Setting up
uninter-
rupted
recording in
Mac OS X.

Remember, these energy-saving features in Windows and Mac OS are quite beneficial — just not when you're recording. Don't forget to restore your energy-saving settings when you're done burning!

Terrific Tips and Tweaks

Although I get into specific recording tips throughout the rest of this book, I beseech you to pay heed to these general tricks that apply to all types of recordings.

Avoid disk-intensive, memory-hungry behemoths

Follow this advice while you're recording, anyway. In other words, if you don't have a burnproof drive, launching programs like Microsoft Outlook, Adobe Photoshop, or Macromedia Flash during that burn is *not* A Good Idea. They simply take up too much system memory and thrash your hard drive too actively to cooperate well with optical storage.

Give your recording software some elbowroom

Is Mac OS 9.2 your recording environment of choice? Do you have at least 64MB of system RAM? Then I strongly recommend that you reserve additional application memory for your recording software, which can use the memory for all sorts of good things.

If you're using Mac OS 9.2, follow these steps to increase the memory allocated to your recording program:

1. **From the Finder, click the recording program's icon once to highlight it. Click the File menu family and choose the Get Info item.**

2. **Click File and select Get Info from the menu.**

3. **Click Show and choose Memory to display the dialog box shown in Figure 6-13.**

Figure 6-13:
Make room!
Under Mac
OS 9.2,
allocating
extra
memory is
A Good
Idea.

4. **In the Preferred Size text box, enter a larger amount of RAM.**

   As a rule, I tend to double the figure, but you should add at least 1024K, or 1 megabyte, of extra memory.

5. **Click the Close button to close the dialog box and save your changes.**

Speed up your hard drive

Here's a great tweak for PC owners running Windows 98 and Windows Me that can help your hard drive's performance! Follow these steps:

1. **Right-click the My Computer icon on your desktop and choose Properties from the pop-up menu.**

2. **Click the Performance tab and click File System to display the File System Properties dialog box (see Figure 6-14).**

Figure 6-14:
Vroom,
vroom!
Suddenly
your hard
drive acts
more like a
sports car!

3. **Select Network Server from the Typical Role of This Computer drop-down list box. Drag the Read-Ahead Optimization slider to Full (if it's not there already).**

4. **To save your changes, click OK to exit the File System Properties dialog box and click OK again to return to the desktop.**

   Note that you may have to reboot after this step.

Beware the flagged-out laptop

Laptop owners can be proud of their computers, but a loss of battery power has caused the premature demise of many a recording session. If you're using a laptop to burn a CD or DVD while you're on the road, use your AC adapter if at all possible — and if not, make doggone sure that your battery is fully charged and can last for at least 30 minutes. Also, remember that most laptops automatically switch to standby mode if their battery power levels drop below a certain point, so don't cut things too closely!

Chapter 7

Getting Ready for the Ball

*A*t this point, you may be ready to throw caution to the wind and start burning 1s and 0s (zeros) — and I can't say that I blame you because I cover a huge amount of ground in this book, and you may not have even recorded a single disc yet! However, I want to devote just one more chapter to preparations: in this case, steps you should take to make your finished discs

✔ Faster during loading and reading

✔ Better organized

✔ Easier to use

✔ Easier to search

See? This stuff is worth another chapter's wait. I promise! I especially recommend that you take care to follow the guidelines in this chapter when you're creating a disc for distribution or creating an archive disc that you will use often over the next decade or two.

Picking a Jazzy Format

I mention formats as features in Chapter 2. The *formats* a recorder can burn are criteria you could use to tell just how high a particular recorder ranks on the evolutionary scale. In this section, I show you how you can make use of those different formats. Remember: Certain formats are the right choice for certain jobs.

Data, lovely data

Data — pure binary 1s and 0s (zeros). Your computer lives on the stuff, and that's what data CDs and DVDs are for. If you're storing only data or program files — no digital audio — this is the disc format for you. These discs fall into one of two standards: the Yellow Book (for data CD-ROMs manufactured in a factory) and the Orange Book (for data CD-ROMs burned with your CD recorder). Some specialized types of discs I briefly mention in Chapter 5 of this book — for example, DVD movies, Video CDs, and photo slideshow CD-ROMs — are specialized types of data discs.

Use a data CD or DVD when you want to

- Store computer files and programs in the same folder or directory hierarchy as on your hard drive.
- Take advantage of the maximum storage space for data.
- Run programs directly from the disc.
- Load data (like a Word document or a spreadsheet) directly from the disc.
- Save multimedia files, like digital video and digital photographs, as pure data.

In case you're wondering, your computer's CD-ROM or DVD-ROM drive is the best playback solution for *any* kind of disc because it can read both audio CDs and data CD-ROMs (or DVD-ROMs) without blinking. Your audio CD player can't return the favor, though. Don't try to read a standard data CD-ROM in an audio CD player: If you hear anything, it's likely to be a screeching wail that will drive away every living thing within a square mile. I'm not kidding; even plants try to escape.

Sweet audio for the ears

Unlike a data disc, a disc recorded in audio CD format — also called *Red Book* — can store only one type of material (in this case, digital audio). However, it does this really, *really* well; so well, in fact, that an audio CD player doesn't recognize anything unless it's either Red Book or a subset of Red Book (like a CD Extra disc, which I discuss in Chapter 11).

You can use a number of different sources for audio tracks, including

- MP3 files
- WAV files (a Microsoft Windows standard)
- AIFF or AAC files (Macintosh standards)
- WMA files (another Windows standard)

Unlike with a tape cassette, however, you can't record your voice directly onto an audio CD. Instead, you have to record your material (usually as an MP3 or WAV file), and then record that disc in audio CD format later.

Are you a musician who uses a Musical Instrument Digital Interface (or MIDI for short) instrument or composes in MIDI format? You can record your compositions on an audio CD as well, but you still have to create an MP3 or a WAV digital audio file on your hard drive with your MIDI software. After the music is in one of these digital formats, you can burn it to an audio CD just like any other MP3 or WAV audio. (Of course, the latest MIDI composition programs can do all this behind the scenes, allowing you to record your masterpiece to an audio CD from a menu command.)

Remember that older standard audio CD players can't read a CD-RW. Use only CD-R media when you're recording CDs unless you're sure that the finished discs will be played only on an audio CD player that supports CD-RW media!

Man, this band is *horrible!*

Okay, let me get this straight: You have just recorded your first audio CD from that huge selection of Slim Whitman MP3 files you're so proud of, and the burn seemed to go like butter. You got no error messages, the songs sounded perfect when you previewed them, and your new drive churned the disc out in less than three minutes. Excellent! Hold on, though — when you try playing your new disc in your car audio CD player, you get either a screeching wail that sounds like a catfight under an outhouse, or nothing. I mean, absolutely *zip*. What went wrong?

This is the classic of all classic problems: You mistakenly recorded a data disc format rather than the audio CD (Red Book) format! Those files are still in MP3 format, and they can be played by using Winamp or another MP3 player program — but *only* on your computer. To play those songs with your audio CD player, you have to record them again. This time, make sure that you choose Red Book or digital audio or audio CD format (whatever your recording software calls it) when you set up the recording.

Alternatively, you may have recorded an *MP3 music disc,* which is very similar in format to the

data disc I just described. However, these discs are now supported by many personal CD players, home stereo systems, and car audio systems. The advantage to an MP3 music disc is the storage space you get: Because the songs are recorded in their existing MP3 form, they take up a lot less space than the same songs recorded in Red Book (digital audio) format. Unfortunately, if the audio CD player you're using doesn't support MP3 music discs, the effect is usually the same as trying to play a regular computer data disc.

Oh, one other possibility exists: If your audio CD player doesn't recognize your new CD but your computer's CD-ROM drive (or your recorder) *does* play it, you have rebelled against tradition and used a CD-RW rather than a CD-R. Of course, this particular rebellion is in vain if you're using an older audio CD player because a player that's four years old or older probably can't read a CD-RW. However, that same disc should play fine in an audio CD player that *does* support CD-RW media. (And come to think of it, you haven't really wasted a disc because you can reformat that CD-RW and use it again. Whew!)

Time for a Mark's Maxim that can save you time and trouble:

Use an old-fashioned CD-R whenever you want to record a disc for a standard audio CD player!™

Straddle the line with mixed mode

There's always an exception, right? (Just like those spelling rules you used to memorize.) In this case, you *do* have a way to record both data and digital Red Book audio on the same recordable CD: I'm talking about *mixed-mode* format, which is used for multimedia discs and games that need programs, digital video, and high-quality audio on the same compact disc. As you can see in Figure 7-1, mixed-mode discs have two tracks: The first contains data, and the successive tracks are digital audio. Pretty sassy, don't you think?

Because that first track is a data track, however, you still can't play a mixed-mode disc in your audio CD player. This is the opposite of another type of dual-purpose wonder, the *CD Extra disc,* where the audio tracks come first, followed by data tracks. You *can* play a CD Extra disc in your audio CD player — I venture into this territory in Chapter 11.

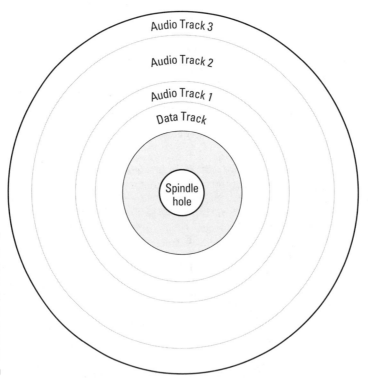

Figure 7-1:
Who says data and audio can't mix? (They separate like oil and vinegar.)

Why aren't all discs recorded in mixed-mode format? Of course, there's not much point in it if you're recording only files and programs or recording only digital audio. Other caveats apply:

- ✔ **Less operating system-friendly:** Older versions of DOS, Windows, the Mac operating system, and UNIX can't read mixed-mode discs. (Then again, DOS is fading into an indistinct memory for most of us; I use a command line only for Linux these days.)

- ✔ **Less compatible:** Older, read-only CD-ROM drives may be able to read only the first or last track on a mixed-mode disc.

- ✔ **Decreased capacity:** Working the magic of mixed mode takes anywhere from 3MB to 19MB of wasted space. Most of that space is required in order to separate the data track from the first audio track. Therefore, don't use mixed-mode format if you need to squeeze every possible pit from your recorded CD.

Use a mixed-mode CD-ROM when you want to

- ✔ Store both computer files and digital audio on the same disc.
- ✔ Run programs and load files directly from the data track.

Throw caution utterly to the wind with packet writing

I crow enough about packet writing — or, as it's more properly called, *Universal Disc Format* (UDF) — in this book that you may already know that it's one of my favorite topics. Packet writing makes it easy to record what you want, when you want it, using any recordable CD or DVD (rewriteable or not). Heck, you don't even need to open Easy CD & DVD Creator first to write a UDF disc with Drag-to-Disc. Just drag and drop as you always do, or save directly to the disc from within your applications. If you can do it with a floppy disk or a hard drive, you can do it with packet writing.

Packet writing even allows you to delete files you have written — in a fashion, anyway. The directory entries for the files you're deleting are overwritten, after which the unwanted files effectively vanish. This situation can make it appear that you've erased them completely and regained that space, like you would with your hard drive, but that's not the case: They still take up space on the disc; you simply can't reach them. (Of course, if you're using a rewrite-able disc — that's CD-RW, DVD+RW, DVD-RW, or DVD-RAM — you can always erase the entire disc and start over.)

Also, you should remember that all recordable media must be formatted before you can use it with a UDF program, like Drag-to-Disc. Naturally, after you've filled up a CD-R, you can't reformat it and use it over again, but (as I mention earlier) you can reformat a rewriteable CD or DVD recorded with packet writing. You lose all the data on the disc, of course, but that makes packet writing a great choice for one-shot discs.

Drawbacks to packet writing? Only a couple exist: You can't record a Red Book audio CD by using packet writing, and older operating systems (before Windows 98 and Mac OS 8) can't read UDF discs without a separate loader program.

"Disc-at-Once? Track-at-Once? Why Not All-at-Once?"

If you really want to act like a computer technotype at your next party, walk over to a group of your friends and jovially inquire, "So, folks, which recording mode do you use with your audio CDs?" It always gets me a laugh. (I don't get invited to many parties.)

Anyway, this question is indeed a valid one. The recording mode you use helps determine the compatibility of your finished disc and how much data or audio it can contain. Therefore, I cover the three common recording modes now so that you're ready to answer my question if we attend the same gala bash.

Meet you at the track

In *Track-at-Once* recording mode (or, as it's technically known, CD-ROM Mode 1), each data or audio track is kept primly separate from the others: No co-ed mingling here! As you can see in Figure 7-2, your recorder turns off the laser write head between tracks.

On the positive side, Track-at-Once mode is supported on every recorder, no matter how old, and can be read on any CD-ROM or DVD-ROM drive. That's why it's the default recording mode used by most recording programs. Unfortunately, those gaps left by the laser when it toggles off can cause a distinctive *click* noise between each track on an audio CD — whether you hear it depends on the audio CD player, but it can be excruciatingly irritating. Therefore, Track-at-Once is best used for data CD-ROMs.

Do it all at once

Disc-at-Once recording mode is the best pick for audio CDs. That's because your recorder's laser is never turned off, and the entire disc is written at once (as illustrated in Figure 7-3). You don't hear a click between tracks, no matter what type of audio CD player you use.

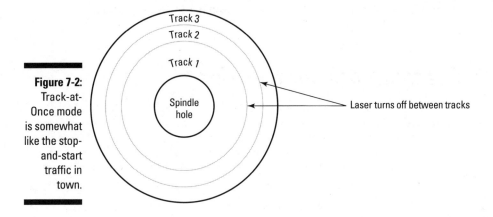

Figure 7-2: Track-at-Once mode is somewhat like the stop-and-start traffic in town.

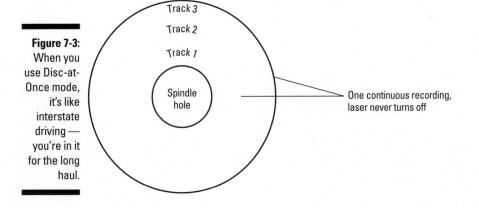

Figure 7-3: When you use Disc-at-Once mode, it's like interstate driving — you're in it for the long haul.

Disc-at-Once mode has three drawbacks: First, truly antique CD recorders (ones that are older than 5 years or so) can't write in Disc-at-Once mode, so if you own an older drive and you try to select Disc-at-Once in your recording software, you will probably find that you can't select it. Second, your disc takes longer to record in Disc-at-Once mode. Finally, Disc-at-Once recording may occupy more temporary hard drive space because — depending on your recording software — your computer may have to create an image file of the entire disc before it can begin burning.

Multipurpose multisession

Multisession recording (or to be technically correct, CD-ROM/XA Mode 2) allows you to add more than one separate session to a disc (think of a chapter in a book), each of which can be read just like a different CD, as shown in Figure 7-4. You can record sessions at different times, too, which makes multisession recording particularly handy for incremental recordings over weeks or months.

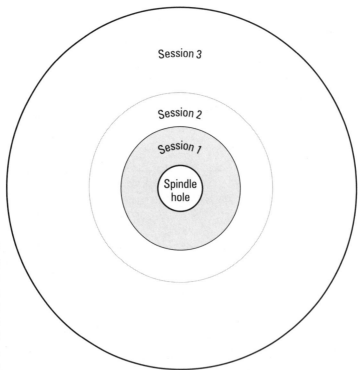

Only Session 1, 2, or 3 can be active at one time

Figure 7-4:
Use
multisession
when you
want a
gaggle of
virtual discs.

Again, compatibility is an issue: Multisession mode is not supported on many older, read-only CD-ROM drives, and you need a separate program that can switch between sessions to read all the material on the disc. Also, multisession discs can't be properly read in audio CD players.

Long Filenames Are Your Friends

While I'm discussing the decisions you must make before recording a data CD-ROM or DVD-ROM, I think that now is the right time to mention the five major file systems. A *file system* is a specific set of naming conventions and a data layout that . . . Whoops, there I go again, letting loose the programmer technical troll within me. (Sorry about that.)

To keep this simple, a file system determines

- What type of computer can read your disc
- The allowable filenames and their length
- The total number of subdirectories (or folders) that can appear on the disc and what arrangement they can take

The five major file systems are

- **Microsoft Joliet:** Supported since Windows 95, Joliet is now by far the most common file system used on PC CD-ROMs. Joliet provides the long filenames and folder names that the Windows crowd now finds indispensable, and those names can include niceties like periods, spaces, and most of the characters on your keyboard. A notable exception is the \ (backslash) key, so don't try to use it. If you're burning a disc on a PC for a PC running Windows, you have little reason to use anything else.

- **UDF:** Universal Disc Format is a fancier name for packet writing, but it's also a file system. UDF is usually the file system of choice for burning data DVDs and DVD-Video discs, since it can handle individual files over 1GB with aplomb.

- **HFS:** If you own a Macintosh, most of your Mac-only discs use the Hierarchical File System (HFS). Some programs allow a Windows system to recognize and read HFS discs (and, in the same vein, you can find Mac extensions that allow Mac OS 8 and earlier to read Joliet discs). Both Mac OS 9.2 and Mac OS X can read Joliet discs without any help, thank you very much.

- **Hybrid:** Hybrid discs contain both a Joliet session and an HFS session and can be read on both PCs and Macs.

- **ISO 9660:** Finally, I come to the oldest file system still in use. ISO 9660 has been around since the dawn of the CD-ROM, and virtually every operating system ever shipped can read it (including heretics like UNIX, Linux, Solaris, and OS/2 Warp). Unfortunately, this high level of compatibility is caused by a strict file and folder naming convention, so you don't find long filenames on an ISO 9660 disc. (You're back to the DOS standard of eight-character filenames and three-character extensions.) Also, you can store a far fewer number of files in each directory.

Which one should you use? Luckily, this question is one that basically decides itself. For a PC disc, I strongly recommend Joliet; Mac owners can rely on HFS. Folks recording cross-platform PC or Mac discs should use the Hybrid file system. Hollywood types recording DVD-Video discs should choose UDF. Finally, if you're looking for the widest possible distribution among the largest number of different computers and operating systems, go with the perennial favorite, ISO 9660.

The Right Way to Organize Files

Yes, Virginia, there is indeed a right way to add files to a data, mixed-mode, multisession, or UDF CD-ROM! Smart organization makes finding that certain data file for your tax return easier — which is especially useful if you're being audited tomorrow. No matter what sort of data you're recording, I urge you to heed this oft-repeated Mark's Maxim:

Take the time to think things through!™

Believe me. I have spent many years — numbering in the decades now — organizing my data. As an author and consultant, I can't afford to waste time digging through an entire binder of 250 discs, trying to figure out what was burned where. Therefore, heed my words when I say:

- **Use every character of those long filenames!** The ability to use long filenames is the primary reason why you should use the Joliet file system whenever possible. You may know now that the file named AHARCAKE you just burned is Aunt Harriet's fruitcake recipe, but will you remember that after 5 or 10 years?

- **Put your files in folders!** This problem is a common one with hard drives, too. Storing all your files in the root directory (like the C drive) results in the worst kind of anarchy (the computer kind!). Also, file systems such as ISO 9660 can handle only a certain number of files in any directory or folder, including the root directory. The solution is simple: Create new folders in the root directory of your CD layout and give the new arrivals logical names, and then organize the files within the folders (more on this in a second).

✔ **Use a logical file arrangement.** You can help yourself in years to come when you're searching for files by organizing them in a Spock-ian fashion: That is, stick files of the same type or files that relate to the same topic together in one folder. Or, if you have enough files and you have the time, you can do both with folder names like Pictures of Fluffy in 2002. Think of the fun you can have! (Okay, I need another Diet Coke.) Anyway, when you combine a folder arrangement like this with long filenames, you can suddenly locate that needle in a haystack — and you can still find it three years from now.

✔ **Use file-cataloging software.** Some shareware and commercial disc cataloging programs can store the names and locations of every file on a drive. These programs create indexed databases of each CD-ROM you record. With one of these utilities, searching for a single file among 20 of your personal library discs is as simple as using the Windows Search feature. Your operating system may also allow you to search an entire disc. For example, Mac OS 9.2 features Sherlock, and Mac OS X includes the powerful Find feature, as shown in see Figure 7-5. You can use both to search not only for filenames but also strings of text *inside* documents!

Figure 7-5:
I use Mac OS X to find everything but my socks.

Of course, you may not want to spend this kind of time if your disc holds two or three 200MB video clips and nothing else — but it sure helps when you have 300 files to store on one CD-ROM.

"Thumbnails? You're Kidding, Right?"

Not the human body kind of thumbnails! I mean the postage stamp-size pictures that represent larger JPEG, TIFF, and bitmap images stored inside a folder. (You may have seen thumbnails in Windows XP, which can be set to show image thumbnails within Windows Explorer.) When you use a program like Paint Shop Pro (www.jasc.com) that can generate these munchkins, you can build a catalog of thumbnails that make it easy to scan dozens of images in seconds (using the most sophisticated optical hardware ever designed, the Human Eye. . . patent pending, I'm sure). After you have found the right image, just double-click the thumbnail to load it. Figure 7-6 shows a screen chock-full of thumbnails that I'm searching through with Paint Shop Pro.

If you also want to catalog your other multimedia files — like sound files and video clips — you can use Jasc Media Center Plus at www.jasc.com. Like digital images, the multimedia thumbnails in this program allow you to preview your stuff by just clicking the icons.

No matter what program you use, the trick to remember is that you must generate the program's catalog and add it to the disc layout so that it can be recorded along with the rest of the material. (No sense in keeping the catalog file on your hard drive for 100 years, unless, of course, you use this disc every day.)

Figure 7-6:
Scanning
more than
100 images
takes only a
few seconds
with
thumbnails!

Converting Files for Fun and Profit

Before I end this chapter, here's a riddle for you: If you have burned a CD-ROM or DVD-ROM of photographs from your digital camera in JPEG format (which most cameras produce) and you're using a Macintosh, what have you done wrong? (Because this chapter is about convenience and ease of use, consider that a clue.)

Technically, the answer is "nothing" — until you try to use those images in many Macintosh applications. You see, some Mac programs that use graphics favor images in TIFF format. Of course, you can use an image editor like Photoshop to open those JPEG images and convert them to TIFF format each time you use them, but talk about a time-wasting hassle! In this case, you would have made a wise decision if you converted all those files to TIFF format before you recorded them so that you can simply pop the disc into your computer and load photos directly from it. (Don't worry if you didn't get that one — it was extra credit.)

With this example in mind, I want to devote this last section to format conversions: which common formats work best in what situations and which programs work best when converting files to other formats. The idea is twofold: You want your material in the form you use it most, and you also want that material to be recognizable and usable in years to come.

What exactly is a *format?* A computer programmer would tell you that a file format is an arrangement of data that corresponds to specific byte positions and data element lengths. (Whew. Thank goodness my days of writing COBOL are over.) We flesh-and-blood humans can simply think of a *format* as a language that's recognized by a program for storing and reading files. For example, although an image may look exactly the same when it's displayed in two different formats, one file may be 100K, and another may be 1MB! The difference in size is caused by the format, which determines the way the image data is saved.

You're likely to encounter four major species of formats when you're recording CDs:

- ✔ **Audio:** Without a doubt, the two most popular — and usable — audio formats for saving your recordings are MP3 and Windows WAV. Between the two, MP3 is probably the best choice because WAV files can reach colossal sizes when recording longer songs at higher-quality sampling rates. Also, Macintosh owners have far more support on their systems for MP3 than for WAV. To convert other sound formats to MP3, I use Musicmatch Jukebox Plus (www.musicmatch.com), as illustrated in Figure 7-7. You can download the basic version for free.

Figure 7-7:
Musicmatch
Jukebox
Plus
converts
audio
between
formats.

✔ **Video:** Digital video now generally resides in QuickTime MOV format, Microsoft AVI format, or MPEG format — and surprisingly enough, I'm again not recommending the Microsoft standard. Instead, I archive my video clips in MPEG format, which is recognized by just about every editor on the planet. You can be certain that future versions of your editor will be able to import your clips for new projects. For conversion, I use Adobe Premiere on the PC, which can import all these formats. More expensive commercial programs can handle a wider range of less popular formats, but because I use only the Big Three, Premiere works fine in my case.

✔ **Images:** For archival purposes, select JPEG, TIFF, or Windows Bitmap; the latter two don't use compression that degrades the image, so they offer better quality, but both TIFF and bitmap images are much larger than their JPEG counterparts. JPEG is recognized by most image editors (and because JPEG is the format of choice for Web pages, you have the advantage of being able to copy your archived images directly to your Web site). On the PC side, either Paint Shop Pro (from Jasc) or Adobe Photoshop does the conversion trick. On the Macintosh side, use Photoshop or the classic GraphicConverter from Lemke Software, at www.lemkesoft.de/en/index.htm (see Figure 7-8).

Don't forget that virus check!

As a final preparation before burning, I always run Norton AntiVirus (see the Downloads page at www.symantec.com) and check the contents of those folders that contain the files I have selected — especially for a disc I'm giving to someone else. Can you think of anything more antisocial than sending your friend a virus in a Word document or a program file?

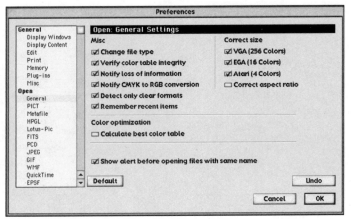

Figure 7-8:
Putting
Graphic
Converter
through
its paces
on the
Macintosh.

✔ **Documents:** I can't think of a better set of tools for importing, converting, and exporting all sorts of document formats than Microsoft Office
(www.microsoft.com). On both the PC and Macintosh, it can read most
of your ancient, hoary document formats for spreadsheets, word pro-
cessing files, presentations, and databases. For archival purposes, it's a
safe bet that saving your documents in one of the standard Microsoft
formats from the Office suite of applications is a good idea.

Part III

Hang On — Here We Go!

The 5th Wave   By Rich Tennant

JERRY AND LYLE ATTEMPT TO LOAD THE NEWEST VERSION OF "TOAST," CD-BURNING SOFTWARE

OK, I got the Sunbeam firewired to the iMac. Try putting the CD in the slot again.

In this part . . .

Are you ready to rock 'n' record, dude? In these chapters, you advance to recording typical audio CDs and data discs with Easy CD & DVD Creator 6 (for the PC) and Toast 6 Titanium (for the Mac). I also show you how to use Drag-to-Disc, a program that takes full advantage of the drag-and-drop convenience of Windows. Even *pie* never had it so easy.

Chapter 8

Taking Easy CD & DVD Creator for a Spin

. . . .

In This Chapter

▶ Recording data discs

▶ Recording audio CDs

▶ Copying an existing disc

▶ Using disc images

▶ Creating multisession CD-ROMs

▶ Erasing a rewriteable disc

. . . .

*I*t's time to crank up Easy CD & DVD Creator on your PC and find out how to make basic data discs and audio CDs! You can consider this chapter the bread and butter of optical recording: These types of discs are likely to make up 90 percent of the recordings burned by most PCs. First, I describe the basic steps for each procedure, and I close this chapter with two projects that illustrate specific tasks.

Interested in recording data and audio discs on a Macintosh? I fill in the details on recording with Toast in Chapter 9.

Recording Data: Putting Files on a Disc

The first disc I ever recorded was a data CD-ROM — ah, the memories! In fact, the first version of Easy CD & DVD Creator hadn't been released yet, and the primitive software I used was anything but automatic or easy to use. In fact, I burned a couple of useless coasters before I finally got everything to work.

Just about everything has changed for the better. Easy CD & DVD Creator shields you from as much of the drudge work of burning a disc as possible. Follow these steps to record a basic data disc with folders and files from your PC's hard drive:

1. **Load a blank disc into your recorder.**

   If you're using a CD-RW, DVD-RW, DVD+RW, or DVD-RAM, it should be formatted (see the section "Erasing a Rewriteable Disc," later in this chapter). Easy CD & DVD Creator detects that you have loaded a blank disc and automatically displays the rather sexy-looking Home window (as shown in Figure 8-1).

Figure 8-1:
Hey, the Home window almost looks like a Macintosh program!

   To run the Home window from the Start menu, choose Start⇨All Programs⇨Roxio Easy CD and DVD Creator 6⇨Home.

2. **Click the funky button marked Creator Classic.**

   The Home program then runs Creator Classic, which is the main recording application within Easy CD & DVD Creator 6.

3. **Choose File⇨New Project⇨Data Disc.**

   Easy CD & DVD Creator opens an empty data disc layout, like the one shown in Figure 8-2.

   If you would rather run Creator Classic directly from the Start menu, choose Start⇨All Programs⇨Roxio Easy CD and DVD Creator 6⇨ Creator Classic.

Figure 8-2:
An empty
data disc
layout, just
waiting
for your
selections.

See the folder tree that fills the top portion of the window? It operates just like Windows Explorer, and you use it to select the folders and files to include in your layout.

4. **To open a folder and display the contents, double-click it; to move up to the preceding directory, click the Up One Level button (which looks like a folder with an up arrow on it).**

You can also use the Select source drop-down list box to navigate to a specific drive or top-level folder on your system. Highlight a folder or file that you want to add by clicking once on the name — you can highlight several by holding down the Ctrl key while you click.

5. **After you have highlighted the folders and files that you want to add in the current directory, click the Add to Project button in the center of the screen.**

Alternatively, you can click and hold the mouse to drag the selected icons from the Explorer tree to the project layout display that fills the bottom half of the window. Oh, and if you look at the bottom of the window, you see a truly nifty bar display that tells you how many megabytes you have used in your layout and how much space remains — programs like this one make me proud to be a technonerd. To switch between different CD and DVD capacities, click the Select Disc Size button, which is conveniently placed to the left of the bar display.

The great file and folder hunt

"I *know* I put that file somewhere on this drive!" Brothers and sisters, I feel your pain — searching for one document in the midst of 50 directories and 30,000 files is not my idea of a fun way to spend an afternoon. If you agree, click the Find Files or Folders button (the button with the folder and the magnifying glass) next to the Select Source Files list box to call for help from Easy CD & DVD Creator.

First, choose the drive that you want to search by clicking the Look In drop-down list box. (Boy, those Windows programmers in Redmond sure know how to label their fields.) Then, select your search criteria:

The filename: Even if you know only a part of the filename, you can enter it in the Named field. (Don't forget to enable the Include Subfolders check box if you want to search the folders below the specified location.)

A word or phrase in a file: Search for all files containing a certain string of text by entering the text in the Containing Text field.

The file's time and date stamp: Click the When Was It Modified tab. You can specify a search for files created or modified within the last week, month or year. Alternatively, click Specify Dates and type the beginning and ending dates in the From and To fields.

The size of the file: Click the What size is it tab and choose its minimum or maximum size. You can select one of the predefined sizes (less than 100K, less than 1MB or more than 1MB), or click Specify size in K and type the target file size yourself.

When you're ready to go, click Search. Good luck, Mighty Hunter!

6. **If necessary, repeat Steps 4 and 5 with other folders until all the files that you want added appear in the layout display (as shown in Figure 8-3).**

    You can drag and drop in the project layout display, too, so it's easy to arrange files in different folders or in the root directory of the disc if necessary.

    Arrgh! It never fails: You're almost finished designing your project layout, and your mom calls (either on the phone, or from the kitchen). Luckily, you can save your current project within Easy CD & DVD Creator. Choose File⇨Save Project List, enter a filename in the File Name field, and click Save. (To copy the current project under another name, choose File⇨ Save Project List As instead.) When you're ready to continue with your project, run Easy CD & DVD Creator, choose File⇨Open CD Project; highlight the project file and click Open to load it.

    You probably won't be satisfied with a name like 010803_0203 for your disc — I don't blame you! Therefore, why not change it? Click once on the disc name, and then change the name just like you would rename a file on the Windows desktop. Remember that you are limited to a certain number of letters, depending on the file system you're using, so keep your name short.

Figure 8-3:
The Data
Disc project
layout is
rapidly
filling up.

7. **Everything squared and ready? Houston, you're go for recording! Click the Big Orange Disc-on-Fire Button in the lower-right corner of the window.**

   The program presents the Record Setup dialog box you see in Figure 8-4. For a simple data disc, the program's default hardware settings should work just fine.

8. **Check to make sure that the correct drive and recording speed are listed.**

9. **If you want to be extra careful, you can click the Details button to display the advanced settings, and then enable the Test and Record radio button. Although it takes twice as long, Easy CD & DVD Creator performs a test recording first, and if the test is successful, you can perform the recording.**

   If a problem occurs, you save a blank disc from becoming a coaster. After you have become comfortable with your recorder, however, I recommend that you pick Record and press onward.

10. **You can make more than one copy of your disc by specifying the number in the Number of Copies field.**

How do you "test" a CD-R?

"Hang on, there, Mark — you said that I could use a CD-R, DVD-R, or DVD+R only once. How can my recorder test the disc without messing it up?"

Easy! If you remember my discussion of lasers in Chapter 1, you remember that your recorder can toggle between two power levels; when you test a layout, your recorder acts like it's burning the disc, when in fact the laser is toggled to the lower power setting. At this lower setting, the beam doesn't affect the dye layer (or the crystalline layer, if you're using a rewriteable disc).

The result is a safe test: Easy CD & DVD Creator can still detect whether it would encounter an error while recording, but if errors are detected, you don't lose your blank disc!

Figure 8-4:
Don't let these settings scare you — this is a walk in the park!

11. **If you can enable the Buffer Underrun Prevention check box, do so with all haste — this action turns on your drive's support for burn-proof recording.**

12. **If you're recording in Track-at-Once mode, you can choose one of these options:**

   • **Don't Finalize Session:** Leaves the disc open so that you can record more data later without creating a multisession disc. However, until you finalize either the session or the disc, you can read this disc only in your recorder. If this field is grayed out, either your drive or the file system that you chose doesn't support this option.

- **Finalize Session, Don't Finalize Disc:** Closes the current session so that the disc can be read in any CD-ROM or DVD-ROM drive; however, the disc itself is not finalized, so you can write additional sessions and create a multisession disc.

- **Finalize Disc:** The entire disc is closed, so you can't write any further sessions. (You can consider it write-protecting the disc.) I typically use this option if I'm recording in Track-at-Once mode.

13. **Click OK to start the wheels turning!**

If you used the Windows Start menu method of running the Home window and you haven't already loaded a blank disc in the recorder, the program automatically ejects the tray and demands that you feed it one.

The Burn Disc Progress dialog box appears, as shown in Figure 8-5, and you can watch the fun. After the disc has been recorded, you can optionally run Label Creator or just quit and try out your new toy.

Congratulations! You're the proud creator of a brand-new data disc.

Figure 8-5:
This is it,
Bucko!
You're
burnin'!

Recording Your Music

Remember to rip and record only what you've bought, or what's legally available on the Internet. Likewise, don't copy commercial software and blithely hand it over to those who didn't pay a penny for it. I won't turn into a lawyer and start talking unintelligible legalese, but honor the copyrights of the musicians and software developers that worked the long hours. Please.

These days, I find myself recording audio CDs primarily from MP3 files — however, Easy CD & DVD Creator can also

✔ Copy both individual tracks from existing CDs (in a process sweetly called *ripping*).

✔ Copy an entire existing audio CD. (Find out more on this in the next section, where I show you how to clone things with CD Copier.)

With your permission, then, I show you how to create the Ultimate Motorhead Mix CD (or, if you prefer, the Absolute Best of Alvin and the Chipmunks):

1. **Load a blank disc into your recorder, which automatically displays the Home screen.**

   Yes, I'm saying it again: *Do not use a CD-RW when recording a standard audio CD for use in a stereo system unless the player is designed to play CD-RWs!* Are you getting tired of that sentence yet? (How about these italicized sentences?) Anyway, you can't say that I didn't warn you.

2. **Click the Creator Classic button in the Home window.**

3. **Choose File⇨New Project⇨Music CD.**

   If you'd rather create an MP3 music CD (and your audio CD player supports MP3 music discs), choose File⇨New Project⇨MP3 Player Disc instead. You can then add up to 700MB of MP3 files from your hard drive because an MP3 music disc is actually a data disc (not a true audio CD). MP3 music discs store MP3 songs in their native format, so you can get several hours of listening pleasure on a single CD! (Remember, however, that you can't play an MP3 music disc in an audio CD player that doesn't support the format . . . you hear absolutely zilch.)

4. **Now it's time to add tracks from the Easy CD & DVD Creator screen shown in Figure 8-6. You can select one of these options:**

   • **Add MP3, WAV, or WMF files:** Use Explorer view in the upper-left half of the screen to locate folders where your audio files are stored.

   • **Rip tracks from another CD:** Load a disc into either your CD-ROM or DVD-ROM drive or your recorder and then select that drive from the Select Source drop-down list box to display the tracks. To load other tracks from other audio CDs, repeat the process.

   If you don't have a track listing for the disc you have loaded, just double-click on a track in Explorer view in the upper-right half of the screen. Easy CD & DVD Creator displays the Preview player, and you can listen to the track before you add it to your layout.

5. **Click once on each track that you want to add.**

   To choose more than one track from the same source, hold down the Ctrl key as you select each track name.

Figure 8-6:
New music
CDs get
their start
on this Easy
CD & DVD
Creator
screen.

6. **After you have selected your tracks from the source folder or disc, click the Add to Project button (which looks like an arrow pointing down) in the center of the window to add them to your project layout. (Alternatively, you can drag the music files from the Explorer view and drop them on the layout at the bottom of the screen.)**

7. **Continue repeating Steps 4 through 6 until your track layout is complete — or until you have packed every second of your blank disc!**

    You can tell how much time you have used on your disc by checking the Estimated Time bar at the bottom of the screen; it tells you how much time the current track list needs and the remaining time you can fill on both a 74-minute and 80-minute CD-R.

8. **Arrange the tracks in your layout as you like by clicking a track name to highlight it and dragging it to the new position in the track list.**

9. **Although it's not necessary, I recommend that you enter both a name for your new disc in the New Disc Title field and the artist's name in the Artist Name field.**

    Need to change or add a name for a track? Just click the entry to highlight it and click again to edit the New Disc Title field.

10. **Ready to burn those hip 1s and 0s (zeros)? Click the Big Orange Disc-on-Fire Button at the right lower corner of the window.**

    If you're loading tracks from an audio CD, Easy CD & DVD Creator prompts you to load the pesky thing when it's necessary so that the tracks can be copied and converted.

    The program displays the Record Setup dialog box.

11. **If necessary, select your recorder and select the fastest possible recording speed.**

12. **You can clone multiple copies of your new music disc by clicking the arrows next to the Number of Copies field.**

13. **Enable the Buffer Underrun Protection check box if your drive supports burnproof recording.**

14. **To add a little technowow touch to your new audio CD, enable the Write CD-Text check box!**

    Many audio CD players (and most CD player programs for your computer) display CD-Text while the disc is playing, which includes the disc name, artist name, and each track name.

15. **If your recorder supports Disc-at-Once mode, select it (to prevent clicks between tracks). Otherwise, choose Track-at-Once mode and choose the Finalize Disc option.**

16. **Click OK, you music-producing mogul! If your recorder is empty, Easy CD & DVD Creator yells for you to load a blank disc.**

    The program displays the Burn Disc Progress dialog box (which has already popped up in Figure 8-5), allowing you to monitor the 1s and 0s (zeros) as they're shoveled into the furnace and onto your disc. When the recording is done, you have the choice of running Label Creator if you want to print a fancy-looking label or a set of jewel box inserts.

Time to grab your headphones and jam to your latest creation!

Copying a Disc

In this section, I describe how you can copy an existing data disc (both CD-ROMs and unprotected DVD-ROMs) or an audio CD. Rather than take the time to crank up Easy CD & DVD Creator, Roxio provides you with a separate program named Disc Copier; it can clone a disc by using just the recorder. If you're lucky enough to have either a read-only CD-ROM or DVD-ROM drive or a second recorder in the same system, you can even copy drive-to-drive and whip out a copy in record time!

Follow these steps to copy a disc:

1. **Choose Start➪All Programs➪Easy CD and DVD Creator 6➪Disc Copier to display what's shown in Figure 8-7.**

Figure 8-7:
You're on
the road to
Duplication
City with
Disc Copier.

2. **Click the Source drop-down list box and select the drive in which you have loaded the disc that you want to copy.**

   It can be any drive on your system that can read a disc, including your recorder.

3. **Click the Destination drop-down list box and select the recorder that will burn the disc.**

   Remember that it can be the same as the Source drive.

4. **Checking the advanced settings (see Figure 8-8) before you begin the copy is a good idea, so click the Options button.**

5. **You can select the Test, Test then Copy, or Copy option. Because I'm familiar with my equipment, I skip any testing and jump right to the real thing. However, Test then Copy does the trick as well (it just takes twice as long), and you won't lose a blank disc if something is SNAFU.**

6. **If you want more than one copy of the original disc, click the arrows next to the Number of Copies field and select, well, the number of copies!**

7. **Using the Buffer Underrun Prevention feature (or burnproof, as we know it) whenever possible is a good idea, so enable the Buffer Underrun Prevention check box if your drive supports it.**

8. **Click the Big Orange Disc-on-Fire Button at the lower-right corner of the window to unleash the fearsome power of your laser, and be prepared to load a blank disc if you're using one drive to copy.**

Figure 8-8:
Preparing to
tweak Disc
Copier.

Using a Disc Image

From time to time, you may find that you need multiple copies of a disc, but you don't want to produce them all at one time. Perhaps the data will change within a few weeks or you're preparing discs for sale or distribution, but you don't know how many copies you need.

This situation is where a *disc image* comes in handy. Think of it as a complete CD or DVD saved as a single file to your hard drive. In fact, you can even create a disc image for later burning without a recorder! I know that sounds screwy, but when you're on the road with your laptop or you're at the office and you don't have your external recorder with you, you can create a disc image file instead. After your computer and external recorder are reunited, recording that disc is a snap.

However, you have to look at the downside: The disc image takes up all the space of its optical sibling, so each disc image you save on your hard drive takes up the space the data occupies on the recorded disc. Therefore, saving anywhere from 800MB to 5GB of free space on your drive (depending on the type of disc you're burning) is a good idea if you think that you need to create a disc image.

Follow these steps to create a disc image with Easy CD & DVD Creator:

1. **Choose Start➪All Programs➪Roxio Easy CD and DVD Creator 6➪ Creator Classic. (Alternatively, you can use the Home window, as I demonstrate earlier in this chapter.)**

2. **Choose File➪New Project and choose the type of disc you need from the pop-up submenu.**

3. **Build your project layout as you normally would.**

4. **Choose File➪Create Disc Image, which opens the Create Disc Image File dialog box that you see in Figure 8-9.**

Figure 8-9:
Choosing a moniker and a location for your disc image.

5. **Navigate to the folder on your hard drive where the image is saved, type a name for your image file, and then click Save.**

Sit back and watch the fun as the disc image is recorded. The image filename carries an ISO extension.

Later, when you're ready to record the disc, the process is just as easy:

1. **Choose Start➪All Programs➪Roxio Easy CD and DVD Creator 6➪ Creator Classic to run the program.**

2. **Choose File➪Record Disc.**

   The Record Disc from Image File dialog box appears, as shown in Figure 8-10.

3. **Navigate to the location of the disc image that you want to record. Highlight it and click Open.**

4. **Make any settings changes necessary (as I show you earlier in this chapter) and click OK.**

5. **Load a blank disc, and the recorder does its stuff.**

Figure 8-10:
Selecting an
existing disc
image to
record.

Using Multisession Discs

As I mention in Chapter 2 of this book, multisession discs have fallen out of favor with the arrival of the UDF format (also called packet writing). Both allow you to record a disc, use it, and then record additional information on it. With a UDF disc, however, you get the same versatility without the extra twists and turns of multisession recording. For example, you don't have to run Easy CD & DVD Creator to record another session, and you don't need a separate session-selection program (which allows you to choose which volume you're going to read).

However, I'm a thorough guy, and you may someday have to make a multi-session disc for some specific application — therefore, allow me to cover multisession recording in this section.

Keep in mind that not all drives on the planet can read multisession discs! Use them only when a standard single-session CD-ROM doesn't do the trick.

Two different types of multisession discs exist, and Creator Classic can burn them both:

- ✔ **Incremental:** Use an incremental multisession disc when you know that you want to add data to an existing session later. As you can see in Figure 8-11, successive sessions can add material or "delete" existing material by overwriting it. (Sorry, Charlie, it doesn't mean that you get that space back — your drive simply can't read it any longer.) Because the data in the preceding session is imported into the new one, you don't need a session-selection program. Your drive simply reads the latest session that you burned.

- ✔ **Multivolume:** In a multivolume multisession disc (See Figure 8-12), all the sessions are kept chaste and separate, and they can't be updated like the data on an incremental disc. You need a session-selection program to switch from one volume to another (and you can read from only one session at a time).

Session 2 contains all the data in Session 1 as well. Duplicate files and directories from previous sessions are overwritten.

ABC	DEF	12345	6789	Blue	Green	Becky	Huck
Session 2							

Recorded data added: DEF, 6789, Green, and Huck.

ABC		12345		Blue		Becky	
Session 1							

Figure 8-11: Use an incremental multisession disc to update things.

Data you've deleted from the previous layout is not included in the new incremental session; although it still exists in Session 1, you can't access it.

ABC	DEF	12345	6789		Green	Becky	Huck
Session 2							

Recorded data added: DEF, 6789, Green, and Huck.
Data to be deleted: Blue.

ABC		12345		Blue		Becky	
Session 1							

Figure 8-12: Never do the sessions on a multivolume multisession disc intermingle!

Session 2 is totally separate from Session 1 — both can be accessed, and no data is overwritten.

	DEF		6789		Green		Huck
Session 2							

Recorded data added: DEF, 6789, Green, and Huck.

ABC		12345		Blue		Becky	
Session 1							

To burn an incremental multisession disc, make sure that you record the first session on the disc by using the Joliet file system, and select these options on the Record Setup dialog box:

- ✔ **The Track-at-Once recording method**

- ✔ **The Finalize Session, Don't Finalize Disc option** (creates a first session, but doesn't close the disc permanently)

When you're ready to record again, follow these steps:

1. **Choose Start⇨All Programs⇨Roxio Easy CD and DVD Creator 6⇨ Creator Classic to run the program.**

2. **Load the original disc in your recorder.**

3. **Choose File⇨New Project⇨Data Disc.**

4. **Add files to the layout as you normally would, and the data in the first session is automatically displayed.**

5. **Finish your recording as usual.**

    When Creator Classic displays the Record Setup dialog box, remember to select the Finalize Session, Don't Finalize Disc option if you want to update the session again in the future! If you're all done (and you're *sure* about that), I recommend that you click the Finalize the Disc radio button.

Erasing a Rewriteable Disc

After you have finished with a CD-RW, DVD-RW, DVD+RW, or DVD-RAM, do you simply chuck it in the nearest wastebasket? No! Instead, you can erase the entire disc at one time (you have no way to erase only part of the disc — it's either all or nothing) and use it all over again.

To erase a rewriteable disc with Easy CD & DVD Creator:

1. **Load the offending rewriteable disc into your recorder.**

2. **Click on the Select source drop-down list box and choose your recorder.**

3. **Click the Disc menu and choose Erase Disc, which displays the dialog box shown in Figure 8-13.**

Figure 8-13: Is that a quick or full disc erasure?

You can choose a quick erase or a full erase. I agree with the good folks at Roxio and recommend a quick erase in most cases.

When do you use the Full Erase option? I guess that sometimes you want to be absolutely sure! However, if you're trying to record by using a rewriteable disc and Easy CD & DVD Creator reports errors with the disc's formatting or TOC (table of contents) information, you probably have to erase the disc to make it usable again. This can happen if a recording session is interrupted by a power failure or if Easy CD & DVD Creator should — perish the thought — crash on you.

Click Start to begin the process — and take a break for a soda or a cup of java if you have selected the Full Erase option.

Project: Developing MP3 Fever

Friends, I have a hankerin' to hear the King — that's right, Elvis Aron Presley himself. The trouble is, I have all my Elvis songs in MP3 format on my hard drive and I want to listen to them in my '64 Cadillac's audio CD player! If you're in the same boat, you have come to the right project: burning a *Best of Elvis* audio CD. (And yes, neighbors, I own the original commercial CDs for the music that I use in this project! I just ripped the tracks into MP3 format for this demonstration.)

1. **Choose Start⇨All Programs⇨Roxio Easy CD and DVD Creator 6⇨ Home.**

2. **Click the Creator Classic button in the Home window.**

3. **Choose File⇨New Project⇨Music CD.**

4. **Click the Select source drop-down list box and select the drive where your MP3 files are living. Use Explorer view in the upper-left half of the screen to navigate to the right folder.**

5. **Hold down the Ctrl key and, in the right pane of the Explorer view, click the MP3 files that you want to add.**

   As you can see in Figure 8-14, I have chosen six songs by Elvis from an entire folder of MP3 files.

6. **Click the Add to Project button in the center of the screen — it looks like an arrow pointing down. Figure 8-15 shows the tracks as they appear in the bottom window.**

Figure 8-14:
Man, that's some great music — I pick only the best.

Figure 8-15:
The track list is taking shape.

7. **If you want to add songs from another folder, repeat Steps 4 through 6.**

   Personally, I think that these are the King's best songs, so let me stop here. As you can tell by the bar display at the bottom of the screen, these tracks take up about 13 minutes and 27 seconds, and I have about 66 minutes and 31 seconds of additional space on an 80-minute blank disc.

8. **You can click and drag the track names to rearrange them. I want my disc to start out with "Jailhouse Rock," so I click and drag the entry from Slot 5 to Slot 1.**

9. **Click in the New Disc Title field and enter a name for your disc.**

10. **Click in the Artist Name field and enter the name of the performer or band.**

11. **As you can see in Figure 8-16, the disc layout is ready to record, so click the Big Orange Disc-on-Fire Button.**

    The Record Disc dialog box appears.

12. **I need only one copy of this disc, so I leave the Number of Copies field set to 1.**

Figure 8-16:
Everything is set to record.

13. Even if your audio CD player doesn't display CD-Text, you may encounter one in the future. Therefore, I always recommend that you enable the Write CD-Text check box for an audio CD.

14. My recorder supports Disc-at-Once recording, so I definitely want to select the Disc-at-Once option. (If this field is grayed out, your recorder doesn't offer Disc-at-Once — use Track-at-Once mode with the Finalize Disc option instead.)

15. Click OK to start the wheels turning and then load a blank disc.

16. When the recording is finished, you can run Label Creator (for help, turn to Chapter 14). Otherwise, eject your disc and enjoy your Elvis!

Project: Archiving Digital Photographs

Got a number of family photos you have taken with your digital camera? Why not burn them to a data CD-ROM and free up that hard drive space for other programs? Here's how you can burn a basic archive of digital images:

1. Choose Start⇨All Programs⇨Roxio Easy CD and DVD Creator 6⇨ Creator Classic.

2. Choose File⇨New Project⇨Data Disc.

3. Click the Select Source drop-down list box and navigate to the drive where your images are stored. To move to another folder, use Explorer view in the upper-left half of the screen.

4. Click one or more filenames while you hold down the Ctrl key.

5. Click the Add to Project button in the center of the screen — that's the arrow pointing down — or drag the highlighted files to the bottom window. As you can see in Figure 8-17, my images now appear in the data project layout.

6. To select more images, just repeat Steps 4 through 6 until you have added all the photos that you want (or, of course, until the disc is full). Use the bar display at the bottom of the screen to keep track of how much space remains.

7. To create a new folder in your project layout, right-click on the disc title in the Layout window in the lower-left corner and choose New Folder from the pop-up menu. The new folder appears with the name highlighted; type a name for the new folder and press Enter to save it. To move images in and out of folders, click and drag the filenames wherever you want them.

   In this example, I have created a folder named Our Dogs, and I have dragged three images into it.

Figure 8-17:
Adding
photographs
to a data
CD-ROM
layout.

8. **Click the disc title to highlight it and click it again to type a new name — I used Photos 2004 for this disc.**

9. **The final disc layout appears in Figure 8-18. Click the Big Orange Disc-on-Fire Button!**

   The Record Disc dialog box appears.

10. **If you don't want multiple copies, leave the Number of Copies field set to 1.**

11. **Select the Disc-at-Once option if you can; if not, use Track-at-Once mode with the Finalize Disc option.**

12. **Click OK to start the wheels turning and then load a blank disc.**

13. **When the recording is finished, you can run Label Creator (for help, turn to Chapter 14); otherwise, eject your disc and hand your photo disc to Grandma!**

Because you finalized this disc, you can't write to it again. If your drive supports packet writing, Chapter 10 shows how to create a UDF disc that you can add files to in the future.

Figure 8-18:
Everything
is set to
record.

Chapter 9

A Step-by-Step Guide to ... Toast?

I don't even own a toaster, but I use my Toast to burn all the time! (Try explaining that to your friends.) In the Macintosh world, however, that sentence makes perfect sense. Compared to Easy CD & DVD Creator, Toast 6 Titanium for the Macintosh (from Roxio) is a lean, mean, and exceptionally attractive recording machine. As you may guess, the program's menu system and appearance are radically different from its Windows sibling, and it has a number of Mac-specific features. (If you're running Mac OS 9.2, you're out of luck. Toast 6 Titanium runs only under Mac OS X — progress marches on.)

In this chapter, you take a look at both the basics of recording and many of the advanced options available within Toast.

Putting Files on a Disc

Toast can create two different types of Hierarchical File System (HFS) discs:

✔ **Mac OS Standard CD:** If your disc will be used on older Macs using System 7 or earlier — those before Mac OS 8.1 — you should use this standard disc.

✔ **Mac OS Extended CD:** Macs running Mac OS 8.1 or later can take advantage of the Extended file system, which allows faster performance and provides a bit more room on the disc for your data.

Therefore, if compatibility is in question, always use the Mac OS Standard CD version of HFS because both older and newer Macintosh operating systems can read it. (Also, as you see later in this chapter, some types of discs require the Mac OS Standard CD file system.)

To record a simple data disc with files from your Macintosh's hard drive:

1. **Double-click the Toast icon on the desktop to launch the program and display the stylish Toast screen shown in Figure 9-1. (Talk about classy!)**

Figure 9-1:
Didn't I tell you that Toast is a spiffy program?

The Record button

2. **Click the Data tab at the top of the screen.**

3. **To select which type of data disc you want to record, click the Advanced button on the Disc Options drawer (in the upper-left).**

   Toast displays the different types of discs that you can record in the selected category. For a basic Macintosh-only data disc, you should enable the Mac Only option. By default, Toast records a Mac OS Extended CD; to record a Standard HFS CD, click the HFS Standard check box to enable it.

   To hide or display the Disc Options drawer, click the button to the left of the Data tab. (In Figure 9-1, it appears to the left of the words "Mac Only" — in the main Toast screen, not in the Disc Options drawer.)

4. **Drag and drop files and folders from the Finder window into the Toast main window.**

Note that the program keeps track of both the number of files in your layout and the approximate amount of space that it uses on the disc. (Check out that nifty gas gauge bar graph that encircles the Record button!) You can toggle between CD and DVD displays on the usage bar graph display by clicking the CD or DVD button next to the Record button.

5. **Repeat Step 4 until you have added all your files and folders or until the disc layout is filled to capacity.**

   You can click and drag filenames to move them into and out of folders, just as you would in the Mac OS X Finder window when you're using List view. To add a new folder, highlight the parent folder (or the CD itself) and click the New Folder button at the bottom of the screen. To remove a file or folder — just from the layout, mind you, *not* from your drive — highlight the unwanted item and click Remove at the bottom of the screen. Figure 9-2 illustrates a typical disc layout that I have created on my system.

Figure 9-2:
Ready to
record with
Toast!

6. **Load a blank CD into your recorder.**

7. **Click the Big Red Record Button.**

8. **The Record dialog box appears, as shown in Figure 9-3.**

   If you need more than one copy of the disc, click in the Number of Copies field and type the desired number. By default, Toast selects the highest recording speed that your drive supports.

Basic Advanced HI-dt-st RW/DVD GCC-4120B

Recorder: HI-dt-st RW/DVD GCC-4120B

Status: CD — Not writable

Write Speed: Best

Number of Copies: 1

Eject   Cancel   Record

Figure 9-3:
To write one
copy or a
thousand —
that is the
question.

9. **Click the Advanced button at the top of the dialog box.**

Here, you determine whether you want to finalize (or close) the disc:

- To write a single session and leave the disc open for later recordings, make sure the Close Disc check box is disabled. (This action is the same as selecting the Finalize Session, Don't Finalize CD setting in Easy CD & DVD Creator.) You can read the disc in your Mac's CD-ROM drive, but you can create a multisession disc by using this disc in the future.

- Enable the Close Disc check box to write the session and finalize the disc so that it can't be written to again. This action corresponds to selecting the Finalize CD setting in Easy CD & DVD Creator.

You can choose to test the recording by enabling the Simulation Mode check box, but note that this selection does not automatically record the disc if the test completes successfully.

If your Mac's recorder supports burnproof recording — and all Macs made in the last three years or so do — make sure that you enable the Buffer Underrun Prevention check box. With Buffer Underrun Prevention turned on, you can continue to use your Mac while it's burning without fear of ruining the disc. *Sassy!*

10. **Click Record.**

While recording, Toast displays a progress bar. After the recording is complete, the program automatically verifies the finished disc against the original files on your hard drive. Because this process takes several minutes, you have the option of ejecting the disc immediately and skipping the verification step.

Recording an Audio CD

Although Apple has released programs like iTunes that can burn audio discs, I still prefer to record audio CDs on the Macintosh with Toast; it gives more choices and more control over the finished disc. To record an audio CD from files on your hard drive and existing audio CDs, follow these steps:

1. **Double-click the Toast icon on the desktop to launch the program.**

2. **Click the Audio tab at the top of the screen.**

3. **Add tracks in either of two ways:**

   - **Add existing sound files you have already saved to your hard drive:** For example, drag AIFF or MP3 files to your layout by dragging the files into the Toast window.

   - **Add tracks from an existing audio CD by loading it into your CD-ROM drive and double-clicking the disc's icon on the desktop to display the track icons:** Drag the desired track icons from the audio CD window into the Toast window. (These tracks have a tiny CD icon to indicate they're being ripped from an existing audio CD.)

   If you plan to copy the majority of tracks from an existing CD, just drag the entire disc icon to the Toast window, and you can load all the tracks at one time.

4. **To create an MP3 music disc with the MP3 files you've added, enable the MP3 Disc option in the Disc Options drawer.**

   If the Disc Options drawer is hidden, click the button to the left of the Data tab. Naturally, you can add only MP3 files to an MP3 music disc project.

5. **You can rearrange the tracks in any order you want by dragging them to their new positions. To rename a track, click on the track name to highlight it and click again to open an edit box. Type the new name. To hear a track, highlight the track name and click the eminently familiar-looking Play button at the bottom of the screen. To remove a track, select the offending track and click Remove. Finally, you can change the length of the pause before a track by clicking the current value — by default, it's two seconds — and choosing a new value from the menu.**

   If you're using files from an existing audio CD and you only have one optical drive on your Mac system, you have to *export* (a more dignified word for rip) any tracks you're copying from other discs before you record your new audio CD. This export step eliminates any possible problems that your drive may encounter if you try recording directly from the discs themselves.

6. **Highlight each track you have added from another disc and click the Export button at the lower-left of the Toast window.**

   Toast displays a Save As dialog box that allows you to pick the folder where the extracted audio is saved. The tracks are saved as AIFF files.

7. **Load a blank CD-R into your recorder.**

8. **Click the Big Red Record Button, which displays our old friend the Record dialog box.**

9. **For a standard audio CD, click the Advanced button and make sure that the Close Disc and DAO (short for Disc-at-Once) options are both enabled.**

10. **Click Record.**

I swear that this is the last time I say this — it really is, folks — *do not use a CD-RW when recording a standard audio CD unless you're sure that the audio CD player supports rewriteable media!* Using a CD-RW in an older audio CD player that doesn't support rewriteable media will likely result in stark silence (and a blinking error message from your CD player). If you do actually hear anything, your CD player is probably producing something that sounds like an enraged moose. (And yes, for you Monty Python fans, a moose once bit my sister. . . .)

After your audio CD has been recorded, you can regain hard disk space by deleting the extracted audio tracks you saved. Or, if the notion is attractive to you, keep them for another recording, or use them with your iPod.

Ooh! It's a Hybrid!

Next, turn your attention to an important type of disc that's easily recorded with Toast: a PC/Macintosh hybrid disc that can be read on both systems. The Mac portion of the disc uses the HFS file system, and the PC portion uses either Joliet or ISO 9660. This disc type is a perfect way to distribute files and programs to a wide audience, especially games, educational material, clip-art libraries, multimedia files, and fonts (all of which are often shared between PCs and Macs).

Note that unless you're running special software, only the native format portion of the disc can be read by either operating system. (Geez, I need a soda. In plain English: The Macintosh can read only the Mac information on the disc, and the PC can read only the PC portion. Sorry about that.)

To create a hybrid disc, follow these steps:

1. **Gather the Mac-only files you want to record and move them to a separate volume (either a separate hard drive partition or a removable disk, like a Zip disk or a temporary partition, which I show you how to create in the next section).**

   If you have any files that should be visible on both Macs and PCs, copy them to the volume as well.

2. **Double-click the Toast icon on the desktop to launch the program.**

3. **Click the Data button at the top of the screen.**

4. **Click the Advanced button in the Disc Options drawer, and then select the Custom Hybrid option. Toast displays the screen shown in Figure 9-4.**

Figure 9-4:
The beginnings of a Mac/PC hybrid disc.

If you're just looking for a single disc offering one set of files that both types of computers can read, eschew the Custom Hybrid format: Instead, click the Basic button on the Disc Options drawer and choose the Mac & PC option. This format creates a simple cross-platform disc that can be read on both Macs and PCs. A Mac & PC format disc is only suitable for sharing simple data files. Unlike a true hybrid disc, a Mac & PC format disc doesn't support any operating system specific features for either type of computer.

5. **Click the Select Mac button.**

6. **From the Select Volume dialog box, click the volume that you created in Step 1 in the list and enable the Optimize on-the-Fly check box. Click OK to return to the main screen.**

7. **Click the Select ISO button to display the ISO 9660 dialog box, as shown in Figure 9-5.**

Figure 9-5:
Yes, Mac folks can communicate with PC folks — sometimes.

8. **Drag and drop to the ISO 9660 dialog box the files that should be read on the PC.**

   You can click on the CD title or a folder name to rename it — files are automatically renamed to conform to the ISO standard. Click the New Folder button to add a new folder, and feel free to drag files and folders around to rearrange your ISO layout.

9. **After you're finished adding ISO files, click the Settings tab. From the Naming drop-down list box, select Joliet (MS-DOS + Windows), which allows long filenames. Click Done.**

10. **Okay, let's burn this puppy! Choose File⇨Save As Disc Image. Toast prompts you for a location to save the image file. (I generally pick the desktop because it's easy to find.) Click Save to create the image.**

11. **Click the Copy button at the top of the screen. This time, select the Image File button from the Disc Options drawer.**

12. **Click the Select button, choose the image you created in Step 10, and click Open.**

13. **Load a blank disc into your recorder.**

14. **Click the Big Red Record Button.**

Mounting an image (and not on the wall)

From time to time, you may want to take advantage of the absolutely nifty ability to mount a disc image on the Mac OS 9.2/X desktop, just like it was a gen-u-wine piece of CD-ROM hardware. You can open the mounted disc and even run programs and load files from it. Your Mac applications can't tell the difference, and you don't have to dig through dozens of CDs to find the one that holds the files you need. (You are likely to use a mounted disc image only for data discs because you can listen to audio tracks just by extracting them as AIFF or MP3 files.) As long as you have the available hard drive territory, you can keep a disc image on tap for any contingency.

To create a disc image, build your data CD layout as usual, as I describe earlier in this chapter. (Make sure that you have at least 800MB or 900MB of free hard drive space if your image will reflect a full disc.) Then, rather than burn the layout, choose File⇨Save As Disc Image. From the Save Disc Image As dialog box, click on the target folder in the list to select it, type a new name (if necessary), and click Save. Toast acts just as though it's writing to a disc; when it's done, however, you have a brand-spanking-new disc image file.

To mount the file, double-click it. Toast automatically launches and presents you with two buttons: Select and Mount. Click Mount, and you're ready to go. (After the volume icon appears on the desktop, you can quit Toast.) The mounted volume stays on your desktop until you reboot your Macintosh or drag the volume icon to the Trash. Enjoy!

15. Click the Advanced button and make sure that the Close Disc option is enabled.

16. Click Record to begin the fun.

17. After the recording has finished, you have the choice of allowing a verify action or ejecting the completed disc immediately and skipping the verification step.

Let Your Video Do the Talking

Toast 6 Titanium allows you to create your own Video CDs, Super Video CDs and DVD-Video discs — after a fashion, that is. Unlike iDVD, you don't have creative control over menu creation and what goes where — Toast does it automatically — but if you're looking for basic transportation for your digital video clips and digital photographs, you can't get much easier than this application!

Video CDs (commonly called VCDs) can be shown on your computer with the proper VCD player application; most standalone DVD players can also handle Video CDs. Super Video CDs (or SVCDs), on the other hand, display significantly better video quality, but there's a caveat or two: An SVCD stores less than a VCD, and most older DVD players won't recognize the format. Therefore, use the Video CD format whenever possible to ensure the best possible compatibility.

To create a Video CD or Super Video CD, follow these steps:

1. **Double-click the Toast icon on the desktop to launch the program.**

2. **Click the Video button at the top of the screen.**

3. **Click the Advanced button in the Disc Options drawer, and select the Video CD or Super Video CD option.**

   If you're creating a disc for use in the United States, make sure you choose the NTSC option.

4. **To add basic menus to the disc automatically, enable the Create VCD Menu check box.**

   Personally, I leave this option disabled and simply allow the video clips to run sequentially — remember, the more video clips you add, the more cumbersome (and harder to navigate) your menus become.

   I always recommend that you click the Video Quality drop-down list box and select High quality — you get less recording time on the disc, but the video on the finished disc looks much better.

5. **Drag and drop video clips to the content window (see Figure 9-6).**

   Alternatively, you can click the Add button to select the video clips from a standard Open dialog box. To remove a clip that arrived by accident, select the clip and click Remove.

   To import digital video directly from your DV camcorder, plug it in — Toast displays a DV camcorder icon in the content window. Click Import, and sit back while Toast creates the video clip! (Just make sure you have enough hard drive space to hold the imported clip . . . the digital world can get cumbersome.)

6. **Add photographs (or an entire folder of photographs) from your hard drive by dragging them into the content window.**

   You can drag images from a Finder or iPhoto window; Toast labels a folder as a slideshow and displays the number of images each slide-show contains.

   Here's a neat trick: Click the Advanced button in the Disc Options drawer, and enable the Add Original Photos checkbox. Toast will create a separate folder on the final disc that will contain all of the photos that you add to your VCD/SVCD project. When you load the disc into a computer, you can copy those images directly from the disc onto the computer's hard drive. (If you use this feature, your discs will both display *and* store your images!)

7. **Load a blank disc into your recorder.**

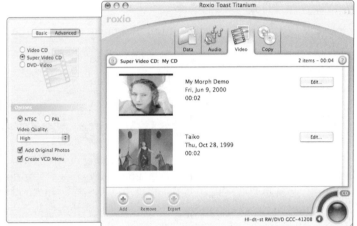

Figure 9-6: Adding the hottest video clips to my new SVCD project.

Can I burn DVD-Video discs with Toast?

Yes, Virginia, Toast can handle basic DVD projects — however, don't expect many frills. (Forget creating fancy animated menus and embedded content.) I recommend that you take the easy route, and follow the same steps I used for VCDs and SVCDs. You'll end up with a DVD-Video disc that plays video clips and slideshows on your computer and DVD player . . . but you won't be able to directly manipulate the contents of the VIDEO_TS folder. A DVD movie must conform to the DVD-Video standard, which uses a very specific set of directories (and is recorded in UDF format). If that sounds like ancient Sumerian to you, there's no need to read any more of this sidebar!

Hey, you. Yeah, you, the DVD wizard who wants to burn a DVD-Video disc. Actually, you *can* hotwire Toast to produce a bona fide DVD-Video disc with your own VIDEO_TS files. (Forgive me if I get a bit technical here for the DVD wizards.) You need to burn the project as a data disc instead, and you have to prepare the contents of the VIDEO_TS folder separately, because Toast doesn't allow you to directly author DVD content.

To create the necessary layout, click the Data tab, and click the Advanced button in the Disc Options drawer — pick the DVD-ROM (UDF) option, and then drag your prebuilt VIDEO_TS folder into the content window. (Remember, most older DVD players also require an AUDIO_TS folder for everything to work, even if the AUDIO_TS folder doesn't contain anything.) Now you can burn the disc. Naturally, I recommend that you use a DVD-R for the best possible compatibility with all DVD players.

8. **Click the Big Red Record Button . . . and wait.**

Unfortunately, digital video takes time to *encode* (a fancy-pants term that describes the conversion of your digital video into a form that can be recorded). How much time? Well, pardner, that depends on the size of the video clips, the quality setting you've chosen, and the speed of your Mac — but don't be surprised if you can take a break for lunch before the Record dialog box appears.

9. **Finally! Click the Advanced button and make sure that the Close Disc option is enabled.**

10. **Click Record and relax.**

Project: Creating a Temporary Partition

As I mention earlier in this chapter, while discussing custom hybrid discs, recording with Toast sometimes requires you to create a temporary partition as a separate volume on your Mac desktop. In fact, you can use the Mac Volume disc type to record the contents of a temporary partition as a complete disc.

In the following steps, I show you how to create a temporary partition to store the Macintosh files for a hybrid disc:

1. **Double-click the Toast icon on the desktop to launch the program.**

2. **Choose Utilities⇨Create Temporary Partition to display the Create Temporary Partition dialog box, as shown in Figure 9-7.**

Figure 9-7:
With a
temporary
partition,
I feel
so . . . self-
contained.

Create Temporary Partition

Name: Fortisque

Size: 160 MB

On: Disk Wolfgang (1.4 GB free)

Format: Mac OS Extended

Cancel   OK

3. **Click the Name field and enter a volume name for the partition.**

In this example, I chose Fortisque. (I have my reasons.)

4. **Click the Size field and enter a partition size in megabytes (the default is 650MB).**

   Naturally, this size can't be larger than the amount of free space on the drive that you select in the On drop-down list box. I have only about 150MB of Mac files to record on this hybrid disc, so I show you how to create a 160MB partition on my hard drive. Leaving about 10MB of breathing space on your temporary partition is always a good idea. This allows you to add a forgotten file or two more without running out of room.

5. **If you need a Mac OS Standard disc, select it from the Format drop-down list box.**

6. **Click OK.**

   As you can see in Figure 9-8, Fortisque has suddenly appeared on my Mac Desktop.

   Don't you wish that it was that easy to add permanent storage space to your system?

   After the partition has been created, you're ready to drag your Mac files into it.

After you're done with the partition, you can delete it by dragging it to the Trash.

Figure 9-8:
Ah,
Fortisque,
there
you are!

Project: Recording a Backup DVD-ROM

Toast can burn with DVD-R/W and DVD+R/W drives, so it makes a good quick-and-dirty recording program for creating backups. The storage space on a DVD-R makes backing up a decent-size drive easy, using only three or four discs. You don't get a full 4.7GB — a 4.7MB disc provides only about 4.25GB when you use the Mac OS Extended format — but it's still nothing to sneeze at.

You, too, can burn a simple DVD-ROM backup for your hard drive files. Follow these steps:

1. **Double-click the Toast icon on the desktop to launch the program.**

2. **Click the Data tab.**

3. **Click the Advanced button in the Disc Options drawer and enable the Mac Only radio button.**

When you're backing up data, compatibility with other computers usually isn't a big deal. Therefore, I heartily recommend that you enable the Compressed check box in the Disc Options drawer. To safeguard your data, you can also enable the Encrypted option, which will prompt you for a password. Security is a good thing, but here's a stern Mark's Maxim:

> **Brothers and sisters, if you can't supply that password, you won't be able to read anything from the disc!™**

4. **Click and drag the desired files and folders into the content window.**

5. **Load a blank DVD-R into your DVD recorder.**

6. **Click the Big Red Record Button, which presents our old friend the Record dialog.**

7. **Click the Advanced button and make sure that the Close Disc option is enabled.**

Because a backup is such an important procedure, I also recommend that you enable the Verify Data check box. Toast takes additional time to check the disc after the recording is complete, but isn't your peace of mind worth that extra step?

8. **Click Record and grab another soda.**

Note that Toast can also write a data layout to a DVD-RAM, but the entire disc is automatically reformatted first, and the data is recorded as a read-only disc. If you want to record data to the disc again using Toast, you lose the current contents of the disc when it's reformatted. Sorry about that — but then, if you're using a DVD-RAM drive for backups, like I do, automatic reformatting really isn't a problem!

Chapter 10

Using Drag-to-Disc: Avoid the Hassle!

*O*kay, I trumpet the advantages of the Roxio Drag-to-Disc throughout the first half of this book, and it's time to deliver the goods. What makes Drag-to-Disc so hot? Here are the facts:

✔ You have no need to open any recording software ahead of time. Just drop a Drag-to-Disc disc in your drive, and everything's taken care of for you automatically.

✔ The Universal Disk Format (or UDF) recording mode — also known as packet writing — used by Drag-to-Disc is almost as reliable and foolproof as burnproof recording. You can safely record data on a Drag-to-Disc disc while you're working in another application under Windows.

✔ You can add files at any time without creating a multisession disc.

✔ Drag-to-Disc works with CD-Rs, CD-RWs, DVD-R/Ws, DVD+R/Ws, and DVD-RAMs.

✔ All popular operating systems can read a UDF disc.

Eager to find out more? This is the chapter for you — I put Drag-to-Disc through its paces.

"Whaddya Mean, 1 Have to Format?"

Hey, I didn't say that Drag-to-Disc is perfect, did I? This program has only two drawbacks:

- ✔ You have to format a disc before you can use it.
- ✔ You can't create mixed-mode or standard audio CDs with Drag-to-Disc.

I can't do anything about the latter — Drag-to-Disc prompts you to launch Creator Classic if you're moving digital audio files to your disc — but the program automatically formats a disc for use with Drag-to-Disc when you drag files to it within Windows Explorer.

If your drive doesn't support this automatic formatting option (or if you want to use compression, which I cover in a paragraph or two), you can follow these steps to manually format a blank disc in Windows XP:

1. **Load a blank CD-R or CD-RW into your recorder.**

2. **Choose Start⇨All Programs⇨Roxio Easy CD & DVD Creator 6⇨Drag-to-Disc to display the Drag-to-Disc window shown in Figure 10-1.**

   You can also double-click the Drag-to-Disc icon in the system tray to display this screen.

Figure 10-1: All roads to Drag-to-Disc start here.

3. **Press Alt+F to display the Format Options dialog box shown in Figure 10-2.**

4. **It's time to give your disc a name. Enter in the Volume Label field a descriptive volume name that has 11 characters or fewer.**

   You see this label displayed in the same places as your hard drive names, including Windows applications, within Windows Explorer, and within My Computer.

Figure 10-2:
Choosing a
volume
name and
enabling
compression
for a disc.

If you suddenly decide to rename your Drag-to-Disc disc later — if you change your significant other, for example — click in the Drag-to-Disc window and press Alt+R, and then type the new name.

You can also choose to use compression on your Drag-to-Disc disc, which means that files can be reduced in size and you can pack additional stuff on the disc. Woohoo! Roxio says that the compression ranges anywhere from 1.5:1 to 3:1. As with a Zip archive, the compression you achieve depends on the data you're adding to the disc. I like to enable this check box because the more space I have to add files, the better. However, this action can limit the number of computers that can read the disc, as you find out from my description of the Eject options later in this chapter. Don't use compression if you want any computer to be able to read the disc!

To read a compressed Drag-to-Disc disc on another computer, you have to have either Drag-to-Disc installed or you have to install UDF support (which is already included on most PCs running Windows 2000 and Windows XP).

5. **If you're formatting a rewriteable disc, select the Format type by clicking the desired option.**

   Drag-to-Disc offers two types of formatting for rewriteable media. *Quick formatting* takes only a few minutes, but you must have Drag-to-Disc installed to read the disc. *Full formatting* can take up to 90 minutes (depending on the speed of your drive and the capacity of the disc), but the resulting disc can be read on any PC running Windows 2000 or Windows XP, even if Drag-to-Disc is not installed on that machine.

6. **Click OK to set the wheels in motion.**

   Drag-to-Disc displays the dialog box shown in Figure 10-3 while it's working.

   When the disc has been formatted, Drag-to-Disc displays the volume name in the Drag-to-Disc window, which you see in Figure 10-4.

Figure 10-3:
I'm
formatting
as fast as
I can!

Figure 10-4:
You're ready
to use Drag-
to-Disc!

Double-click My Computer, and you can see your new drive. Although it appears to be a CD-ROM or DVD-ROM, it's ready to store data and read it. The Drag-to-Disc icon in the Windows system tray now sports a fashionable miniature red padlock, which tells you that you have loaded a Drag-to-Disc disc.

Depending on the brand and model of your recorder, you may not be able to eject a Drag-to-Disc disc using your drive's Eject button like you can with a regular read-only disc. Don't worry, though: I cover the procedure for safely ejecting a Drag-to-Disc disc later in this chapter.

Just Add Files and Stir

"So what programs do I run to use a Drag-to-Disc disc?" Programs? You don't need 'em! Drag-to-Disc works behind the scenes, so you can forget that it's there. Just read, create, copy, and move files to your Drag-to-Disc disc in the same way you use your hard drive or a floppy disk. You can save to the disc within your applications, drag and drop files, or use a file management program like Windows Explorer.

You can also keep tabs on the status of your Drag-to-Disc disc by checking its Properties page: Double-click My Computer to display your drives, right-click the Drag-to-Disc drive icon, and choose Properties from the pop-up menu. Figure 10-5 shows the Properties for the disc that I show you how to format in the preceding section.

Figure 10-5:
Viewing the properties for a Drag-to-Disc disc.

As you can see, the file system is listed as Drag-to-Disc-R, with compression enabled. You can see that this disc has approximately 719MB of free space remaining. Remember, though, that it's a guesstimate because the rate of compression can vary depending on the type of data you're storing.

That's it! Of all the recording programs I cover, Drag-to-Disc is definitely the easiest to master: There's literally nothing to it.

"Wait — I Didn't Mean to Trash That!"

When you delete files from a Drag-to-Disc CD-RW, DVD-RW, DVD+RW, or DVD-RAM, the files are deleted and you recover the space those files used. When you delete files from a CD-R, DVD-R, or DVD+R Drag-to-Disc disc, the files are no longer accessible, but you don't regain the space.

Unfortunately, you can't undelete files from a Drag-to-Disc project by using the Windows Recycle Bin — after they've been deleted, those files are long gone, pardner. If a Drag-to-Disc project disc is damaged or corrupted, however, you can use ScanDisc to attempt to recover the files from it — more in the section "Whoops, I Can't Read This Disc" later in this chapter.

Eject, Buckaroo, Eject!

A Drag-to-Disc disc has one side that's a little tricky: You may not be able to simply eject a Drag-to-Disc disc like any other mundane CD-ROM or DVD-ROM. (In fact, the Eject button on your recorder may be disabled!) Drag-to-Disc has to take care of a few housekeeping tasks, like updating directory entries and preparing the disc for reading.

Go ahead and give the Eject button a poke, but if it doesn't work, you can always follow these steps to eject a disc by using the Drag-to-Disc window:

1. **Right-click the Drag-to-Disc icon in the system tray to display the pop-up menu, and then choose Eject Disc.**

   Alternately, display the Drag-to-Disc window (as I show you earlier in this chapter in the section "Whaddya Mean, I Have to Format?"), and click the Eject button. You can also right-click on the drive icon in the My Computer window and select Eject.

   If you're using a non-rewriteable disc, Drag-to-Disc displays the Eject Disc dialog box that you see in Figure 10-6. You can enable or disable three check boxes to determine how the disc is prepared when it's ejected:

   - **To read the disc on a computer with UDF support (or Drag-to-Disc installed):** Disable the Make This Disc Readable on Any CD or DVD Drive check box. The disc is closed so that computers that can read UDF version 1.5 can read the disc — this includes Windows 2000, Windows XP, Mac OS 9.2, and Mac OS X. With this option, you can either leave the disc open so that you can write more to it later, or you can enable the Protect Disc So That It Cannot Be Written to Again check box (which I describe in a second) to finalize the disc permanently.

   - **To read the disc on any computer:** This option creates an ISO 9660 disc that can be read on just about any computer. (Note, however, that you can't use this option if you have elected to compress the data on the disc.) Again, you can leave the disc open and write to it again later, or you can enable the Protect Disc check box to finalize the disc.

   - **To allow further recording:** If you want to continue recording later (for example, you need to read something else or record an audio disc with Creator Classic and you need the drive), disable the Protect Disc So That It Cannot Be Written to Again check box. You can't read the disc on anything other than a recorder running Drag-to-Disc, however, so it's effectively out of commission until you reload it.

Figure 10-6:
Preparing to
give your
Drag-to-
Disc disc
the boot.

2. **Click OK to eject the disc.**

Depending on the option that you chose, you may have to wait while the disc is finalized, but Drag-to-Disc shows you a progress dialog box to let you know how things are going.

Do you usually pick the same Eject options for your CD-Rs, DVD-Rs, and DVD+Rs? If so, you can choose an Eject setting that Drag-to-Disc will apply to all discs in the future. Click the Drag-to-Disc window and press Alt+S to display the Settings dialog box, then choose the desired Eject settings. Click the Advanced Eject Settings button to specify whether non-rewriteable discs should be prepared with the UDF 1.5 or ISO 9660 file format, as I described earlier in this section.

Adding Files to an Existing Disc

If you have ejected a non-rewriteable disc, you can reload it and write additional data as long as

✔ You didn't choose the Protect Disc So That It Cannot Be Written to Again check box.

✔ Additional space remains on the disc.

When you reload a non-rewriteable Drag-to-Disc disc, the program may have to open a new session and read the files that it already contains. This process can take a few moments, depending on whether you decided to close the disc or leave it as is. However, after the disc is back in the drive, you can use it normally.

Erasing a Drag-to-Disc Disc

Like Creator Classic (which I explore like Jacques Cousteau in Chapter 8), Drag-to-Disc allows you to completely erase CD-RW, DVD-RW, DVD+RW, or DVD-RAM media. To erase a disc:

1. **Click in the Drag-to-Disc window, or right-click the Drag-to-Disc icon in the system tray to display the pop-up menu.**

2. **Click Erase Disc from the pop-up menu.**

   Drag-to-Disc requests confirmation that you really want to erase the disc.

3. **Click Yes.**

Sit back while the disc is erased, or go grab yourself another soda.

"Whoops, I Can't Read This Disc"

In case something nasty occurs and you encounter problems with a Drag-to-Disc disc (for example, if you're hit with a power failure while copying files to the disc), the program offers a ScanDisc feature that can recover files and fix some errors. Note that this program should not be confused with Windows ScanDisk, which is used only with hard drives and floppy disks.

To scan a Drag-to-Disc disc for errors, follow these steps:

1. **Click in the Drag-to-Disc window, or right-click the Drag-to-Disc icon in the system tray to display the pop-up menu.**

2. **Click Launch ScanDisc.**

   Drag-to-Disc displays the dialog box shown in Figure 10-7.

Figure 10-7:
Running
ScanDisc
on an ill
Drag-to-
Disc disc.

3. **Click Scan to begin.**

   Drag-to-Disc provides a progress bar while it works. If the program finds
   problems, you're prompted for confirmation before the program gathers
   recovery information.

4. **Click Yes to continue. (Naturally, this is a definite choice.)**

   If files can be recovered, ScanDisc allows you to copy them to another
   drive.

5. **Click the Destination Drive drop-down list box to select the target
   drive, and then specify the target folder in the Destination Folder list.**

6. **Click Copy to attempt to recover all files and folders.**

Each recovered file is renamed with a generic filename, so you have to open
each file manually to determine what it is, and if it was recovered successfully.
(I know this stinks worse than an angry skunk in a closet if you have dozens
of files, but there's no other choice. Such is technology.)

Project: Creating a New-Employee Disc

Here's the deal: Suppose that you work in the human resources division of
your company and it's your job to provide new employees with all the information they need. However, your office doesn't have an intranet (that's
another book entirely), so you hit on the idea of a New Employee CD-ROM
that contains all sorts of company clip art, press releases, document templates, and the company president's recipe for Heavenly Hash Browns. Your
coworkers often take these discs on business trips, too. Your discs are popular because they save plenty of hard drive space on laptops.

That's a great idea, but it has one problem: Your company is continually
requesting that new material be added to the discs, and some information is
soon out of date and needs to be deleted to make sure that it doesn't get
included in a company document accidentally. You need a way to add more
data to a disc and be able to selectively delete information whenever you
want. Hey, that's the definition of a CD-RW Drag-to-Disc disc! Follow these
steps to create the perfect employee disc:

1. **Choose Start⇨All Programs⇨Roxio Easy CD & DVD Creator 6⇨
   Drag-to-Disc to run Drag-to-Disc.**

2. **Load a blank CD-RW into your recorder.**

3. **Press Alt+F to format the disc (as I demonstrate in the section
   "Whaddya Mean, I Have to Format?" earlier in the chapter).**

   Depending on your recorder, you could do this automatically . . . but this
   disc may need compression to hold that huge hash browns recipe.

   4. **Name the disc (ACMECO, for example), and because you're assuming that all computers in your company are running Drag-to-Disc or using an operating system that recognizes UDF discs, enable compression to make room for as much data as possible.**

   5. **Click OK.**

   6. **After the disc is formatted, double-click the My Computer icon on your desktop. Drag to the recorder icon all the company files that you want to add to the disc to copy them.**

      After all the files have been recorded, it's time to eject the disc.

   7. **Right-click the Drag-to-Disc icon in the system tray and choose Eject from the pop-up menu.**

Pass the disc with pride to your next new employee — and whenever you need to update the contents of the disc, just pop it back in the drive and start copying and deleting files!

Part IV
So You're Ready to Tackle Tougher Stuff?

The 5th Wave   By Rich Tennant

"You'll just have to get used to burning CDs without them screaming in agony for eternity."

In this part . . .

*H*ere I show you how to create the mystical optical
pets known as CD Extra discs, video CDs, and even
a digital photo album and slideshow disc. I also demonstrate how to transfer your music from albums and cassettes to audio CDs. I show you how to create a detailed,
professional appearance for your discs — inside and
out — with informative labels and box inserts along with
an HTML menu system that makes your discs easier to
use. Finally, I'm going into DVD storage and I'm taking
you with me!

Chapter 11

Heavy-Duty Recording

· ·

In This Chapter

▶ Creating a mixed-mode disc

▶ Mastering albums and cassettes to CD with AudioCentral

▶ Adding special effects with AudioCentral

▶ Designing a bootable CD-ROM

▶ Creating a slideshow photo CD

▶ Designing a Video CD

▶ Recording an album to a CD with AudioCentral

▶ Recording a standard mixed-mode disc

▶ Recording a bootable CD-ROM

▶ Recording an enhanced CD Extra disc

▶ Recording a slideshow photo CD with PhotoSuite

▶ Recording video with DVD Builder

· ·

"*A*ll right, troops — if you have been following along in this book, you know that I've been easy on you. I've covered the simple stuff, and you can burn simple data discs and audio CDs until the cows come home. But what if you need to burn a mixed-mode disc? Or record favorite albums and cassettes on audio CDs? Or even record a DVD for use in your DVD player? Those are heavy-duty recording jobs, Private. Have *you* got what it takes?"

Of course, you do. Luckily, those are the specialized discs that I cover in this chapter! You may not use them often, but when you do, you can hold your head up high and say, "I know how these are made. Step aside, and let the expert show you how it's done."

It's Data, It's Audio, It's Mixed!

Ever felt like you need both digital audio and computer data on the same disc? If so, consider mixed-mode format. You can burn two different types of mixed-mode discs — the one you select depends on the material you're recording and what device will play it.

Putting data before your audio

I mention standard mixed-mode discs in Chapter 7. They're great for discs that need to combine both digital audio and computer data, but aren't meant to be used in a standard audio CD player. These discs can be played only in a computer's CD-ROM or DVD-ROM drive.

Typically, the program is installed from the first track (the data portion), which is closest to the spindle hole. After the program is running, it plays the audio tracks that follow: That's why most sophisticated computer games now use mixed-mode format: because the game program can load movies and data files from the first track and still access the digital audio tracks while you're blasting the aliens from Planet Quark.

The extra behind CD Extra

As you can see in Figure 11-1, a CD Extra disc turns regular mixed-mode format on its head: One or more audio tracks come first, followed by a data track. The big attraction here is for musicians; a CD Extra disc can be played in both a standard audio CD player (which really can't tell the difference because the data is at the end) and a computer's read-only CD-ROM or DVD-ROM drive. This, folks, is the definition of neat!

Groups such as the Rolling Stones, the Red Hot Chili Peppers, and the Squirrel Nut Zippers have popularized the CD Extra disc with their fans. Although the format costs a minute or two of disc space (the blank space that's necessary to separate the tracks), the band's music can share the disc with a multimedia presentation of the latest music video or still pictures of a recent concert — or even lyrics to the songs.

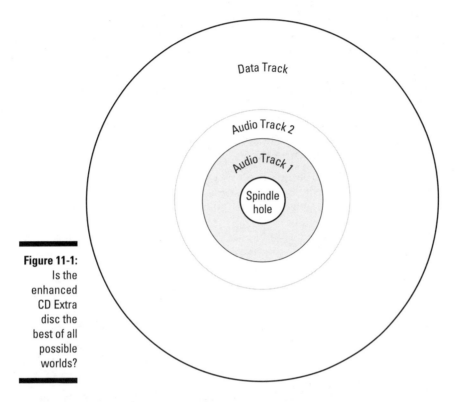

Data Track

Audio Track 2

Audio Track 1

Spindle hole

Figure 11-1:
Is the
enhanced
CD Extra
disc the
best of all
possible
worlds?

Doing Vinyl with AudioCentral

AudioCentral is the all-encompassing audio player, editor, and recording application that ships with Easy CD & DVD Creator 6. It involves a little more work than copying an audio CD or recording a new disc from MP3s. In effect, you can consider AudioCentral's analog recording feature (which is part of the AudioCentral Sound Editor program) to be the bridge between your existing music collection (vinyl albums, cassettes, and even antique media, like 8-track cartridges and reel-to-reel tapes) and the permanence and sound quality of audio CDs. With the right equipment, you can transfer the music from all these types of old recordings to a brand-new audio CD format.

However, let me make one thing perfectly clear: *I recommend analog recording with AudioCentral for only those recordings in your collection that aren't already available on audio CD.* In other words, using AudioCentral's Sound Editor to back up your Boston albums is simply ridiculous! Here's why:

- ✔ **Too much effort:** Why go to the trouble of remastering material that's already available on audio CDs? It's much easier to jump online or walk down to your local record store to pick up a copy of that Police album on audio CD.

- ✔ **Subpar sound quality:** Here's an easy-to-remember Mark's Maxim that never steers you wrong:

  No matter how good your equipment is and how well you have treated your old media, the sound that you achieve is never as good as a professionally mastered audio CD.™

- ✔ **Less than visually striking:** Unless you spent a bundle on a compact disc screen printer, your finished disc doesn't look as good as a commercial disc (and it doesn't have those liner notes or that flashy jewel case liner).

"Okay, Mark — exactly when should I use AudioCentral's Sound Editor for recording?" I would say that if your recording fits these criteria, it's a prime candidate for recording with AudioCentral:

- ✔ **Unavailable on audio CD:** The college band you loved so much that didn't hit the big time — perhaps it produced an album or a cassette, but those never become 1s and 0s (zeros) without your help.

- ✔ **Rare or live recordings:** The one time that Frank Zappa jammed onstage with Ella Fitzgerald? Burn it, and then *please* send me a copy! I would pay a pretty penny for that one.

- ✔ **Personal recordings of you, your family, and your friends:** Your grandparent's family history, or the soundtrack to your 16th birthday party, which your dad recorded.

To use Sound Editor's analog recording features, you need the assistance of your home stereo and the original equipment (sorry, this program's good, but it can't play that 8-track cartridge by itself), and you have to make a cable connection or two. Although I cover the procedure in the section "Project: Recording an Album to CD" at the end of this chapter, you need to connect your stereo's amplifier or tuner to your computer's sound card input jacks. Because computer sound card hardware varies widely between manufacturers (some cards may even need special cables), check the documentation that came with your sound card to determine how to do this.

Adding Effects in Sound Editor

While I'm discussing AudioCentral's Sound Editor application, I should also mention that the program allows you to tweak and improve your older recordings while you're remastering them to audio CDs. For example, you can make use of effects like these:

✔ **Room Simulator:** Where a stereo widening or "shrinking effect is added to music

✔ **DeTuner:** Where that persistent background hum can be eliminated (unless it's part of your 1960s music and it's actually part of the song)

✔ **DeClick:** Where you can clean older, low-fidelity recordings of annoying pops and clicks

I show you how to make use of the audio effects in the section "Project: Recording an Album to CD," later in this chapter.

Giving Your Disc the Boot

I think I've created only one or two bootable discs in my entire burning career — but when you need one, they're absolutely critical. (In both cases, I had to create bootable discs to take care of hardware problems with PCs that wouldn't boot. The drivers, programs, and data that I had to store wouldn't have fit on a floppy, either.) A bootable disc contains everything that your computer needs to complete the loading of a specific operating system. In most cases, the operating system is DOS, Windows, or Linux — including the required hardware drivers for things like your mouse and your CD-ROM drive.

Here's a great stumper for the next so-called computer guru that you meet who claims to know all things binary: In the Windows world, a bootable disc conforms to the *El Torito* standard. Of all the strange names I've encountered in my computer travels, that one even beats the acronym TWAIN (which stands for *Technology Without An Interesting Name*)! My editor's favorite Mexican restaurant was also named El Torito — hopefully, though, they didn't burn anything there.

Let me be honest with you: Creating a bootable CD-ROM is not an easy matter, so it's a project for experienced computer owners. Gathering all this stuff takes careful planning because just a single missing line in your boot files can render the entire disc useless. For this reason, it's good news that Easy CD & DVD Creator requires you to create a floppy boot disk that it can import into your data layout. If your computer can boot from the floppy disk, you know that it can do the same with your bootable CD-ROM. (You can also create a bootable hard drive image and then use that to record, if your hard drive is working.)

I show you how to create a bootable disc later in this chapter. If you decide to record one, make sure that the computer you use it on supports booting from a CD-ROM. Most PCs built in the past three or four years can use a bootable CD-ROM; check your PC's manual. If the documentation doesn't cover this option, follow the instructions provided in your PC's manual to display the BIOS settings and look for a bootable CD-ROM option. (Some older, first-generation DVD-ROM drives don't recognize a bootable DVD-ROM. Luckily, I don't think PC owners need quite that much emergency space yet.)

Creating an Optical Photo Album

Every photo album is optical, of course — but when I use the word, I mean a photo album that's recorded on a CD-ROM or DVD-ROM. The photos in an optical album can be displayed on your computer monitor, saved to your hard drive for use in your documents, or — if you would rather have an old-fashioned hard copy — printed on your inkjet or laser printer.

Easy CD & DVD Creator 6 is thoughtfully accompanied by an excellent Swiss Army knife for your digital images: Roxio's PhotoSuite 5, which you can find at www.roxio.com. You can use PhotoSuite to create optical photo albums and slideshows (with your digital photographs) and video postcards (with your digital video). If you have a Web site, the program can even create catalog pages for your photographs. A visitor to your site just has to click a thumbnail to display the full-size image.

I show you in this chapter how to use PhotoSuite to create an optical photo album that can display your images in a slideshow. See the section "Project: Recording a Photo Disc," later in this chapter.

Recording that MTV Video

The last advanced specialized disc that I discuss is the *Video CD* (commonly called a VCD), which stores digital video in MPEG-1 format. You can watch a Video CD in a Video CD player, a computer CD-ROM drive (with the right software) and most of the latest generation of DVD players. Before the advent of DVD players, Video CDs were the primary method of recording and distributing digital video among computer owners. An enhanced version of the Video CD — called the Super Video CD, or SVCD — provides even better video quality, but an SVCD stores less than a VCD, and SVCDs aren't compatible with all DVD players.

Easy CD & DVD Creator uses a combination of a separate program named DVD Builder to help simplify the creation of a video CD. With DVD Builder, you can burn a professional VCD, SVCD, or DVD, complete with a basic menu system — and I lead you through the process step-by-step in the last project in this chapter.

Project: Recording an Album to CD

I'm the proud owner of a special record album: *Batman and Robin,* recorded in 1966 on the Tifton label and performed by "the sensational guitars of Dan and Dale." You may not believe this, but the guy at my local record shop says that he doubts this classic LP will be released on compact disc any time soon! (In fact, he said something about "a snowball's chance" — I didn't catch the rest.) I have two choices: Either I can continue to play the album and listen to it deteriorate over the next few years, or I can master that music to an audio CD and enjoy it in digital splendor for the next century! (If you think that I'm choosing the former option, you're reading the wrong book.)

Remember that your computer's sound card must be connected to your stereo's amplifier or preamp before you can begin. Follow these steps to master an album to an audio CD:

1. **Choose Start⇨All Programs⇨Easy CD and DVD Creator 6⇨ AudioCentral⇨Sound Editor to display the screen that you see in Figure 11-2. (Sorry, Mac owners, but both AudioCentral and Sound Editor run only under Windows.)**

Figure 11-2: I think that Audio Central's Sound Editor sports an extremely cool interface.

2. **If you're lucky enough to have multiple sound cards in your PC, choose Tools⇨Recording Device to choose which card to use, and then choose the desired sound card from the pop-up submenu that appears.**

3. **Choose Tools⇨Recording Source. Sound Editor displays a pop-up submenu listing all audio inputs (or sources) for this recording; choose the desired source.**

   By default, Sound Editor uses the slightly wacky "What U Hear" setting, which means that the program records what you hear through your stereo's speakers . . . and this is what you need for this project. However, you can also choose other sources, like a microphone or a MIDI synthesizer.

4. **Turn on your stereo system and start playing your album.**

   Optionally, recall the days when the LP was considered state-of-the-art and high-fidelity. Speculate on the future of audio media, and wonder what everyone will be using to record music in another decade.

5. **Click the Enable Record Mode button (which sports a microphone) at the bottom of the Sound Editor window.**

6. **Drag the Recording Level slider so that the input level meters remain green through most of the music, with an occasional foray into the yellow portion of the meter.**

   If the music that you're recording varies quite a bit in volume, make sure that the strongest and loudest passage of music lights the entire green portion of the level meter

7. **Okay, here's the fun part: Start your album over at the beginning and immediately click Record.**

   Sound Editor creates a WAV format sound file in your Clips directory.

   Don't know where your Clips directory resides? By default, it's the My Music folder within your My Documents folder. However, you can change this location by specifying your favorite folder within AudioCentral: Choose Tools⇨Options, and then click the CD Options tab to display the settings shown in Figure 11-3. Click the Change button in the Copy Settings section, select the desired location on your system, and then click OK. Click OK on the Options dialog to return to AudioCentral.

8. **When the album is over, click Stop (the button bearing that attractive square) at the bottom of the Sound Editor window.**

9. **Click the Enable Record Mode button (which sports a microphone) at the bottom of the Sound Editor window.**

Figure 11-3:
Selecting
the folder
where
Sound
Editor parks
your music.

10. **If you like, you can also apply some effects to your new recording. Choose Edit⇨Select All, and then choose Tools⇨Apply Effect to Selection.**

    Sound Editor displays a settings dialog box for the effect you're adding (like the Room Simulator dialog box, shown in Figure 11-4), where you can fine-tune the effect to your taste.

11. **Choose File⇨Save Playlist to assign an artist and album title to the audio file that you just created, and click Save.**

That's it! You can now exit Sound Editor and listen to your new digital audio files with your favorite MP3 or WAV player. After you're satisfied with the results, follow the instructions in Chapter 8 for recording a typical audio CD from MP3 and WAV files.

Wow, Dan and Dale never sounded so good! Next, I think I'll try that live bootleg album of the Dick Nixons.

Figure 11-4:
Adding a
Church
effect
to "the
sensational
guitars of
Dan & Dale."

Project: Recording a Bootable CD-ROM

Suppose that you work as a computer repair technician for a company and you want to create a test CD-ROM that can boot an absolutely *clean* (or default) installation of DOS or Windows. You include diagnostics programs on this CD-ROM, so it becomes a basic software-toolkit-on-a-disc for your travels throughout the building. (If this sounds like firsthand experience, believe me — it is!)

This situation is the perfect time to use a bootable CD-ROM. As long as all your company's computers can use a bootable disc, you can guarantee yourself a stable environment (what techies call a *vanilla boot*) for diagnosing troublesome hardware toys.

This type of disc requires more preparation than the others that I cover in this chapter, and I strongly recommend that *only experienced PC owners and technicians should attempt to burn a bootable CD-ROM.* With that said, you should prepare a floppy disk that boots your system with exactly the same configuration as you want for the bootable CD-ROM. Make sure that it contains the CD-ROM driver, too!

Follow these steps to create your bootable disc:

1. **Choose Start⇨All Programs⇨Easy CD and DVD Creator 6⇨Creator Classic to run the program.**

2. **Choose File⇨New Project⇨Bootable Disc.**

   Creator Classic opens the dialog box that you see in Figure 11-5.

   Things can get really hairy really quickly at this point — although you can create several exotic types of bootable CDs, I stick with the easiest (and most compatible) type.

3. **Click the Bootable Disc Type drop-down list box and select Floppy Disk Emulation (1.44MB).**

   Leave everything else on this dialog box as is.

Figure 11-5:
The
beginnings
of a
bootable CD.

4. Load into your 1.44MB floppy drive the floppy disk that you have pre-pared and click OK.

After churning for a few seconds while the system files are read, the bootable CD-ROM layout shown in Figure 11-6 appears. Note the two files that have already been added to the layout: *BOOTCAT.BIN and BOOTIMG.BIN must not be erased or moved!* They're the files that make this puppy bootable.

Figure 11-6:
Check out
the all-
important
BOOT files
for this disc!

5. If you just want the disc to boot your PC (without reading additional files from the disc), you can skip ahead to Step 8. Otherwise, you can locate and highlight more data files by using the same method that you use to select files for a data CD-ROM (which I demonstrate in Chapter 8).

6. Click Add (the arrow pointing downward in the middle of the window) to add the files and folders to the data portion of the layout.

7. Repeat Steps 5 and 6 until you have finished adding files to the layout.

8. Click the Big Orange Disc-on-Fire Button and start the recording as you would any other data CD-ROM. (Again, for more information on the settings available when recording a data disc, you find the details in Chapter 8.)

Project: Recording a Mixed-Mode Disc

Suppose that you need to record a selection of multimedia clips to carry with you on a business trip — some are video clips that you need to store only for the ride, but some of the clips are digital audio that you need to hear to practice your presentation. One solution would be to burn two discs — one, a data CD-ROM for the video clips, and the other, a traditional audio CD. A mixed-mode disc, however, allows you to combine both these types of content on a single disc.

Follow these steps to create a mixed-mode CD:

1. Choose Start⇨All Programs⇨Easy CD and DVD Creator 6⇨Creator Classic to run the program.

2. Choose File⇨New Project⇨Mixed-Mode CD to display a special mixed-mode layout shown in Figure 11-7.

   Make sure that the data CD icon is selected at the lower-left side of the screen, under the Mixed-Mode CD Project label — it looks like a tiny disc with a file folder. (By default, Creator Classic assigns the data portion of your disc with a string of numbers for a name, but you can change that — more on this in the step or two.)

3. Locate and highlight the data files by using the same method that you use to select files for a data CD-ROM. (For the details on selecting files, visit Chapter 8.)

4. Click Add (the downward-facing arrow in the middle of the window) to add the files and folders to the data portion of the layout.

5. Repeat Steps 3 and 4 until your data layout is complete, as shown in Figure 11-8.

Figure 11-7:
A blank
mixed-mode
CD layout in
Creator
Classic.

Figure 11-8:
The data
part of this
mixed-mode
layout
is now
complete.

TIP

Don't forget to click the data CD label and name the data portion of the CD-ROM something descriptive. (Alternately, you can type the new name directly into the Disc Name text box.) The default name, which is built by using the current date and time, is rarely what you want.

6. **Click the music CD icon next to the Empty Audio CD Project label (lower-left side of the screen) to add the digital audio tracks. (The icon looks like a disc with a musical note.)**

   As you can see in Figure 11-9, the lower-right portion of the screen changes to the familiar audio CD track layout.

7. **Locate and highlight the MP3, WAV, or WMF digital audio files that you want to record, just as you do in designing a standard audio CD.**

   Remember to watch the free-space display at the bottom of the screen to make sure that you don't run out of space while adding audio files.

8. **Click Add (that's the down arrow in the middle of the window) to copy the files to your track layout.**

9. **Repeat Steps 7 and 8 until your audio track layout is complete, as illustrated in Figure 11-10.**

Figure 11-9: Whoa! Now you've switched to digital audio — on the same disc.

Figure 11-10:
I think this
disc is ready
to be
burned,
don't you?

10. **Click the Big Orange Disc-on-Fire Button and finish the recording, just like with a typical data CD-ROM. (Consult Chapter 8 for information on selecting options for a data CD-ROM.)**

Project: Recording a CD Extra Disc

As you may have guessed, I could also have created the disc that I showed you how to burn in the preceding project by using a CD Extra disc. Like a mixed-mode disc, a CD Extra (or Enhanced) disc can hold the same unique combination of digital audio tracks and computer data. The big difference is that you can play the audio tracks from a CD Extra disc in your standard audio CD player, and you need a computer's CD-ROM drive to access the digital audio on a mixed-mode disc. That's great for adding that video of your garage band to that *Best of Deep Purple* disc you burned!

Follow these steps to record a CD Extra disc:

1. **Choose Start⇨All Programs⇨Easy CD and DVD Creator 6⇨Creator Classic to run the program.**

Documenting your CD Extra discs

CD-Text is a nice feature that allows many audio CD players to display the CD title and the artist and track names while you listen. That's all that most people need. However, a CD Extra disc can store even more reference information describing the audio tracks, including the artist name, CD title, and publisher. If your audio CD player can't show this additional stuff, your computer probably can when you play the disc in your CD-ROM drive.

If you want to store this extra information, you must enter it after you have added your tracks (see Step 5 in the section titled, "Project: Recording a CD Extra Disc"). Choose File⇨ Project Properties, which displays the Project Properties dialog box, and click the Enhanced CD tab to display the dialog box shown in the following figure. Click the Created and Published drop-down boxes to select dates from a miniature calendar; the other fields can be entered by just clicking in the field and typing away. Click OK to save the information that you entered and return to the CD Extra layout.

Personally, I don't use these fields, and you don't have to enter any of this stuff — but the fields do come in handy when you're recording a disc that will be used as a master for a manu-facturing run, or a disc that will form part of an ongoing archive.

2. **Choose File⇨New Project⇨Enhanced CD. Again, Creator Classic has a special layout screen for a CD Extra project, as illustrated in Figure 11-11. If the music CD icon (next to the Empty Audio CD Project label at the lower left of the screen) isn't already selected, select it now.**

3. **Locate and select the MP3, WAV, or WMF digital audio files to record, just as you do in designing a standard audio CD.**

4. **Click Add (that familiar down arrow in the middle of the window) to copy the tracks to the audio CD portion of the layout.**

5. **Repeat Steps 3 and 4 until you have added all the audio tracks that you want.**

6. **Click the volume label for the data CD icon at the left side of the screen and change the label to something descriptive. Type the new label into the Disc Name text box.**

Figure 11-11:
A CD Extra
project
layout.

Leave the CDPLUS and PICTURES folders as they are. Don't delete these folders or add files within them, because they're used in conjunction with the audio tracks on the disc! (You can find out more about this topic in the nearby sidebar, "Documenting your CD Extra discs.")

7. **Locate the files and folders to add in the usual manner by using the Explorer display in the upper half of the screen, and highlight them.**

8. **Click Add (that handsome arrow pointing down in the middle of the window) to copy the selected files and folders to the data portion of the layout.**

9. **Repeat Steps 7 and 8 until all the files that you want are added. Figure 11-12 shows a finished data layout for your CD Extra disc. Note the location of the data files in the layout.**

10. **Click the Big Orange Disc-on-Fire Button and finish the recording as you would with a typical data CD-ROM.**

Figure 11-12:
The finalized
audio and
data layouts
for your CD
Extra disc.

Project: Recording a Photo Disc

Aunt Harriet canning preserves. Pictures of the kids at Christmas. Those
home inventory photographs. 'Nuff said! Whatever the subject of your digital
images, you can create a photo disc with PhotoSuite that can be viewed on
any DVD player (or a PC with a DVD viewing program).

Follow these steps to burn a photo disc:

1. **Choose Start⇨All Programs⇨Roxio Easy CD and DVD Creator 6⇨
   Applications⇨Roxio PhotoSuite 5 to run the program, which displays
   the screen shown in Figure 11-13.**

2. **Create a new album for your slide show disc. Move your mouse pointer
   over the View, Organize & Archive button at the left side of the window,
   and then click the View & Organize button that magically appears in the
   middle of the window. Click the Create New Album button at the left of
   the window and type a descriptive name for your album (see Figure
   11-14), and then click Create.**

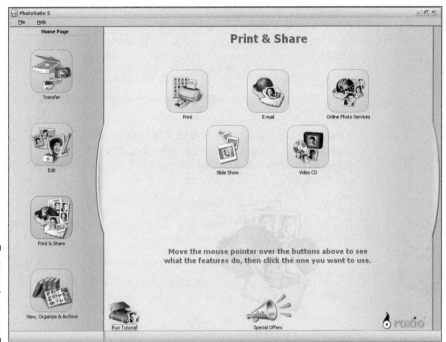

Figure 11-13:
PhotoSuite
waits for
the action
to start.

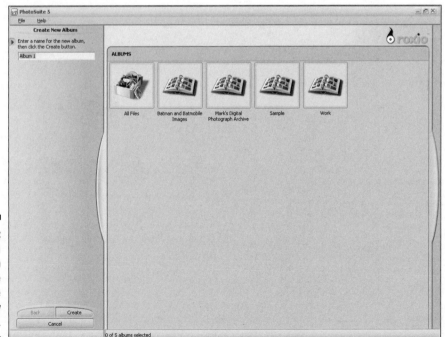

Figure 11-14:
Creating a
new album
to use
for the
slideshow
project.

Now you're rewarded with an empty album window. Remember, you don't *have* to create a new album just to record a slideshow disc, but it does help keep things tidy — for example, you can easily delete the album later.

3. **Click the Add Photos button from the panel at the left of the window.**

   PhotoSuite displays the thumbnail-laden Add dialog box that you see in Figure 11-15.

4. **Navigate to the folder that holds the images you want to add to the album. Click an image to highlight the filename; to add multiple images, hold down the Ctrl key while you click. Click Add to add the selected images to the album.**

   Figure 11-16 shows the thumbnail display for an album.

5. **Repeat Steps 3 and 4 until you have added all the images that you want to include on your photo disc.**

   To view an image in full-size mode, double-click the thumbnail image.

6. **If you like, you can rename an image: Click the thumbnail to select it, and then click the caption and type the new caption.**

   When your album is just right, you're ready to create the slideshow.

Figure 11-15: PhotoSuite makes it easy to add images to your slideshow album.

Figure 11-16:
The photo album is rapidly filling up with thumbnails.

7. **Click the Done Organizing Albums button to return to the PhotoSuite main menu. Move your mouse over the Print & Share button, and then click the Video CD button in the Print & Share screen.**

   You're given the option of creating a Video CD from photos, or from an existing slideshow.

8. **Click the Create Using Photos Only button, and then click Next.**

   PhotoSuite displays the screen that you see in Figure 11-17. The program comes with a number of menu templates; click a template name to display it in the window.

9. **After you've selected a template, click Next to continue.**

10. **Click the Add More Photos button to display the Add dialog box. To add all images in the album that you created earlier, click the My Albums button and choose the album that you just created from the drop-down list at the top of the Add dialog box. Click the Select All button in the Add dialog box toolbar and click Add. Click Next to continue.**

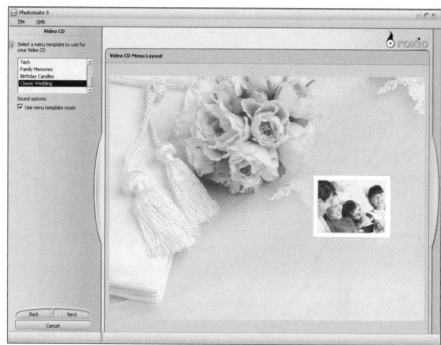

Figure 11-17:
Defining the
look for a
Video CD
menu.

11. Drag the image thumbnails into the order that you want them to be displayed. Click Next to continue.

At this point, PhotoSuite allows you to name your slideshow presentation, change the default delay of 5 seconds between slides, and add a single digital audio file (in WAV, MIDI, WMA, or MP3 format) that plays in the background during the show (see Figure 11-18).

You can also record a track from an existing audio CD, or record your voice with a microphone. Click the Record button, and then choose a recording quality setting (and, if you're ripping a song from an audio CD, choose the perfect track). After the recording is complete, you can listen to it before you decide whether it should be saved to disc.

If you've packed a large number of images into your layout (or you've added a huge sound file) and you're a little worried about the elbow-room on your Video CD, click the Calculate Disc Size button to display the approximate space that you've used so far. You should be able to add at least 600MB of material to your Video CD without fear of running out of storage space!

Figure 11-18:
Adding
a little
background
tune from
Old Blue
Eyes.

12. If you want to add a background audio track from an existing audio file, click the Browse button to select the file. If you would rather skip the audio accompaniment, leave the Background Sound drop-down list box empty. Click Next to continue.

13. PhotoSuite displays the menu preview screen that you see in Figure 11-19. Click in the title text box and type the menu title, and then click the buttons on the nifty remote control to preview your photos. When everything looks (and acts) just right, click Next to continue.

14. Time to burn! Load a *blank* CD-R into your recorder — don't use a disc with an existing session. Click the Record button to start the process, and watch PhotoSuite load Creator Classic take care of the burn (see Figure 11-20). Talk about teamwork!

To watch your slideshow, just load the disc into your DVD player! You can also view the disc on your PC with most DVD viewing programs.

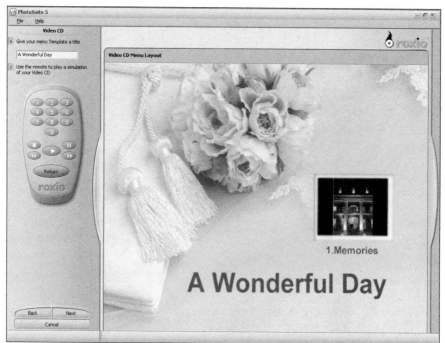

Figure 11-19:
Previewing
a great gift
to the
newlyweds.

Figure 11-20:
PhotoSuite
calls on
Easy CD &
DVD Creator
for the
burning
chores.

Project: Recording a DVD Movie Disc

To end this chapter on advanced recording, I show you how to create a DVD-Video of a child's birthday party. Suppose that you edited a series of short video clips with Adobe Premiere and you've saved them in MPEG format on your hard drive. The DVD should show the clips in order.

Follow these steps:

1. **Choose Start⇨All Programs⇨Easy CD and DVD Creator 6⇨DVD Builder to load the program. As shown in Figure 11-21, the wizard runs automatically. Select the Create a DVD Builder Project radio button and click Next to continue.**

2. **Click the button for the type of disc that you want to create — a VCD, SVCD, or DVD-Video disc — for this project, and then click the Import Files button to use existing digital video clips from your hard drive. Click Next.**

Figure 11-21:
The opening gambit used by DVD Builder.

Note that you can also capture a digital video stream from a DV camcorder or analog input (like a VCR). If you're adding still images to your project, you can also include existing images from your hard drive, or capture digital photographs directly from your digital camera. For right now, just add existing video clips, but you can switch to these other sources whenever you like. *Sassy!*

3. **The Import Files dialog box appears, as shown in Figure 11-22. Navigate to the folder in which you stored your MPEG files and digital photographs. Hold down the Ctrl key and click the desired clips and images, and then click the Add Files button.**

Figure 11-22:
Choosing
video clips
for the
project.

DVD Builder automatically checks the quality of each clip, and alerts you if a clip is not well-suited to a VCD, SVCD, or DVD project (see Figure 11-23). If a clip is tagged as okay for a particular kind of disc, you get a green light — if it's likely not to work, you get a red light. (Software designers get paid a lot of money for ideas like these.) You can choose to add an offending clip to your project anyway (with the idea of burning a disc type that can use the clip) or just click Cancel and not add the clip at all.

Figure 11-23:
This clip
works with
VCD and
SVCD, but it
may not be
suitable for
DVD.

> **File Quality**   ✕
>
> The 'D:\Batman Convention.mpg'   **Add Anyway**
> file may not display correctly on your TV.
>   **Cancel**
> VCD   SVCD   DVD
> ◉   ◉   ◉   **Help**
>
> ☐ Don't show this dialog again   **Details >>**

4. **Click the Add Anyway button (if necessary), and DVD Builder adds the item to your disc layout as a thumbnail-size icon.**

   Note that the layout has two sections, as shown in Figure 11-24: the Intro section on the top right, which contains a cool, old-fashioned count-down reel clip by default, and the Main Menu section on the bottom right, which displays a button for each movie clip that you add as a separate item. (Hence the tabs for Movie A, Movie B, and so on.) A single item can hold multiple video clips and still images, depending on where you drag the thumbnail.

5. **Add the rest of your clips and still images: Click one of the buttons at the top of the DVD Builder window (Video Capture, Image Capture, or Import Files). Naturally, if you want to use existing files from your hard drive, click Import Files and repeat Steps 3 and 4.**

   Note that DVD Builder keeps track of the amount of space that you've used with a bar display at the bottom of the window. You can toggle the estimated space between the different types of discs by clicking the Disc Size Status button at the left of the bar; click the type of disc that you want to record, and the status bar changes to reflect the capacity of the specified disc type.

Not quite sure about the contents of a video clip? Just double-click the clip's thumbnail icon to watch it in the Preview window, complete with the familiar controls from a typical DVD player program — these include pause, advance/rewind one frame, and jump to the next chapter (if your clip contains discrete chapter markers).

If you add a clip or image by mistake, right-click the item to display the pop-up menu and choose Delete to remove the element from your project.

Figure 11-24:
Selecting the order in which items will appear.

6. **Now drag each item into the desired frame. To automatically create a new menu button on the Main Menu screen, add the item to the next empty Movie tab. To add an item to the sequence for an existing button, drag the item to the empty frame at the end of the sequence.**

Who wants a spiffy menu with a title like *Main Menu* or button captions that read *Movie A* and *Movie B?* Double-click the Main Menu thumbnail icon (directly under the words Main Menu, to the right of the Movie A tab), and it appears in the Preview window — now you can click any text item, and DVD Builder displays the dialog box that you see in Figure 11-25. If you like, you can even change the look of the text item by clicking the Select Font button and selecting a different font from the list that appears. When your text looks just right, click OK, and the change is reflected in the Preview window.

Figure 11-25:
Changing
the text on
your menu
adds
pizzazz.

Select Font

| 2004 Chicago Batman Convention | Select Font |

OK   Cancel   Help

7. **Before committing your project to disc, click the Change Menu Themes button at the bottom of the DVD Builder window. A scrolling strip appears at the bottom of the window (see Figure 11-26). Double-click a theme thumbnail to apply it to your project.**

If you decide you like the original theme, just click the first thumbnail in the strip, and all will be as it was.

8. **Ready to preview your disc? Click the Preview icon to view the entire sequence — it's the button with the TV and tiny remote control at the bottom right of the DVD Builder window.**

The program displays the high-tech control panel that you see in Figure 11-27, complete with familiar controls like the buttons on a DVD player. You can navigate by using the buttons on the control panel, or just click directly on your menu buttons with your mouse pointer. To display the Intro sequence again, click the Intro button at the top of the control panel.

Figure 11-26:
Choose a different theme to build the right mood.

Figure 11-27:
Previewing the goods before you record.

9. **When you have finished your preview, click the Close button on the control panel (the button with the X at the top right corner) and click the Big Orange Disc-on-Fire Button to continue.**

   From the Burn Project dialog box (which you see in Figure 11-28), you can select which type of disc you want to record. In most cases, you want to burn your project immediately, but you can also create a disc image for later recording.

10. **To record now, click the radio button for the type of disc that you want, load the correct type of media (a CD-R, DVD-R, or DVD+R — always use a write-once disc for use in a DVD player), and click OK to display the familiar Record Disc Setup dialog box.**

11. **Finish the recording as you would do for a standard data disc layout, as I describe in Chapter 8.**

Figure 11-28: Choosing recording options for a DVD project.

Chapter 12

BAM! Add Menus to Your Discs!

*Y*our cell phone uses a menu. Your computer programs use menus. Some cars now use menus to display information to the driver. I'm sure that someone somewhere is trying to add a menu to bathroom fixtures — all in the name of those two powerful deities, Convenience and Ease of Use. (And as a dedicated owner of that most necessary of machines, The TV Remote Control, I'm all for convenience and ease of use!)

In this chapter, I show you how you can add a professional-looking point-and-click menu system to your recorded data CD-ROMs and DVD-ROMs — without spending a fortune on strange programs, dedicating half of next year to learning any strange scripting language, or hiring some strange programmer for half of next year's income to do it for you. (If you like, you can send your thanks to mark@mlcbooks.com — there's nothing better than e-mail from happy readers!)

Everything Uses Menus These Days

Can you imagine buying an application or a game program, installing it, and discovering that it had no menu system? Why, you would think that our civilization had returned to the archaic Dark Ages of DOS, with commands you had to type by hand. That's why I add, for one reason or another, a menu to about half the discs I burn. I think that any disc that falls into one of the following categories needs a menu onboard to make it, well, more convenient and easier to use.

(By the way, I still remember about 90 percent of those archaic DOS commands. Who knows when I may need them again, but I'm too nostalgic to forget my first PC operating system!)

Discs chock-full of images, video, and sounds

If you want to display digital photographs, play sound clips, or show video clips, you have come to the right place. *Hypertext Markup Language* (or HTML for short) provides support for all these files, and they sound and look as nice as they do when you receive them over the Internet (just much, *much* faster). Whoops, I almost forgot: You can add cool extras, like Flash animation, Adobe *Portable Document Format* (or PDF) files, and Java applets to your HTML menu, too.

Discs burned to distribute to others

Convenience and ease of use are both doubly important when you're recording a disc for distribution. As a shareware author, I can attest that what seems to you like a piece of cake to use can be a hunk of lead the size of an anvil to a computing novice. For example, rather than try to figure out what program to run and where it is on your disc, your customer may decide to chuck your demo CD-ROM into the trashcan.

Besides making your disc easier to use, an HTML menu system allows you to pull out all the stops for a professional first impression: Your menu can make liberal use of graphics, music, and even video (*without* requiring a connection to the Internet) while providing the point-and-click functionality everyone wants. A multimedia menu tends to draw people; as anyone in advertising can tell you, using eye candy helps to deliver the message.

Discs with Internet links

If an Internet connection is available, your discs can offer direct links to your online Internet presence. You can take visitors directly to your Web site, prepare an e-mail message that's automatically addressed to you, and load resources from your Web server (like the latest program update or your latest newsletter in PDF format).

Discs with text files galore

If you take the time to convert your text into HTML (which I demonstrate to you later in this chapter), you can display them directly within the friendly confines of a Web browser, complete with links to other documents, search commands, and basic text formatting.

Discs that include a Web site

Yes, Virginia, you can indeed store an entire Web site on a disc, complete with every graphic, sound, and animation found on the Internet site. (The only thing that would have to be left by the wayside would be streaming video because it requires a connection to the Internet for you to download.) Because Netscape Navigator, Microsoft Internet Explorer, and Apple Safari can all load a Web page from a CD-ROM or a hard drive rather than from a Web server, anyone with a browser can visit your site — just by loading your disc.

Discs with dozens and dozens of folders

If your disc has only one or two folders, no big whoop (although you're still betting that the person who has your disc knows how to use Windows Explorer or will read your printed instructions). But what if your disc has nested directories three or four levels deep and that person has to dig for a specific piece of clip art or a certain Adobe Acrobat PDF file?

With an HTML menu, you can provide hyperlinks that automatically open these files or download them directly to the computer's hard drive for later use — no digging, no searching and, very likely, a satisfied customer.

Designing Menus (But Not for Food)

What's the secret to designing a good menu? What elements should it have? Of course, the appearance of your menu is completely up to you — and the flexibility of HTML makes it easy to add a menu that's as flashy or mundane as you like. However, I can provide you with a few guidelines that apply equally well to any disc menu:

   ✔ **Plan your menu in advance.** Before you run your HTML editor, sit down with a piece of paper and a pencil (remember those?) and write down precisely what commands your menus should include and how many menus you need. For example, if you need only an e-mail link, a couple of text links, and a download link, you can place all those on one menu. If you're selling different products and you want each to have its own page, make notes of what commands each page needs.

✔ **People like consistency.** Think of the best sites that you find most attractive on the Web: I bet that each site has its own graphic design elements (like buttons, separation bars, fonts, and incidental graphics) that set it apart. Those elements work only when they're used consistently, so avoid a hodgepodge of different looks. Also, decide ahead of time what common controls should be on every page. For example, if your menu has more than one page, don't forget to plan the navigational controls you need. As with a standard Web page, you need links to advance a single page or send your user back to the home page — and it's a good idea to add a link to back up a single page, too.

✔ **"What's my motivation?"** Okay, sorry about the actor-speak. Ask yourself what kind of an impression you want to make on the people using your disc. Do you need the multimedia pizzazz, or would your purpose be better served with a simple menu and a few animated images? If you're recording a disc just for reference purposes, for example, your family, friends, or customers probably don't need anything fancy — clarity and speedy retrieval are more important. A demo disc that offers a product, on the other hand, may pull out all the stops and offer plenty of eye candy.

✔ **How will the information be used?** Will the information on your disc be viewed directly within the browser (like a PDF or HTML text file), or do users have to download programs and data to their hard drives first? It's always a good idea to add text to your menus that helps guide novices if something has to be done.

Whether your menus are plain and simple, somewhat attractive, or downright Hollywood, they must be arranged in a logical manner. If your disc offers primarily a catalog of images, why put the links to the sample images on a secondary menu? Your menu system should save as many mouse clicks as possible, so it's always helpful to "put the best stuff in the window."

Using HTML for Your Menus

HTML (short for *Hypertext Markup Language*, as though anyone really worries about it anymore) is just plain neat. When it was first developed, it was heralded as the beginning of a new age of communication as the foundation of the World Wide Web; and indeed, it has proven to be exactly that. HTML could rest on its laurels for the rest of history, known as nothing but the cornerstone of the Web.

But a great concept like HTML is hard to contain to a single facet of the computing world: Software developers and engineers have this funny habit of using something that works well in ways that the original designers would have never considered. For example, HTML has now become the basis of today's disc-based help and documentation; many applications, utilities, and games now ship with no printed manual. The entire manual is saved in HTML format to the disc itself. (In fact, that was what prompted me to develop my first HTML menu for a disc, sometime back in the hoary days of 1996: I was fascinated by my first experience with an on-disc HTML manual.)

So why does HTML make such a good foundation for a disc menu system? Reflect, good reader, on these facts:

- ✔ **Free, free, *free!*** That got your attention, didn't it? Not only are Web browsers generally free, but you can also choose from a wide range of free HTML editors (with a generous handful of inexpensive shareware editors around to boot). Probably the best known of these HTML editors is Microsoft Front Page. Even programs like Microsoft PowerPoint and Word can create simple Web pages.

- ✔ **It's available on everything.** HTML is such a pervasive force these days that every operating system either displays it or includes a browser; that includes the Big Three (Windows, the Mac operating system, and Linux) as well as strange and wonderful beasts like BeOS, OS/2 Warp, and Solaris. Because operating systems now install a Web browser automatically, you're also virtually assured that your customers can use your menu. If, in some cosmic irregularity, they haven't installed a browser, you can even include the distribution versions of Netscape Navigator or Microsoft Internet Explorer on the CD itself.

- ✔ **Friends and customers already know how to use it.** These days, the vast majority of folks already know how to use their Web browsers, and those browsers can automatically display common multimedia file formats; no need to manually run external programs. (I know a friend who's uncomfortable with any programs other than Outlook Express and Internet Explorer, and even he could use your disc.)

- ✔ **A complete menu toolbox.** HTML has evolved into a powerful language, complete with tools to display formatted text; search that text for specific words and phrases; play movies, music, and sounds; display images; link files; copy files from disc to hard drive; send e-mail; and visit other Web sites. Whew!

- ✔ **A normal person can understand HTML.** Compared to a serious programming language like C or Visual Basic, understanding HTML is a walk in the park. To be honest, you really don't need to study it anyway because a good HTML editor can create a menu without your writing a single line of code. (For example, I use Netscape Composer in the menu project at the end of this chapter.)

✔ **You can use third-party plug-ins to add even more features.** Need Flash animation for your HTML menu? How about specially written Java applets? (If you don't know what either of these is, feel free to ignore them.) If you can program in Java or you have an application to build Java applets for you, your menus can run these toys with a click of a mouse (or automatically with the menu).

"So how do I add the menu system I create to my disc layout?" That's the simplest part. The HTML files that you create (along with the files they use, like graphics and sounds) are copied to a separate folder that you create in your CD layout. The person using your disc can open the folder manually and double-click the top-level HTML menu file, or you can create a shortcut (in Windows) or an alias (in the Mac operating system) in the root directory that loads the top-level menu.

While I'm discussing HTML within specific margins in this chapter, you can find out all the details of the language and what it's capable of in the book *HTML 4 For Dummies,* 4th Edition, by Ed Tittel and Natanya Pitts (published by Wiley Publishing, Inc.).

Mentioning Animation

If you're interested in animating your menus, I recommend these two methods:

✔ **Animated GIF images:** You can use Animation Shop 3 (from Jasc) to create animated GIFs. It's simple stuff, but all browsers can display them without additional plug-ins, and they can add basic animation to a title or a background. Figure 12-1 shows Animation Shop 3 at work; it's a steal at $40, and you can buy it directly from Jasc at their Web site (www.jasc.com).

✔ **Macromedia Flash:** Flash MX 2004, from Macromedia (www.macromedia.com), is the standard for creating interactive animation for HTML pages. Unlike with an animated GIF image, you can control what happens and what runs when your customer clicks a Flash control or animation. Flash animations can use sound, images, and graphics that you have drawn yourself and imported from your favorite drawing program. If you have visited a Web site recently that uses fancy drop-down menus, they were likely created in Flash. The latest version even adds support for MP3 music.

Figure 12-2 illustrates the Flash design environment. Although Flash takes some time to master and costs about $500, I often recommend it to folks who are looking for professional-quality Web animation. If you take the time to study the program, Flash can produce browser-based games, deliver interactive education, and — oh, I forgot — create CD-ROM menus worthy of Microsoft or Adobe.

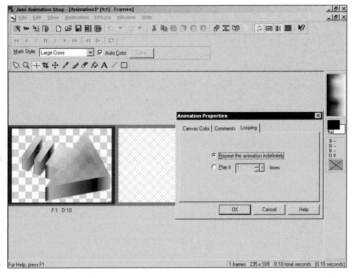

Figure 12-1:
Creating an
animated
GIF in
Animation
Shop 3.

Figure 12-2:
Putting
Macromedia
Flash
to work
creating
serious
animation.

I don't go into detail on Flash, but Gurdy Leete and Ellen Finkelstein do, in their book *Macromedia Flash MX 2004 For Dummies,* (published by Wiley Publishing, Inc.).

For those with knowledge of HTML

I often make quick changes to Web pages with Windows Notepad — it's easy to modify a word here or there or change the color of a font. However, I use a CareWare HTML editor when I'm designing or making major changes to an existing page, and I can heartily recommend it as a powerful addition to your HTML toolbox. The program, Arachnophilia, was written by Paul Lutus. You can download your copy at www.arachnoid.com/arachnophilia/. (It comes in flavors for all versions of Windows.)

Arachnophilia offers support for format templates, tables, keyboard macros, a global search-and-replace feature, page frames, and much

more. It even includes a built-in ftp client for transferring Web pages and files. The program can display with its internal browser a preview of a page you're developing, too. The following figure shows Arachnophilia at work on my personal Web site. Note that this is not a WYSIWYG (short for What You See Is What You Get) HTML editor per se (like Front Page), so you do need knowledge of the HTML language.

(By the way, CareWare is a simple concept: Simply repay the author with deeds of kindness in your general area, and be thankful for what you have. It's a great program at a great price.)

Project: Creating a Disc Menu with HTML

Time to get your hands dirty with HTML. I show you how to create a typical basic disc menu for a distribution CD-ROM that I can send to customers. The program is Handsome Prince 2.0 ("Turns a regular guy into a mate fit for a princess"), and you need to add these functions to your menu:

- ✔ A link to download the program from the disc to the computer's hard drive
- ✔ A link to the READ ME file so that it can be read directly from the disc
- ✔ A link to send e-mail
- ✔ A link to the program's support Web site

Because the customer has already bought the program, you don't need anything flashy — a simple menu that offers fast access to the program and the other links is perfect. I use Netscape Composer, the free HTML editor that ships with Netscape Navigator (www.netscape.com), to show you how to create the menu. Follow these steps:

1. **Choose Start⇨Programs⇨Netscape 6⇨Netscape 7.1 to run Navigator.**

2. **From the Navigator menu, choose File⇨New⇨Composer Page.**

   The Netscape Composer screen shown in Figure 12-3 appears.

3. **First, select a title for the page: I typed** Handsome Prince Version 2.0. **Click and drag to select the text, and then choose Format⇨Font. I use the Helvetica font. Choose Format⇨Align, and choose Center from the pop-up menu.**

   You now have a dramatic-looking title for the CD-ROM menu, as you can see in Figure 12-4.

   Now you create a line to separate the title from the rest of the menu.

4. **Press Enter twice and choose Insert⇨Horizontal Line to add the bar (see Figure 12-5).**

Figure 12-3:
Netscape
Composer
(before your
inspiration
hits, that is).

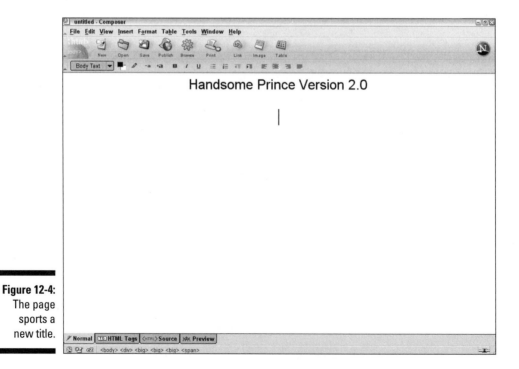

Figure 12-4:
The page
sports a
new title.

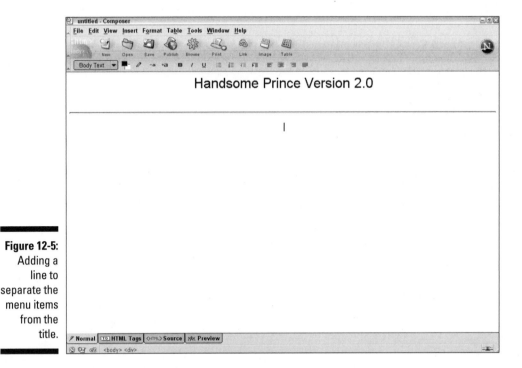

Figure 12-5:
Adding a
line to
separate the
menu items
from the
title.

5. **Add the first link — a download link for a file (for example, HPRINCE2.EXE). Click the Link icon on the toolbar to display the Link Properties dialog box (see Figure 12-6) and type the link description (I used the words** Copy Handsome Prince 2.0 to your hard drive) **in the Link Text box. Click the Choose File button to locate the file (make sure that you select the All Files view in the Files of Type drop-down list box at the top of the dialog box). Highlight the filename and click Open. Click OK to create your first link, as shown in Figure 12-7.**

Before you celebrate too much, though, you have to change the location of the file you chose because that file will be on a CD-ROM rather than on your hard drive. Right-click the link that you just created and choose Link Properties from the pop-up menu. In the Link Location field, erase the rather cryptic file location that Composer created and just type the name of the file to download (in this case, **hprince2.exe**). Click OK to save your changes. With this change, your browser looks for the file in the same location as the HTML file itself, which is in the root directory of the CD-ROM.

You may be wondering how the program is copied to the hard drive. Because HPRINCE2.EXE is a binary application, your browser knows that it can't be displayed, so you receive instead the familiar prompts asking whether you want to copy it to your hard drive. Neat, eh?

Figure 12-6:
Configuring
the
download
link.

6. **To display the formatted HTML READ ME file (which I show you how to create in the next project), repeat Step 5.**

For this example link, type the title **Read the Handsome Prince 2.0 READ ME File** in the Link Text box and select the README.HTM file from the files and folders on your hard drive.

If you need to remove a link, highlight the link text by clicking and dragging, and then choose Format⇨Remove Link.

Figure 12-7:
You're in
business
with your
first item.

7. **Now you need the e-mail link. You enter this code directly: Choose Insert⇨HTML to display the dialog box that you see in Figure 12-8. Type this text into the box:**

```
<A HREF ="mailto:mark@mlcbooks.com">Send An Email to the
              Author of Handsome Prince</A>
```

Figure 12-8:
Entering
HTML code
directly into
Composer.

8. **Change the e-mail address (the part immediately following the** `mailto:`**) to your address and click Insert.**

   Voilà! Your menu is shown in Figure 12-9 with its new e-mail link.

   Again, things are about as automatic as they can get. If the computer using your disc is connected to the Internet, clicking this e-mail link in a Web browser connects the user's computer to the Internet and displays the user's default e-mail program, complete with a new message already addressed to you.

9. **Press Enter twice and repeat Step 6 to create your Web site link. This time, type this text:**

```
<A HREF ="http://www.mlcbooks.com">Visit the Handsome
            Prince Support Site</A>
```

10. **Change the Web address (the part immediately following the** `http://`**) to your Web site address. Click Insert.**

    Your new disc menu now includes the basic functions (as shown in Figure 12-10).

Figure 12-9:
Wow, man,
dig that
crazy
e-mail link.

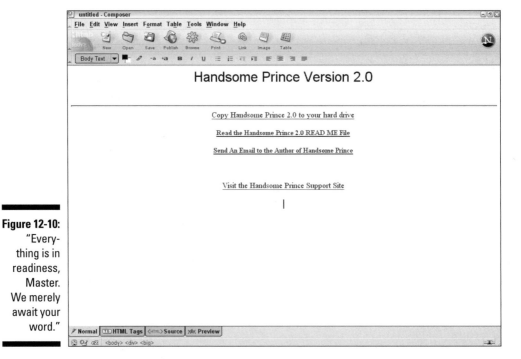

Figure 12-10:
"Every-
thing is in
readiness,
Master.
We merely
await your
word."

Before you declare things finished, how about sprucing up the background a little bit?

11. **Choose Format⇨Page Colors and Background to display the dialog box that you see in Figure 12-11. Enable the Use Custom Colors radio button and click the Background color sample box. Composer displays a grid of possible colors you can use. Select a color that coordinates well with the black and blue of the text (like a light orange or gray), and then click OK to change your background color.**

Figure 12-11:
Selecting
text and
background
colors for
the menu.

12. **To save your page, choose File⇨Save As. Composer prompts you for a title to be displayed on the title line of the Web browser; I typed** Handsome Prince 2.0 CD-ROM. **Click OK. From the Save Page As dialog box, select the folder where the menu should be saved. Type a descriptive name (I suggest something like** MENU.HTM) **and click Save.**

Because your files reside on a CD-ROM, you must make sure that the locations of any linked files match the locations they have within the CD layout. In the example, HPRINCE2.EXE must reside in the root directory, just like the MENU.HTM and README.HTM files. If these files are in different folders, your download link doesn't work.

13. **To test your menu, open your browser, choose File⇨Open to display a standard Open dialog that lists the files and folders on your system. Then locate and select the HTML menu file.**

Figure 12-12 illustrates the menu as displayed within Internet Explorer. Don't forget to check all the links and make sure that they work.

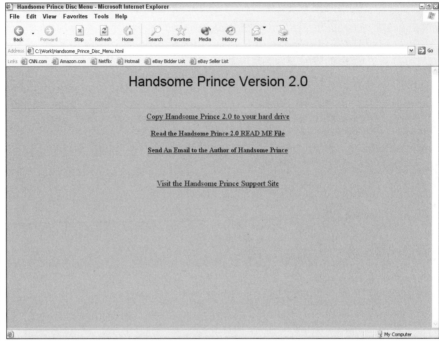

Figure 12-12:
Viewing
the fruits of
your labor.

Project: Converting a Text Document to HTML

Personally, I like viewing text as a file within a browser. It somehow seems more of an elegant solution than just opening Windows Notepad. When you need to show a text file within your CD-ROM menu, though, converting that text to HTML becomes a requirement because no View a Text File command exists. For a simple text file, like the READ ME file for Handsome Prince 2.0, Microsoft Word makes the conversion easy.

Because Word does a simple conversion job, you have to use an HTML editor to add graphics, add a table, or change a dotted line to a solid separator bar (like the one you used in the preceding project). Even if you have to add graphics and special formatting in another program, however, Word makes a great conversion tool for the text.

Follow these steps to convert a text file to HTML with Word:

1. **Choose Start⇨All Programs⇨Microsoft Word. From the Word menu, choose File⇨Open, which displays the standard File Open dialog with the files and folders on your system. Navigate to the location of the original text file and double-click to load it.**

Your text file should look something like Figure 12-13.

Figure 12-13:
Opening
a text
document
in Word —
nothing up
either
sleeve.

2. **Because HTML text can be formatted with bold and italic text, take a moment to change to either bold or italic any text that needs a little emphasis. Select the text you want and click either the Bold or the Italic button on the Word toolbar.**

TIP

Avoid the Underline text attribute because it can be easily mistaken for a link in the finished HTML file. Also, you don't need to choose an alternative font because a simple HTML file uses the default font set by the browser's configuration.

3. **After the text is italicized and bolded as you like, choose File⇨Save As. The Save As dialog box appears. Navigate to the location where you want to save the file and choose Web page from the Save As Type drop-down list box.**

4. **As shown in Figure 12-14, the Save As dialog box for a Web page has an additional field that you should fill in. Click the Change Title button and type a descriptive title. (The new title is displayed in the browser window.) Click OK to return to the Save As dialog box.**

Note that the title is not the same as the filename, which you should enter now. I use the filename README.HTM, from the preceding project.

5. **Click Save to begin the conversion.**

Figure 12-14:
With an
HTML Web
page, you
get a title
thrown in
for free.

6. **After the file has been saved, choose File➪Exit to exit from Microsoft Word and return to Windows.**

Figure 12-15 shows the finished HTML file README.HTM loaded in Internet Explorer. Not a bad job!

Figure 12-15:
The finished
READ ME
file dressed
as a Web
page.

Chapter 13

Storing Megastuff with DVD

---

*W*hether it holds 90 minutes of digital video or it's simply crammed full of backup files, a DVD recordable disc is a wonderful thing — only current prices are holding most technotypes back from investing in a DVD-R/W, DVD+R/W, or DVD-RAM drive. But those prices have already fallen from $1,000 to less than $300 for a fast DVD-R/W drive, and the cost of blank media has dipped more than 50 percent over the past two years. It's simply a matter of time until DVD recorders pack the shelves at your local discount store; they will replace the CD-RW drives that are now standard equipment on today's PCs and Macs.

My job is clear: I must prepare you for the rigors of DVD recording so that you're ready for the coming wave of new hardware! It's a daunting job, but, well, it's not *really* all that daunting. If you're interested in backing up your system or simply saving 4.7GB of data at once, burning a DVD is a process similar to burning a CD-R or a CD-RW. I show you how in this chapter.

If you're interested in mastering a DVD with digital video for use in your home DVD player or your computer's DVD-ROM drive, you are indeed walking into an unfamiliar land — but this chapter shows you the way there!

Let me be honest with you (as always): This isn't a book about either digital video editing or DVD authoring. The topic for this particular tome is recording CDs and DVDs, and I need all the space that my editors give me just to tackle those topics! However, if the basic introduction to editing and authoring in this chapter is enough to pique your interest, I recommend *iMovie 2 For Dummies*, written by Todd Stauffer, and *Digital Video For Dummies,* 3rd Edition, written by Keith Underdahl (both published by Wiley Publishing, Inc.).

What's Involved in Recording a DVD-R or DVD+R?

In short, the same four things required in order to burn a CD-R are involved in recording a DVD-R or DVD+R:

- A recorder
- A blank disc
- Your source material
- The appropriate recording software (either UDF/packet writing, a DVD authoring program with built-in burning capabilities, or a full-blown mastering program similar to Easy CD & DVD Creator or Nero 6)

With this close resemblance to the now-familiar process of CD recording, what gives DVD recording that James Bond feeling — at least at the time this book was written? Here are a number of reasons:

- **Prices are still high.** The painful side of DVD-R/W, DVD+R/W, and DVD-RAM recording simply *starts* with the high cost of the drive. Then you're hit with the cost of the blank media! A single DVD-R sets you back $1 or $2, and a typical DVD-RAM is a hefty $15. The higher the cost, the less appealing DVD recording remains to average computer owners.

- **DVD standards are still evolving.** "Should I invest in DVD-RW, or is there something just around the bend? Will my DVD player read the discs that I record?" Unfortunately, far too many question marks still surround the different DVD formats, and many computer owners are holding back another six months to a year, hoping for one to become a clear winner.

- **Perceived value.** At this point, many folks just don't feel that they *need* the space offered by recordable DVD. DVD is attractive for digital video and system backups, but 700MB per CD-R is still a fair chunk of territory (at a mere pittance of a price, too).

- **DV is only just becoming a mainstream technology.** As DV camcorders continue to drop in price and Uncle Milton decides to try out digital video editing, DVD recording is sure to heat up (pun intended). Right now, the analog camcorder and the VHS VCR are still King of the Mountain.

The Heavy Stuff: Introducing DVD Authoring

If you have been reading up on DVD technology, you know that DVD *authoring* (that's the process of creating an interactive DVD-ROM title, usually involving digital video, still images, and custom-written programs) and DVD burning go hand in hand.

Authoring a disc involves a little bit of flowchart design (the creation of a logical menu system), a little bit of artistic talent (the development of a distinctive look and feel for the buttons, images, and background), and at least a basic knowledge of digital video. Of course, the DVD-Video discs that you buy at your local video store are authored by professionals who use hardware and software packages that cost many thousands of dollars. You may be surprised, however, at the results that *you* can achieve with the right software, as you see in the iDVD project at the end of this chapter. (My first DVD amazed my family. After they played with the menu system for several minutes, I was such a hit that I could have sold them oceanfront property in Kansas.)

Although the recording is only a small part of the authoring process, I want to give you a small taste of two authoring programs. iDVD 3 is a free package that's exceptionally easy to use, and DVD Studio Pro 2 is a full-blown professional authoring package that sets you back $500. (If that's not a wide price range, I don't know what is.) Both these programs were developed by Apple (www.apple.com) and run exclusively on the Macintosh, but PC folks get about the same treatment at the low-end price point with MyDVD 5 Deluxe from Sonic for $70 at www.sonic.com. Coincidentally — wink, wink — MyDVD works very much like iDVD 3. Go figure.

Welcome to the world of iDVD

iDVD 3, a Mac OS X application, ships with the current crop of high-end G4 and G5 Macs that offer the DVD-R SuperDrive. Because iDVD is aimed squarely at novices, it has only a small selection of the more powerful features offered by more expensive authoring applications. For example, iDVD automatically creates your disc's menu system, and you're limited to full-screen video. But, friends and neighbors, the kids at the local elementary school are now using iDVD. It's easy — and if it's easy, *normal* people will try it!

DVDs created with iDVD are limited to displaying digital video and still images (using a slideshow format). These displays are organized into media folders (which, in turn, can hold subfolders). I especially like the fact that discs created with iDVD take advantage of the DVD player remote control (even though you don't have to know anything about how your DVD remote functions). It's all taken care of automatically by iDVD, leaving you free to concentrate on where to put what and how it should look.

An iDVD disc can contain up to about 90 minutes of digital video (DV) or a combination of DV and slides. After you have completed your design, you can use the program's Preview mode to try out your disc before you burn it (complete with a virtual remote).

For a guided tour through the process of creating a DVD-Video disc with iDVD 3, check out the project at the end of this chapter.

Letting loose with DVD Studio Pro

On the other end of the spectrum, you have a heavyweight of DVD authoring: DVD Studio Pro 2 includes commercial features, like Macrovision copy protection, support for today's popular widescreen aspect ratio, a total of nine possible camera angles, MPEG format support, region coding, and much more. You have complete control over your menu creation, with layered images taken from Adobe Photoshop. Unlike with iDVD, you choose what actions are taken when the different buttons are pressed on the DVD player's remote control. Whereas iDVD 3 can use only one audio track — the audio from the video itself — a high-end package like DVD Studio Pro allows as many as eight tracks, so you can mix music with your DV.

As with iDVD, you get a Preview mode with DVD Studio Pro, so you can double-check all your work before burning. Speaking of recording, that too is supported internally. As extra options, you can also write your completed project to a disc image or DLT tape.

If you're already well-versed in digital video editing, you should feel right at home using DVD Studio Pro 2 (and you should be better prepared for the high prices for DV hardware and software). If you have just bought your Macintosh and you have never shot a frame of DV, I recommend that you pass on both the complexity and the price. This package will likely take you places where you don't want to venture, so stick with iDVD 3 (or, on the Windows side, MyDVD 5).

Let UDF Do the Work

Here's another of my patented Nuggets o' Knowledge, a Mark's Maxim for rewriteable recording:

> **What works with CD-RW usually works just as well with DVD-RW or DVD+RW.**™

(Look out — you could soon see this catchy phrase on bumper stickers and T-shirts.)

In this case, what works is *Universal Disc Format* — or UDF, otherwise known as your old friend *packet writing,* which is compatible with Mac OS 9, Mac OS X, and all versions of Windows 98 (and later). A number of great programs are available for both Windows and the Mac operating system (OS) that implement the Holy Grail of UDF. These applications allow you to use your recordable DVD drive as a 4.7GB floppy (isn't *that* a mind-boggling idea?) except that your DVD recorder is much faster and much more reliable and holds a heck of a lot more.

For DVD packet writing, I use Roxio's Drag-to-Disc, which I cover in stunning detail in Chapter 10. Of course, you can also run the full-blown Easy CD & DVD Creator to build a DVD from a project layout, as I demonstrate in Chapter 8 . . . but it takes longer, and I'm a creature who craves instant satisfaction.

Project: Recording a DVD-R with iDVD

Do you have a DVD-R drive in your Macintosh? Yes? Then you're a self-contained movie studio, and you probably didn't even know it! (Don't worry — you have plenty of time to hit eBay and bid on a beret, a megaphone, and one of those chalkboards with the clacky thing on top.) On the software end, all you need is iDVD 3. (And, as you've probably already figured out, this project gives you a good idea of how to handle things under Windows XP with MyDVD 5.)

In this project, I use iDVD to show you how to create a home video DVD-Video disc that you can watch in almost any standard DVD player. You may be amazed at how easy Apple has made the process and how professional your finished DVD looks. The completed disc features

- ✔ An interactive menu system
- ✔ Separate menus for digital video and a slideshow of still photographs
- ✔ Menu music imported from iTunes
- ✔ An automated slideshow

As a first step, you should convert or export your video in QuickTime format. Both iMovie and Final Cut Pro allow you to export QuickTime movies directly, but you can also use QuickTime Pro to convert video from other formats. If you plan to add digital images, I recommend that they be in JPEG format, which takes up far less room than the same images in TIFF format.

One cool feature of iDVD is its ability to use a digital photograph as the background for your DVD menu system. If you want to do this, make sure that the image you're using is 640x480 pixels. (If necessary, you can resize it with any image editor; I use Photoshop.)

After your source material has been converted to QuickTime and JPEG, follow these steps:

1. **Double-click the iDVD icon in your Applications folder to launch the program, which displays the iDVD project window that you see in Figure 13-1.**

In effect, the project window is the skeleton for your DVD menu, so it's time to put something on those bare bones.

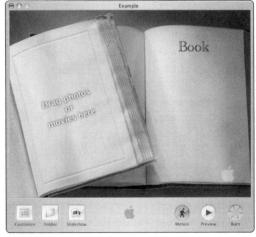

Figure 13-1:
The iDVD project window, ready to receive your creative genius.

2. **Choose Project➪Project Info. Click in the Disc Name field and type the name for your DVD. Click OK to save the change.**

   In this case, I entered **Example**. (Just call me Mr. Imagination.)

   Next, it's time to choose a theme, which includes preconfigured choices for fonts, button styles, and the background image used in your menu.

3. **Click the Customize button in the main iDVD window, which opens the iDVD Theme drawer.**

4. **Click the Themes button at the top of the drawer and scroll through the choices that appear, as shown in Figure 13-2, to choose a theme.**

   For this example, select the Green Linen 2 thumbnail in the list.

Figure 13-2:
Some of the prebuilt iDVD themes that you can choose from.

5. **To use your own background image, click the Settings button in the Theme drawer (see Figure 13-3), drag an image from a Finder window, and drop it into the Image/Movie thumbnail (or *well*) in the Background section.**

   To add a moving background, drag a QuickTime movie into the well instead.

Figure 13-3: Displaying the settings for an iDVD project.

At this point, the blank menu system, shown in Figure 13-4, already looks classier than anything I ever did with my VHS camcorder.

Figure 13-4: The menu after the theme has been applied.

You can also indulge in additional iLife goodness: Click the Photos button in the iDVD drawer and select an image directly from your iPhoto collection.

6. **Click the title text to change it, type the title for your menu, and press Return to save it.**

In Figure 13-5, I've used the title "Our Lazy Crazy Day at the Beach." Man, do I like Apple software!

Figure 13-5:
Changing
the title of
the menu is
child's play.

The theme is, well, themes!

If you want to import your own image as a menu background — or you want to create your own theme and use it for all your future iDVD projects — click the Settings button at the top of the iDVD drawer. As you can see in the following figure, you have much to specify here, including the background image, the position and font properties of your title and buttons, and the shape of your buttons. After you have selected what you like from the Settings panel, click the Save in Favorite button and specify a name for your theme. After it has been saved, you can pick your custom theme for any project.

7. Drag an audio clip into the Audio well in the Settings panel.

What fun is a menu without your favorite background tune? You can drag the audio file from a Finder window, or click the Audio button in the iDVD drawer to choose a song from your iTunes collection (if you're feeling sassy). iDVD recognizes AIFF, MP3, AAC, and WAV sound files.

Next, it's time to add a video clip to the menu. That sounds a tad daunting, but there's nothing to fear with iDVD.

8. Open the folder that contains your QuickTime movies and drag one to the iDVD project window.

As you can see in Figure 13-6, the program creates a custom button using a thumbnail image from the video. The button is automatically centered in the screen for you. Definitely not daunting.

Figure 13-6:
The first video clip appears in the iDVD project.

9. Because the title under the button is less than descriptive, change it: Click once on the text to display the edit box and type a new name.

You can also move the slider that appears above the button to choose the thumbnail image from within the clip. (This is great for clips that begin with darkness or something equally as uninteresting.) Figure 13-7 illustrates the slider. If you enable the Movie check box, the Movie button in the menu becomes animated!

You can move a Movie button anywhere you like on your menu — just click it and drag it to the desired destination; it snaps to the closest position on an imaginary grid. You can turn off this automatic alignment by enabling the Free Position option in the Settings panel.

10. Add additional clips by repeating Steps 8 and 9.

You can add a maximum of six buttons to a single DVD menu screen; personally, I avoid overcrowding a menu by adding no more than four buttons.

Figure 13-7:
You can
select the
image that
appears on
your button,
dude.

11. **Add a separate submenu for your slideshow display of digital images: Click the Folder button to add a submenu button to the project window and change the button name to whatever you like (I typed** Slide Show**).**

You can change the look of your menu buttons another way: Click the Settings button in the Theme drawer, and then select any Movie button you've added to your DVD menu layout. Adjust the button's properties in the Button section of the Settings panel, and voilà! You have a new appearance for your buttons!

12. **Double-click the Slideshow button on your iDVD menu to display the submenu screen. Click the title at the top of the submenu screen to open the edit box, type your title text, and press Return to save it.**

13. **It's time to add the Slideshow button itself. Click the Slideshow button at the bottom of the iDVD window, which adds a button to your submenu.**

14. **Double-click the button that you added; this opens the My Slideshow window. Drag the images that you want to add from their locations on your hard drive into the window, as shown in Figure 13-8.**

Once again, you can add images to your slideshow in another way: Click the Photos button at the top of the iDVD drawer, which displays all the images in your iPhoto Library (as well as the albums that you've defined there). Images can be dragged from the Photos tab to the Slideshow window.

15. **At this point, you need to decide whether you want an automated slideshow or a manual slideshow. If your parents had a slide projector like mine did, this step should really interest you:**

   • **Manual:** For a manual slideshow, leave the Slide Duration drop-down list box set to Manual. It's a good idea to enable the Display < > During Slideshow check box, which superimposes left and right arrows on the image as appropriate. (Although these arrows are optional, they help remind Aunt Harriet how to advance through the photos in a manual slideshow.) The lucky person holding the DVD player remote control presses the right cursor key to move forward through the images and the left cursor key to move backward.

- **Automatic:** The DVD player displays the images automatically (but you can still move forward and backward by using the remote). Click the Slide Duration drop-down list box and select the number of seconds to delay before switching to the next image. If you like, you can still enable the Display < > During Slideshow check box.

Figure 13-8:
Preparing
the contents
of the
slideshow.

16. **How about some audio for that slideshow of your cousin's wedding? Again, you can drag an audio file from a Finder window to the Audio well in the Slideshow window.**

If you're a fan of iTunes, click the Audio button in the iDVD drawer and you can choose that perfect song from your iTunes playlists.

17. **If you want to change the order of the slideshow sequence, click and drag the image that you want to its new spot on the list. After you've finished designing your slideshow, click the Return button to return to the submenu screen.**

Whoops — now that you have added your images, don't forget to customize the slideshow button.

18. **Drag the slider to select one of the images in the slideshow as the button image. To change the button's caption, click it and type your new text; press Return to save it.**

(If you're too cool for sliders, drag one of the JPEG images that will make up your slideshow and drop it on top of the button.)

19. **Care to preview your DVD? Click the Preview button at the bottom of the iDVD window.**

iDVD displays a most cool-looking virtual remote. Note that the slideshow button in the middle of the screen is now highlighted, just as it would be if you were using your DVD player. Use the buttons on the remote to select menu items, and click Enter on the remote to activate the item that's highlighted. When you're done playing with your DVD-to-be, click the Preview button again to return to editing mode (where you can make changes if you like).

You should save your project to your hard drive before you burn it.

20. Choose File⇨Save Project As to display a standard Mac OS Save dialog box. Navigate to the destination folder, type a new name for your project, and click Save.

Okay, you film mogul, you — it's time to record your own DVD!

21. Click the Burn button, which opens to display a glowing fail-safe button. (Kinda nuclear-looking, ain't it?)

Apple doesn't want you to waste a blank disc with an accidental click of your mouse. (Plus, it's one of the neatest animated controls I've ever used.)

22. Click the Burn button again to start the recording process, and load a blank DVD-R into your DVD recorder when prompted.

After the first disc has been burned, you can choose to record additional copies.

23. When the recording is done, eject the disc and pop it in your DVD player.

Or, if you like, you can watch your creation on your Mac with the Mac OS X DVD Player, which you can find in the Applications folder.

I should warn you that iDVD has quite a bit of housekeeping to do to prepare your digital video, so you probably have to wait several minutes before the recording starts. (This preparation time depends on the speed of your Mac, the number of movies that you have added, and how long they are.)

Chapter 14

Adding That Spiffy Touch

. . . .

. . . .

*J*ust how proud are you of your finished discs? I probably should narrow the focus of that question a little: Just how proud are you of the *appearance* of your finished discs?

If you're happy with the sound of an audio CD and your computer can easily read all the information that you recorded on a data disc, you're technically done. If you're distributing your discs to others, though, or you want to include background information on the contents of a CD, I highly recommend that you take the extra step of printing a CD label or jewel case inserts. Heck, for the most professional look, go hog-wild and print a matching set of labels and their accompanying inserts!

In this chapter, I show you how to design and create with Label Creator, and you add that spiffy visual touch that separates a ho-hum burning project from a true masterpiece of art.

How Not to Label Your Discs

Before I get down to the business of adding a stylish, professional look to your recorded discs, allow me to make absolutely, *positively* sure that you don't damage them! You can indeed simply write a title on top of the disc — in fact, most blank discs these days are preprinted with straight lines to help you write neatly — but if you would rather label your discs by hand, please make sure that you avoid any of these writing instruments while marking directly on your silver friends:

✔ **Ballpoint or sharp-tipped pens:** If your writing instrument has a sharp point and it's metallic, don't even *think* about using it to mark your discs! Standard ink is hard to see and simply wipes off most discs. That's not the real danger, though: You could scratch the surface of the disc and damage it.

✔ **Soluble markers:** Although I advise you elsewhere in this book to keep liquids away from your discs, soluble (also called *erasable*) markers are also affected by the oil from your fingertips. In other words, if you happen to brush your finger across the disc, *Ella Fitzgerald* may suddenly become *la rald.* That's not enough information to help me determine who's singing — although, in Ella's case, I don't really *need* a label! Stick with permanent markers, and you get to keep all the words you write.

✔ **Paint pens:** Kids love these newfangled craft pens — your discs, on the other hand, most definitely do not. The solvents in a typical paint pen can damage the clear protective lacquer layer on top of the disc, and the buildup produced by a paint pen can unbalance the disc if it's heavily used. Also, a disc with any type of buildup may be harder to use in your car audio CD player. Can you imagine what loose flakes of paint could do to that $400 CD deck you bought for your Porsche?

Some manufacturers of recordable DVDs advise that you shouldn't apply paper labels at all to their media. Check the instructions that accompanied your blank media to see whether you should add a label to that new DVD-Video disc you just burned!

Of course, I may sound overly cautious, but let me be blunt: I have more than twelve hundred music discs in my collection (some of which are irreplaceable live recordings), and I want each and every disc to last as long as possible! The same goes for data CD-ROMs and DVD-ROMs; any digital camera owner who enjoys the hobby probably would be just as protective of a photo collection archived to CD-ROM.

Hey, You Can Tell a Disc By Its Cover

If you're like me, an audio CD isn't really complete with a simple title and an artist name scribbled on top. That works for a road mix with various artists, perhaps, but I would still like to know the name of each track (as a minimum). For my favorite music — and the rarer recordings in my collections — I like to have much more on hand:

✔ The total time for each track in minutes and seconds — good for determining at a glance how long a particular period of musical nostalgia will last. (For me, it's the '70s.)

✔ For live performances, I add the location and date of the gig and who joined in the jam.

✔ For composers, I include the year of their birth and death.

✔ For jazz groups, I like to keep track of who played what instrument.

Naturally, you can't fit all that (or even a significant part of it) on the CD label. Here's where the extra space provided by jewel box inserts comes in so handy: With the two sides of the front insert and a single-sided back insert, I have all the territory I need to satisfy my historical urges.

Easy CD & DVD Creator doesn't let you down! As part of the package, Roxio provides a great object-oriented visual editor, Label Creator, that's likely to satisfy even the most demanding label and insert fanatic (even those of us who can't produce much more than a stick figure).

The program allows you to

✔ Add straight or curved text — with optional justification — using your choice of fonts

✔ Include your own graphics and images

✔ Use basic shapes like squares and circles in your design

✔ Add cut and fold lines to help keep your geometry accurate

✔ Choose from a number of preset themes, which apply to all elements of your label and cover set

Label Creator can use a huge variety of precut inserts, or you can print to regular paper and use a cutting board to achieve the same results.

Progress marches on . . . if you're using a DVD-R/W, DVD+R/W, or DVD-RAM drive, check out the inserts that the program can create for standard plastic DVD cases. The latest version of Label Creator can even produce labels for those funky mini-discs!

"Hmmm, Can I Label with Duct Tape?"

Disc labels are big business these days: Just visit the software section of your local Maze O' Wires electronics store, and you're likely to see at least three or four different disc labeling packages. Some include only the label design, printing software, and some blank labels to get you started; these labels are applied by hand using a template guide, usually while the disc is held tightly in its jewel case. Other packages include a device to help you precisely align the label with the top of the disc.

I use the NEATO CD labeling system (www.neato.com), which includes the two-piece NEATO label application device shown in Figure 14-1. To use the device, you place your disc upside-down on the spindle (so that the recorded side is facing up) and you put your printed paper label facedown on the base. To apply the label, you simply push the spindle into the base and press down. There's no chance of misalignment, and the finished label is free from bubbles.

CD-ROM, recorded side up

Spindle

Label backing

Figure 14-1:
The NEATO CD labeler device is just that.

After a label is applied to a disc, *never attempt to remove it* (unless the labels that you're using specifically say that you can do so). Virtually all labels are designed to be permanent, and they don't peel off!

I would say that disc labels come in a rainbow of colors, but that would be cliché — how about all the colors of the rainbow instead? You can even get clear labels that allow the color of the disc to show through from underneath — perfect for use with those neon-colored blank discs.

The NEATO system also comes with label design-and-printing software called MediaFACE II (see Figure 14-2), which includes a set of features similar to Label Creator.

Figure 14-2:
Designing a label with MediaFACE II from NEATO.

Project: Creating Jewel Box Inserts

Ready to dive into Label Creator? In this project, I create a custom set of jewel box inserts for a compendium of classic TV show theme songs that I've just recorded from my MP3 collection. The inserts should list each track, the time for each song, and the total time for the entire disc. The example uses clip art of a TV set for the graphic.

Follow these steps:

1. **Choose Start⇨All Programs⇨Easy CD and DVD Creator 6⇨Label Creator to display the program's main window, as shown in Figure 14-3.**

   Make sure that the Front icon is selected in the Cover display on the left side of the screen.

   You can also choose to launch Label Creator as soon as you have successfully burned a disc. Starting the program this way automatically carries the text information from the project layout into your label project.

Figure 14-3: Where it all begins — the Label Creator main window.

If you like, you can use one of the Label Creator standard themes, which provides a common background, entry fields, and a font for you to use. Now it's time to take a look at changing themes.

2. **Choose Format➪Change Theme to open the Change Theme dialog box that you see in Figure 14-4.**

If you hate menus with a passion, you can click the Theme toolbar icon instead, or simply double-click the desired theme thumbnail in the theme strip at the bottom of the window. (Try saying that three times fast.)

Figure 14-4:
Choosing
another
theme for
your inserts.

Notice that Label Creator marks each theme as being either an audio theme or a data theme. Although any theme can be used for any type of disc, these tags indicate which types of fields automatically carry over from a project layout. (Basically, if you choose to use an audio theme with a data DVD-ROM, you have to do more work and create all the fields manually.)

3. **Select a jazzy retro audio theme to match those classic TV melodies: Select 60's [Audio] and watch as the program updates the Preview window. You can continue to check out new themes, but after you're done, select 60's [Audio] again and click OK to accept it.**

If you start Label Creator immediately after recording a disc, all the text information is already loaded into the fields. Because you started the program from the Start menu, you need to import the information from the disc.

4. Load your audio or data disc into your recorder.

I mention earlier in this book that enabling CD-Text is A Good Thing. This is one of the reasons: Label Creator can use CD-Text to import text into a label project at any point in the future.

5. In the Label Creator window, choose Add⇨Disc Contents.

If you have more than one disc loaded on your system, the program asks you which disc to use. Otherwise, it imports the disc information that you entered when you burned the disc. As you can see in Figure 14-5, this includes the title and artist name — the track list for an audio CD appears on the Booklet and Back cover layouts. Remember, you can switch back and forth between the different cover layouts in a project by clicking the buttons at the left of the window.

6. If you want to make a change to any of the fields before you print (for example, to correct a spelling error that you may have made when you typed the text the first time), double-click directly in the field. An edit text box appears, and you can type the information directly in the field. Press Enter to save your changes.

If you make a mistake while you're editing your layout, don't forget that old standby: The Undo button on the toolbar.

Figure 14-5:
It's like magic! All the fields have been typed for you.

7. **To add the clip art, choose Add⇨Picture to display a standard File Open dialog box. Navigate to the location of the clip art (which can be in Windows bitmap or JPEG formats), click the filename to highlight it, and click Open.**

   The graphic appears in its own resizable window.

8. **To change the dimensions of the graphic, move your mouse cursor to any of the square handles on the edge of the window and click and drag to resize the edge. To move the entire graphic somewhere else on the layout, click in the middle of the graphic window and drag it to the spot you want.**

   Figure 14-6 illustrates the futuristic TV object, ready to be resized and relocated.

Figure 14-6:
I can do just about anything with this TV. Aren't computers wonderful?

9. **To add a new block of text, choose Add⇨Text or Curved Text.**

   A text block appears, ready for you to resize and relocate, as you did with your graphics.

10. **To enter the text, double-click the text box to make it an edit text box, and then type something; press Enter to save your changes.**

11. **If you're using precut insert paper, load it into the printer as instructed by the manufacturer.**

    When you're ready to print (or you that you're ready to print), use the Print Preview function first — it can save you one or two sheets of paper!

12. **Choose File⇨Print Preview to display the screen shown in Figure 14-7. If you're satisfied, click Print on the toolbar; if you need to make changes, click Close and return to the layout.**

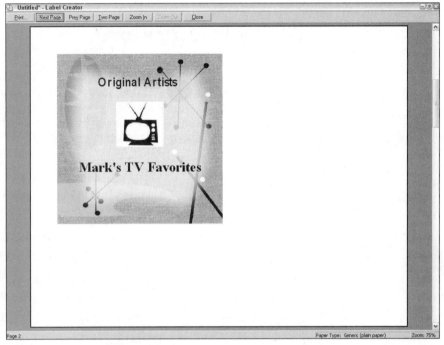

Figure 14-7:
Checking
things out
with Print
Preview
before
printing.

**13. You can also print a back cover insert by clicking on the Back button
in the Cover display on the left side of the screen.**

Because you have already either imported or typed your information,
the back cover layout automatically includes all that text. (Whew!)
Figure 14-8 illustrates the back cover layout for my TV Theme Songs
audio CD.

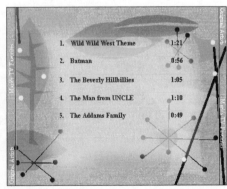

Figure 14-8:
A standard
back cover
layout, with
text already
entered
automat-
ically. Neat!

"Hey, where's my text?"

If nothing shows up when you click the Contents button, Label Creator cannot load any text from the disc. Do you give up hope and throw your hands up into the air helplessly? Not likely! You can add that information in two ways:

✔ **Siphon the Internet:** If the disc is a copy of an existing audio CD, Label Creator automatically does the Internet thing and tries to download the information from a CD database. If this doesn't work, make sure that the Enable Audio Disc Information Download check box is enabled: Choose Edit➪Preferences and click the Internet tab to display the field, as shown in the following figure. Enable the check box (if it's not already enabled) and click OK.

✔ **Start typing:** If Label Creator reports that your disc can't be found in the Internet CD database, you have to manually enter any information that you want printed on the inserts. Choose Add➪Track to open the Add New Track dialog box (see the following figure), and enter just the information you want; it can include the track number, title, and the duration. Click Add Track to save the information to the label layout. Repeat this procedure for each track; after you have finished, click Done. Finally, double-click the words Artist or Title within the main screen to enter the artist name and the disc title. Label Creator opens an edit text box, and you can type the information directly in the field. Press Enter to save your changes.

Project: Creating a CD Label

Now I need to create a CD label for a disc that is a collection of pop tunes for a kid's birthday party. Because I want to give the disc to the guest of honor after the party, it needs to look its best! Follow these steps to create a CD or DVD label:

1. **Choose Start➪All Programs➪Easy CD and DVD Creator 6➪Label Creator to run Label Creator. In the Cover display on the left side o f the screen, click the Disc icon, which opens the layout shown in Figure 14-9.**

2. **Import the disc information by choosing Add➪Disc Contents.**

   For a standard label, this step fills in the track names, the title, and the artist name.

   You could click the Theme toolbar button and select one of the Roxio themes, but in this case you want to use a background of your own.

3. **Choose Format➪Change Background to display the Change Background dialog box, shown in Figure 14-10.**

4. **Enable the Disc Label check box and click the Select a Picture button to display the File Open dialog box.**

   To add an image acquired directly from your digital camera or scanner, click the Acquire a Picture button instead.

5. **Locate your JPEG or Windows bitmap image file. Select the filename and click Open. You see that the background is loaded on the disc label template. Click OK to return to the Label Creator main screen.**

Figure 14-9:
An empty
disc label
layout,
ready for
your artistic
side.

Figure 14-10:
Choosing
a custom
background
for an audio
CD label.

6. **Click the Font drop-down list box in the toolbar and select a festive font. (Note the example of the font that appears to the right of each name in the list.) To increase or decrease the font size, select a number from the Points drop-down list box.**

Remember that the changes you make to the text format and font affect only the text box that's selected (in this case, the Title text box).

7. **Select the Artist text box and choose the same font and point size.**

8. **Add a Happy Birthday message and the date to the disc. Choose Add⇨Text, which adds a new text block to the layout. Resize and relocate the new text block below the spindle hole.**

9. **Double-click the text box to make it an edit text box, type the text, and then press Enter to save your changes.**

The completed label is illustrated in Figure 14-11.

Figure 14-11:
This label
turns a mere
audio CD
into a true
birthday
present!

10. **Load your CD label blanks into your printer as instructed by the manufacturer.**

11. **Choose File⇨Print Preview to check the appearance of the label. If you're satisfied, click Print on the toolbar; if you need to make changes, click Close and return to the layout.**

Part V
The Part of Tens

In this part . . .

Step right up, step right up! Gentlefolk, I offer you valuable tips, guidelines, and advice on CD and DVD recording. You, too, can be a sharp troubleshooter, but be wary of pitfalls along the way. I also point out ten sweet little programs that may become invaluable as a part of your personal CD recording studio.

Chapter 15

Ten Hardware Troubleshooting Tips

*N*othing is worse than a minor hardware problem — except, of course, a major hardware problem. In this Part of Tens chapter, I cover my favorite tips to help you leap over the most common physical troubles with CD and DVD recording: that is, those difficulties that result from your hardware settings, your blank media, and — most important — your drive. Some of these items are mentioned earlier in this book, but they're important enough (and crop up enough) that they should be repeated.

"Why, Of Course the Jumper Is Set Correctly!"

Tip: Check and *double-check* your jumper and DIP switch settings before you replace the cover on your computer.

Let me be honest: Configuring both jumpers and DIP switches is a pain, and both EIDE and SCSI recorder owners are stuck with them. Every drive manufacturer seems to use different settings, and if you're installing an older drive (or one you scavenged from a friend or relative), you may find yourself without documentation on which jumpers need to be moved where. (It's best to ignore the USB and FireWire folks snickering in the background — they have no jumpers to set.)

Unfortunately, those settings mean the difference between your drive working and not working; unlike with horseshoes, you don't get points when you come close with your jumper settings. Therefore:

- ✔ When you're installing an EIDE drive, check any other device on the cable (even if the other device shouldn't have to change its master and slave settings).

- ✔ Check your drive's documentation to make sure that the drive is oriented properly so that its pins match the pins in the manual. (After all, a group of eight pins looks the same when viewed upside down.) Most jumper pin sets are marked with identifying numbers on the circuit board to help you determine which pin is Pin 1. DIP switches are easier to "read" than jumper pins because each switch is clearly marked.

- ✔ Never use a pencil when setting DIP switches, because the lead from the pencil can result in a shorted switch.

- ✔ Save any jumpers that you can completely remove; it's amazing just how precious that little chunk of plastic and metal can be. Stick any spares in your parts bin and cherish them.

- ✔ If you don't have any documentation for an EIDE or SCSI device and you don't know the settings, visit the manufacturer's Web site and look for manuals in text or Adobe Acrobat PDF format.

How You Turn Things On Does Make a Difference

Tip: Turn external drives on before you boot your computer.

Most computer owners figure that they can turn on their computers and external toys in any order, but that approach can cause problems — especially with external SCSI drives, which are particularly sensitive to these matters. As a rule, turn on all external peripherals first, like your printer, scanner, and CD or DVD recorder.

You can easily take care of this problem once and for all: Buy a surge suppressor or UPS (uninterruptible power supply) for your system and plug your computer and all your peripherals into it. Just leave everything plugged in and switched on. Then use the switch on the surge suppressor or UPS to turn everything on at one time. (Think of it as that big master switch that Dr. Frankenstein always pulled to start everything in the laboratory.) Because your external stuff comes on instantly (before your computer even gets started booting up), this method is the same as turning on everything external by hand.

(This little trick is one of those that separates the novices from the power users, so consider yourself initiated.)

Where Did That Click Come From?

Tip: Always use Disc-at-Once recording when you're burning audio CDs.

Although this question indicates a hardware problem, it's not a problem you can solve with a setting change on your computer. If you're hearing irritating clicks between tracks when you play an audio CD, the hardware in question is your audio CD player. This happens with many older players when you burn audio CDs using the Track-at-Once recording method; the click is caused by the gap your recorder leaves between tracks, which your audio CD player detects. To make things even more frustrating, that same CD plays perfectly in other audio CD players and CD-ROM drives.

To avoid the problem altogether, *always* use the Disc-at-Once recording method when you're burning audio CDs. Fortunately, all but the most antique CD recorders (those older than five years or so) are able to record with Disc-at-Once. Because these older drives are as slow as molasses in an Alaskan winter, I strongly recommend that you spend $150 or so and buy a new drive. Not only do you get Disc-at-Once, but you can also see the progress bar moving when you record a disc. (Ever recorded at 2X? I started out with a 2X recorder in the halcyon days of the early 90's . . . that, good neighbors, is the *definition* of the word *plodding*.)

Your Recorder Wants to Play, Too

Tip: Don't forget to connect the audio cable from your sound card to your new drive.

Here's another common problem that I hear all the time: "My recorder works great when I'm burning discs, but if I try to play an audio CD with my CD or DVD recorder, I get nothing."

If you can hear the audio with headphones connected to your drive's headphone jack, you have pinpointed this problem: You forgot to connect the digital audio output cable from your drive to your sound card. Without this cable, the drive can play an audio CD and you'll never hear it. You probably received the cable with your sound card — sometimes, drive manufacturers include one, too. If you have already connected a CD-ROM or DVD-ROM drive to your sound card, use that drive rather than your recorder to listen to audio CDs. Most sound cards have only one of these input connectors.

Driving Miss Data

Tip: Keep up-to-date any hardware drivers required by your drive.

For folks using internal EIDE and SCSI drives, this isn't much of an issue — an internal drive uses the standard hardware drivers that come with Windows or Mac OS. However, external USB and FireWire drives are a different matter entirely. These recorders often use drivers supplied by the manufacturer, and it's possible for other hardware installations to overwrite them accidentally, causing your drive to take a dive.

At least, I *think* it's by accident — sometimes, a typical PC system reminds me of a gladiator's arena. Various pieces of hardware and software battle it out with sword and shield to see who works and who fails. (And then, of course, Microsoft releases a new version of Windows, the arena master lets loose the lions, and *everything* fails.)

Your drive's manufacturer may also release new versions of that hardware driver; these updates can solve problems or improve compatibility with your operating system.

Check your drive's manual for the company's Web site and download the latest drivers directly to your computer; if you're not on the Internet at this time, call the company's tech support line and request that someone send you the drivers on a disk.

Keep Your Firmware on the Cutting Edge

Tip: Flash your recorder with the latest firmware.

That advice may sound somewhat racy, but in this case, the term *flash* means the updating of your drive's internal firmware. Your recorder's firmware stores all the programming for its various functions — much like the BIOS (Basic Input/Output System) stores settings and configurations for a PC. It's called firmware because it can be updated, just like the hardware drivers that I cover in the preceding section. In fact, you update your drive's firmware for many of the same reasons that you update hardware drivers: to fix bugs in your drive's operation, improve the performance of the drive, and even add or enhance a feature or two.

Again, the manufacturer's Web site generally offers firmware upgrades, but if you're without Web access and you're lucky enough to talk to technical support, you can request that an upgrade be sent to you in the mail.

Speed Does Make a Difference

Tip: Use the fastest drive on your system to store images and temporary files.

With all the sky-high X factors wandering around the countryside — 8X DVD recording, and 40X CD recording — it's easy to forget that your hard drive's performance also has a direct impact on the success of your CD and DVD burning. (I mention defragmenting, a way to improve your hard drive's performance, in Chapter 6.)

If you have more than one hard drive on your system, check your recording software and see whether it has a system test that you can run to determine which drive is the fastest. (Easy CD & DVD Creator has this feature: To run the system tests, run Creator Classic and choose Tools➪System Tests.) You can also download hard drive speed-testing programs from Internet shareware sites.

After you have determined which drive is the fastest, configure your recording software to use that drive for its temporary storage area. Also, choose that drive when you're saving a disc image or when you're collecting files in one place before you add them to your CD or DVD layout.

Leave This Cartridge, DVD-RAM, and Seek Your Fortune

Tip: To use a DVD-RAM in a DVD player, jettison the cartridge.

I'm a fan of DVD-RAM — I like to use my drive for backups and DV storage. Once in awhile, however, I burn a disc for use in my DVD player. (It's a third-generation player, so it can read DVD-RAMs.) Most people who try this technique quickly find out that their DVD players can't accept the huge, clunky cartridge that surrounds a DVD-RAM, so they figure that this can't be done.

If you use a DVD-RAM cartridge, you can easily remove the disc from the case for use in tray drives; in fact, the entire front side of the cartridge (by the write-protect switch) is hinged so that it can open. Find the tiny round locking pin at the bottom left of the cartridge; use a pen to punch out the pin and discard it. Locate the release tab on the left front corner of the cartridge, push in the tab with a paper clip, and you can pull the front side of the cartridge toward you.

Keep in mind that the surface of any recordable DVD media (that includes DVD-R/W, DVD+R/W, and DVD-RAM) is much — and brothers and sisters, I do mean *much* — more sensitive to fingerprints and dust than a CD-R or CD-RW. Take the utmost precaution in handling a recordable DVD, and follow this Mark's Maxim to the letter:

> **Never set a recordable DVD on a surface (not even label side down); leave it outside its jewel box or your drive only long enough to transport it back and forth.™**

Take That Cleaning Disc Far, Far Away

Tip: Never, never, never use a CD-ROM or DVD-ROM cleaning disc in your recorder.

They certainly *look* innocent and harmless, hanging on the shelf at your local discount store. But don't be tempted to try a CD-ROM or DVD-ROM cleaning disc in your CD or DVD recorder. These discs typically use a tiny brush on the underside of the disc, which is supposed to sweep dust and dirt from your drive's lens. Unfortunately, they can damage your recorder's read/write lens system (which, by the way, is self cleaning anyway). Those tiny bristles can be pulled loose and stick in your drive, or the brush can scratch the surface of the laser lens.

The best way to keep your recorder clean is to keep the tray closed. Don't leave it open unless you're loading or unloading a disc. If you have an external recorder, wipe it from time to time with a dry, static-free cloth to remove surface dust.

When Your Disc Cries, "I'm Stuck!"

Tip: Use the emergency eject hole to unload a troublesome disc.

Typically, you use the emergency eject hole on the front of your drive if

- ✔ The disc isn't turning in the drive for some reason (perhaps it was loaded off-center in the tray).
- ✔ Your computer's operating system has locked up and you can't eject the tray.
- ✔ You have a hardware driver problem and the tray doesn't eject.

To manually eject the tray, carefully insert a straightened paperclip into the emergency eject hole on the front of your drive and push it gently. This technique may take a few tries because the release button you're trying to press is pretty small. (If this seems a little silly, feel free to hum the theme from *Mission Impossible*.)

Chapter 16

Ten Software Troubleshooting Tips

"**I**t's only software — you can fix it easily, right?" I wish that I had a dime for every time I've heard that question. For some reason, most computer owners seem to feel that a software glitch is automatically easier to solve than a hardware problem. This, dear friends, is about as accurate as Napoleon's assessment of Waterloo. In fact, software incompatibilities can be even harder to track down and solve than hardware problems. Both Windows and Mac OS use dozens of drivers and programs (tactlessly spread out over the entire hard drive in locations dark and mysterious) to control the operation of a single CD recorder. They all have to work together as a team, but sometimes some of these files seem to strike out on their own just to generate headaches for you.

I use this Part of Tens chapter to address the software tips I dispense most often to my family, friends, and consulting customers. Only the latter have to pay anything, but I eat well during the holidays. I cover three or four of these tips in earlier chapters, but they belong in the Top Ten Tips category, so you also find them here.

Device Manager: Checking under the Windows Hood

Tip: Use the Windows Device Manager to check for possible software conflicts.

Most Windows owners have used the Device Manager (see Figure 16-1) from time to time to take care of a specific task — for instance, enabling or disabling auto insert notification, which I cover in the section, "In Case of a Disc Loading, Please Notify Windows Immediately," later in this chapter. You may not realize, however, that the Device Manager also makes a doggone good basic software diagnostic tool. With it, you can check

- ✔ Whether hardware devices and their software drivers are working correctly

- ✔ Whether two hardware devices are "fighting" over the same system resources (which can cause both devices to stop working or your PC to lock up)

- ✔ Whether you have hardware devices that Windows doesn't recognize

Figure 16-1: The awesome glory of the Windows Device Manager.

You can also use Device Manager to change the settings, configuration, and properties for each piece of hardware on your system. To display the Device Manager in Windows 2000 and Windows XP, right-click the My Computer icon on your Windows desktop and choose Properties from the pop-up menu. Click the Hardware tab, and then click the Device Manager button. If a device is causing problems, Windows marks it with either a yellow question mark symbol or a red check symbol. You can display the properties for any hardware device by clicking it to highlight it and choosing Properties.

If another device is attempting to use the same system resources as your internal recorder, display the properties for the offending device and enable the Disable in this Hardware Profile check box at the bottom of the panel. This setting should allow your drive to work (at least you can record while you try to figure out what's wrong). I also recommend trying to remove the conflicting device from your system and allowing Windows to reinstall it. To do this, right-click the device in the Device Manager, click Remove, and reboot your PC.

If you have a copy of Norton Utilities 2004 or Norton SystemWorks 2004, I also heartily recommend the dynamic duo of Norton WinDoctor (shown in Figure 16-2) and Norton Disk Doctor — they're a great combination! Disk Doctor can check your drive for file and folder problems (caused by a power failure, for example), and WinDoctor automates repairs for common software problems that crop up over time (like when a program doesn't completely uninstall).

Figure 16-2:
The
WinDoctor
is in the
house.

Your Image Can Be Everything

Tip: If your older PC and CD or DVD recorder are experiencing Buffer Underrun errors, record from a disc image.

If you're using an older Pentium II or III computer and a recorder without support for burnproof recording, you likely still encounter the dreaded Buffer Underrun error. (You may remember from earlier chapters that a Buffer Underrun error indicates that your PC can't transfer data fast enough from your hard drive to your recorder. The recorder aborts the burn.) Although defragmenting helps, it doesn't solve the problem completely; the more files you record and the smaller they are, the more your computer and hard drive have to work to supply your recorder with the 1s and 0s (zeros) it craves. Buffer Underruns don't happen on every disc, but when they do, they cause a trip to Coaster City.

What can you do (other than buy a new and faster PC or a recorder that offers burnproof recording)? Here's a tip that can keep you going while you save up the cash for a new system: Use Easy CD & DVD Creator to record the project as a disc image first, and then record the actual disc from the image. Your computer has an easier time sending a single large file to your recorder than it does sending hundreds or thousands of smaller files, and you're much less likely to encounter recording errors.

For details on creating a disc image, turn to Chapter 8.

"Hey, Your Session's Open!"

Tip: Don't forget to close a session before you're finished with a disc.

You have no need to be embarrassed about this one. If you wrote a session to a disc and left it open (either because you forgot to close it or you wanted to burn more to the disc later), you can still read the disc in your recorder. However, both your computer's read-only CD-ROM drive and a standard audio CD player will likely spit it back at you. To read the disc, you have to use your recorder.

To close an open session using Easy CD & DVD Creator, load the disc into your recorder, click Disc, and choose the Disc Information menu item. From the Disc Information dialog box (illustrated beautifully in Figure 16-3), click the drive to display the information for the disc, and then click Finalize Session.

Figure 16-3:
Closing an
open
session with
a definite
bang.

"Captain's Log, Stardate, Uh — Hey, Spock, What Day Is It?"

Tip: Use the recording log to help diagnose recurring problems.

The way I see it, the more information you have — and, in the worst case, the more information your technical support representative has — the easier it is to diagnose what's going wrong with your system. Easy CD & DVD Creator can log all error messages to a file in any folder you choose, so you don't have to hover around the monitor with a scratch pad and a pencil to scribble down anything you see.

To enable error logging, click Tools and click the Options menu item to display the Creator Classic Options dialog box, as shown in Figure 16-4. Select the Enable Error Logging check box, and click the Browse button to select the folder where the log will be written. Choose a directory other than the Windows Temp directory (you don't want to lose the log because of a Disk Cleanup operation), enter a filename, like ERROR.LOG, and click Open. Finally, click OK to save your changes and return to Easy CD & DVD Creator.

To open the log, you can use Windows Notepad or any text editor — even Microsoft Word will do, in a pinch.

Figure 16-4:
It's not a
pecan log,
it's not a
cheese
log, it's a
recording
error log!

Don't Use Dated Software

Tip: Always apply the latest updates and patches to your recording software.

As hardware continues to advance, so must your software! Updates to your recording program can fix bugs, add support for new recorders, enhance the performance of the program, and improve the program's compatibility with your operating system.

However, many folks ask me "Do I need to upgrade to the latest version of the software?" Naturally, that costs you cash and, not surprisingly, I recommend that you *not* upgrade unless

✔ You specifically need a new feature that has been added to the new version.

✔ The new version performs significantly better on your current system.

✔ The current version doesn't support your brand-new recorder, and your current version will have no future updates. (Some companies have the nasty habit of dropping *all* support for older versions after one or two newer versions have been released.)

Check the software developer's Web site for updates and patches. Also, many programs now have built-in links to the company's Web site, so your recording software can launch your browser for you and automatically connect to the proper Web page. Woo-hoo!

Validation Is a Good Thing

Tip: If you're recording an ISO 9660 disc or over the network, validate before you burn.

As you may know, recording an ISO 9660 disc (which doesn't accept long file-names and folder names and strictly limits the number of folders you can add to a disc) on a Windows PC usually requires you to rename and move things within your CD layout. An ISO 9660 disc doesn't accept long names for files and folders. Unfortunately, the problems you encounter trying to record a disc are almost never apparent until you're ready to burn — or after you try to read the disc you've just burned (using your PC) on another computer that's running the Linux operating system. Although programs such as Easy CD & DVD Creator warn you about these problems, I've used recording software that didn't give me any warning whatsoever and merrily burned a useless disc.

Another common problem occurs while you're recording files over a network from a remote hard drive. If the drive is suddenly taken off the network or the remote user renames a file or folder before you start the recording, the process rewards you with a fat, juicy error and a lovely coaster as a parting gift.

Obviously, what you need in situations like these is a way to verify that

- ✔ The files and folders arranged in your layout all conform to the require-ments of the file system you have chosen
- ✔ The files and folders that reside on a remote network drive are still avail-able and still bear the same names

Lo and behold, Creator Classic delivers with its validation feature, which you can use with any layout type that includes data files. After you're ready to record and you want to verify that everything is Go for launch, choose File➪ Validate Project. You can watch the fun as the program checks each item in your CD layout; if anything fishy turns up, Creator Classic alerts you with a warning dialog and you can fix it immediately.

In Case of a Disc Loading, Please Notify Windows Immediately

Tip: Know when to enable or disable auto insert notification.

Windows offers a host of small niceties that make your computing life much easier — not the least of which is the ability to automatically run a selected program from a CD as soon as it's loaded. This feature is *AutoPlay,* and many PC owners don't know that they can disable it if they want.

Why would you want to disable AutoPlay? When you're copying tracks or entire discs during a burning session and you load a source CD-ROM, the last thing you want is an installation program automatically starting up! For this reason, many recording programs disable AutoPlay automatically. But talk about a Catch-22: If your recording software disables AutoPlay, you have to install new CD-ROM software by double-clicking the right program. (Sometimes figuring out precisely what you're supposed to run from a game's CD-ROM is a little challenging.) Plus, when you load an audio CD, you have to run your audio CD player program manually.

Therefore, here's how you can disable auto insert notification within Windows XP, as necessary:

1. **Double-click the My Computer icon on your desktop.**

2. **Right-click once on the drive you need to configure to highlight it and choose Properties.**

3. **Click the AutoPlay tab to display the panel shown in Figure 16-5.**

Figure 16-5:
There's the culprit —
your auto insert notification setting.

4. **Click the Content drop-down list box to choose the desired type of disc.**

5. **Enable the Select an Action to Perform radio button, and click the Take No Action icon to disable AutoPlay for the selected disc type.**

6. **Click OK to exit the Properties panel and return to the Windows desktop.**

If you'd like to avoid this hassle, you can click the Prompt Me Each Time to Choose an Action button on the AutoPlay tab — this means that Windows XP will display a confirmation dialog each time you load a disc. (Okay, so this is a bit of a hassle as well, but many people prefer this route instead of disabling AutoPlay entirely.)

Depending on the driver your recorder uses, you may have to reboot immediately after this process.

Slow It Down, Speed Racer

Tip: Use a slower recording speed when you encounter errors.

This advice is one of those basic truths that should be made into a tattoo. If you're encountering recording errors when your new 8X DVD recorder is burning across the landscape at its top velocity, *slow down!* No unwritten law says that you have to record every disc at the maximum speed offered by your drive.

For a number of reasons, your system may not be able to supply data at the top speed supported by your drive — even with burnproof support, your drive may slow to a crawl under certain circumstances. (You won't ruin the disc, though.) You may be multitasking with a woolly mammoth like Photoshop, or you may be recording a slew of tiny 4K files that are thrashing your hard drive. (Consider writing a disc image first, as I explain in the section, "Your Image Can Be Everything," earlier in this chapter.) Also, don't forget that most manufacturers rate their blank media with a top speed; if you're trying to write at 8X with discs rated at only 2X, bad things may happen. Your mileage may vary according to your brand of drive and discs, and whether you're using CD or DVD media.

When All Else Fails, Reinstall!

Tip: In case of massive, horrendous software problems, uninstall and reinstall!

Yes, I know — you and I have heard that litany countless times, but it's *true. It really works.* If your recording software is continually locking up or crashing, uninstall the program: Click Start and choose Settings⇨Control Panel⇨Add/Remove Programs. After you wipe the program from your system, reinstall it. Don't forget to reapply any patches or updates (that is, unless all your troubles started immediately after you applied an update).

Why does this technique work? It's a blanket approach to the problem: When you reinstall, you erase and replace whatever's causing (or at least contributing) to the errors. Potential culprits can include missing or corrupted drivers and shared files, "mulched" configuration files, and even updates to your software that have caused things to go haywire.

No, reinstalling doesn't always work, but it is something you should *always* try.

Overdoing Overburning

Tip: Overburn only when you really need the extra space.

As I mention in Chapter 2 of this book, overburning can squeeze from your blank discs additional megabytes of space (or a minute or two extra for audio CDs) — *if* your CD recorder can reliably overburn. That's a big *if* because both your recording software and your drive have to support this procedure. However, even if you can overburn, keep these tips in mind:

- ✔ Overburned discs are generally unreadable in CD-ROM drives 4 years old or older, and in many audio CD players.

- ✔ Switching media brands can suddenly thwart your attempts at overburning — it depends on the manufacturer.

- ✔ Check with the manufacturer of your drive to determine the absolute limit in megabytes and minutes and seconds you can overburn. (If necessary, a bit of experimentation can tell you this limit.)

With most media, I recommend that you keep almost all your recordings below the 80-minute/700MB limit and overburn only when it's absolutely necessary.

Chapter 17

Ten Things to Avoid Like the Plague

Mother Nature has ways of telling you to stay away from certain plants and animals — you don't want to get involved, usually because of claws, teeth, or poisonous spines. Alternating bands of neon green and orange can't be A Good Thing, right?

Unfortunately, you can encounter lots of really nasty, time-wasting trouble when buying, installing, and using a CD or DVD recorder, and you don't receive any warning beforehand. For example, recording over a network *sounds* like a great idea — until you try it.

In this Part of Tens chapter, I take over as the technoversion of Mother Nature (now *there's* a weird visual image for you) and identify what should be off-limits. Avoid these things like the plague, and you'll thank me!

Antique USB 1.1 Drives

Two or three years ago, shopping for an external drive came down to two choices. You could pick Small Computer System Interface (or SCSI, which was expensive, complex to configure, and quite scary for the average PC owner) or take the easy route and choose a USB 1.1 drive. Many folks opted for Universal Serial Bus (USB) because a USB drive is easy to install and much cheaper than a SCSI adapter card and drive.

In the new millennium, however, a USB 1.1 drive doesn't appear quite so attractive, and you should avoid buying one. Here's what the advertisements for these drives didn't tell you:

- **They're slow.** Compared with USB 2.0 or FireWire, I mean *really* slow: If Dorothy had used a USB 1.1 drive, she would still be in the Land of Oz. Because the data transfer rate is limited to the top speed of a parallel port, virtually all USB 1.1 drives are limited to 4X recording, with a handful of drives capable of a blistering 8X.

- **Forget DVD burning.** You might as well try to burn a DVD-R with a book of matches — a horrible pun, but you get the idea. USB 1.1 simply can't provide the data transfer speeds to burn a DVD at 2X or higher.

Unless you have absolutely no recourse — either you burn with a USB 1.1 drive or you don't burn discs — let these antiques fade away into the hoary pages of history and invest in a USB 2.0 or FireWire recorder.

"Holy Aqueous Tragedy, Batman!" (Avoiding Liquids)

Not much explanation needed for this Mark's Maxim:

Keep liquids away from both your discs and your recorder!™

In a pitched battle, a diet soda always wins. At least you can clean your discs when they have been accidentally dunked — you may have to use a little disc cleaning solution. However, knock your mug of hot cocoa on your external recorder, and you have just created an expensive paperweight.

A Bad Labeling Job Is Worse than No Label

To accurately read a CD-ROM or DVD-ROM, your drive has to control the speed of the disc's rotation, and — oh, there I go with the engineering-speak again. (Insert sound of my palm slapping my forehead.) All you have to remember is that a disc that's badly out of balance is harder to read, so sticking a huge, heavy label on just one side of a disc may render it unusable. This includes large mailing labels, return address labels, and even — gasp — stickers. If a label weighs enough, it throws the disc's balance out of whack. For this reason, many manufacturers of DVD media advise that you never apply a paper label to their discs; check the manufacturer's recommendations before you stick something where it shouldn't go!

The easiest way to avoid this problem is to use CD-ROM/DVD-ROM labels and a labeling device, like a CD Stomper (www.cdstomper.com) or NEATO (www.neato.com) system, which leave your discs in perfect balance after they're applied. Even better, you get quite a bit more space to hang text and graphics.

One note of warning about any label you apply: After it's on your disc, don't try to remove it unless it's specifically designed to come off! Most labels use a permanent adhesive; if you try to peel it off, you will probably rip the label (which can unbalance the disc).

Copy Protection Works

If you're buying a CD or DVD recorder to create backup copies of games or DVD movies, don't expect much success. Most computer CD-ROM games and all DVD-ROM discs are copy protected, and you won't have any luck in duplicating them. (They're also copyrighted, but I don't go into that here.)

Certain programs can remove the encryption from DVD movies, and one or two recording programs purport to duplicate discs. However, a number of different copy-protection schemes are also available and are continually being updated. Therefore, what works on one disc may not work on the next. 'Nuff said.

Don't Settle for a Tiny Buffer

As I mention earlier in this book, the size of your recorder's data buffer has a direct effect on the performance of your recorder — especially when your system is under pressure, like when other programs are running in the background or you're recording at 24X or faster speeds. The larger the buffer, the more efficient the recording process, and the less likely you are to encounter errors during the burn. (If the drive supports burnproof recording, buffer size is somewhat less critical, but you'll still benefit from faster recording with a larger buffer.)

If you're shopping for a recorder, I recommend a drive with at least 2MB; naturally, 4MB or more would be even better. Most older recorders have a scanty buffer of 512K (or even less), so scavengers beware.

"We Interrupt This Network Recording. . . ."

Let me be straightforward and say that this section is a personal vendetta. I was a hardware technician for a large hospital for several years in my hometown of Columbia, Missouri, and one of the other techs I worked with was continually ruining perfectly good discs trying to record over a network. He was using files from a network hard drive as the source, and because of the constant network broadcast messages and servers going up and down, he produced coaster after coaster. Eventually, I recommended that he try packet writing with Roxio's Drag-to-Disc (the subject of Chapter 10), which solved most of the problems. A burnproof recorder can also help alleviate problems with an overloaded network, but it still won't remount a network drive that's disappeared because the server went down!

Of course, you may find yourself forced to record over the network if your recorder is installed in a diskless workstation or an older computer with a tiny drive, but if you have the hard drive space on the computer with the recorder, *please* copy those files to the computer's local hard drive and record them from there.

I can't bear to think of any more innocent silver lives being wasted because the network slowed to a crawl.

How Slow Is Too Slow?

This one's for all the scavengers out there: If you have inherited a 2X or 4X CD recorder, consider passing it on to another friend or family member and shopping for a new drive. "Why, that's heresy to a scavenger, Mark! Of all the folks on this planet, *you* should know that!" It's true, I have scavenged more than my share of unwanted 4MB video cards, keyboards, ISA network cards, and SIMM memory from garage sales and basements. However, you have three good reasons to turn your back on 4X (and perhaps even 8X) CD recorders:

✔ **How much is your time worth?** After you have recorded an entire 680MB disc in 3 minutes with a 24X drive, you're going to wonder whether your 2X or 4X drive is lying dormant in hibernation for 15 minutes (or more) while it's burning a disc.

✔ **Older drives don't have the niceties.** With an "antique" 2X or 4X drive, you are likely to miss out on most of the features I have been crowing about — packet writing, Disc-at-Once, burnproof recording, and even CD Extra discs.

✔ **Their support has dried up.** Good luck in getting support for a 5- or 6-year-old drive: If you're lucky, the manufacturer may still have a firmware update or two on their Web sites, but it's more likely that support for such an old model has evaporated completely.

Of course, that 4X drive can still burn a mighty nice data CD-ROM of the plain variety. Just have your lunch on hand while you wait.

In the DVD recording world, recording speeds are rated much slower, but virtually all drives out there can burn at 2X — if you can afford it, you'll save yourself a heap of time if you opt for a 4X or super-fast 8X DVD burner.

Give Those Discs a Home!

If you have been burning discs for six months or so, you have followed one of two paths:

✔ **The light path:** You have picked up a snazzy CD/DVD binder or a jewel box shelf unit, and your discs are resting comfortably in their protected, dust-free environment. Your audio CDs don't skip because of scratches, and your data CD-ROMs and DVD movies never give you a hint of trouble when you read them.

> ✔ **The dark path:** You have two or three stacks of 20 unprotected discs adorning the front of your monitor, and they're picking up scratches and dust right before your eyes. (Also, you knock over a stack from time to time and wake up your significant other with a scream.)

Do yourself — and your discs — a favor and store them the right way.

Putting the Worthless in High-Tech Cleaning

I mention this in Chapter 1, but it bears repeating: You have absolutely *no reason* to spend $20 or more on a CD cleaning device that looks like a cross between one of da Vinci's flying machines and an automatic bread maker. All you need to clean your shiny round friends is a photographer's lens cloth — any high-density silk material will do in a pinch, too.

If a disc has picked up liquid gunk — I warn you about liquids earlier in this chapter, in the section "Holy Aqueous Tragedy, Batman!" (Avoiding Liquids) — it's a good idea to buy a flask of CD cleaning solution to help clean the toxic waste.

Here's an oft-repeated Mark's Maxim:

> **If you carry your discs correctly and store them responsibly, you simply don't need the Rube Goldberg cleaning contraptions now on the market!™**

Keep 'Em Cool

One thing your CDs and DVDs share with pets and children: Never, *never, NEVER* keep them trapped in a hot vehicle, especially in direct sunlight. Owners of car CD players know how finicky these beasts can be, and no matter what Aunt Matilda told you, discs can warp. (I haven't seen one melt yet, but I'm only 42 years old. There's still plenty of time.)

How can you fix a warped disc? Forget trying to press it back into shape with a thick, heavy hardbound book — coping with the disc is a better idea. Most recorders are more tolerant of a warped disc than audio CD players are, so you may get lucky enough to copy it (or at least create a disc image you can use to record a new disc).

However, it's best to just keep those discs cool in the first place!

Chapter 18

Ten Nifty Programs You Want

1 cover the most popular recording software the world around in this book (Easy CD & DVD Creator, Toast, and Drag-to-Disc) along with a number of specialized programs, like Adobe Premiere and iDVD. With the programs I focus on, you can record just about any type of CD and DVD under the sun.

These tools aren't the only ones you can use, of course; you can swear by other recording programs, for example (I don't cover the software you swear *at*), as well as utilities for converting images, creating thumbnails, editing digital audio and video, and much more. I mention classics like iMovie, WinAmp, and Paint Shop Pro elsewhere, and a host of others are available.

In this chapter, I review my favorite programs that I recommend to everyone with a recorder. I don't present any $5,000 software packages here: Most of these programs are shareware or cheap commercial software, and a few are even free. I think that the programs in this chapter appeal to both novice and experienced drive owners. I've used all these nifty tools on the PC and the Mac, and I bet that you will find them invaluable too!

CDRWIN

Windows CD recording shareware from Golden Hawk Technology
(www.goldenhawk.com)

CDRWIN has been a shareware favorite of the CD recording community for many years. The latest version now handles recordable and rewriteable DVD formats. As you can see in Figure 18-1, the basic interface looks almost comical (pun intended); behind that deceptively simple façade, however, lies a powerful recording engine! Also, the Golden Hawk Technology Web site is a great place to start when tracking down firmware upgrades for older CD recorders. (Think of firmware as the built-in "operating system" for your recorder, which can be updated just like software.)

Figure 18-1:
Don't be
fooled
by the
appearance
of CDRWIN.

At the time I type these words, CDRWIN is an absolute steal at $39, and you get versions for Windows 98, Windows Me, Windows NT, Windows 2000, and Windows XP.

Along with the basic data and audio CD formats CDRWIN can record, it includes these nifty features:

- ✔ Multiple recorder support, which allows you to use as many as 32 SCSI and EIDE drives connected to the same computer to burn copies of the same disc *simultaneously.* (Now you understand the attraction of those SCSI device chains.) For more on SCSI and EIDE drives, flip to Chapter 4.

- ✔ Extraction of specific sectors on a data or audio CD, which comes in handy when copying just a portion of a mixed-mode or CD Extra disc.

- ✔ Support for advanced CD and DVD recorders with the Kodak Disc Transporter, which automates the recording of multiple copies of the same disc.

- ✔ A complete selection of CD-Text fields for each track on an audio CD, including performer, songwriter, composer, arranger, and a custom text description.

- ✔ Extraction of audio files as both WAV and AIFF formats, which makes a difference if you need to send digital audio files to a Macintosh owner.

GraphicConverter

Macintosh image conversion and editing shareware from Lemke Software
(www.lemkesoft.de/en/index.htm)

For Macintosh owners, GraphicConverter represents the classic shareware success story, and it's now available for both the Classic Mac OS 9.2 and Mac OS X (see Figure 18-2).

Figure 18-2:
GraphicCon-verter is a Macintosh image-editing toolbox.

GraphicConverter can import more than 170 different formats of digital images, and it can export almost 75. Although manual and automatic (batch) conversion of image formats is its claim to fame, you can also

- Browse and view a folder's worth of images from within the program.
- View images in a slideshow display.
- Perform basic image-editing chores, like cropping, rotation, reducing and increasing color depth, and adjusting brightness and contrast.
- Whiz through mundane image-management tasks, like deleting, renaming, and moving images from one folder to another.

For a mere $30, the powerful tool GraphicConverter can't be beat!

PowerDVD

Windows Video CD and DVD-ROM player from CyberLink
(www.gocyberlink.com)

In my book, PowerDVD is the best software DVD player available — it demolishes anything from Microsoft (including the Windows XP DVD player) with a lengthy laundry list of features. It can also play Video CDs and MPEG digital video that you have stored on your hard drive. The most impressive PowerDVD features include

- Full support for Dolby Digital decoding and Dolby Headphone playback
- Dual subtitling (which comes in handy if you're studying a new language by watching your favorite movie)
- Digital 4x and 9x zoom
- Closed-caption display
- A screen capture utility
- A neat bookmark feature that lets you jump directly to a specific point in a film
- The neatest and most configurable control panel on the planet (as you can see in Figure 18-3)

You can buy a copy of PowerDVD directly from the CyberLink Web site for $49.95.

Figure 18-3:
PowerDVD is hands-down the best for watching DVD movies on your PC.

Final Cut Pro

Macintosh digital video editor and special effects generator from Apple
(www.apple.com)

If you're serious about DV editing and you're lucky enough to own one of the Apple Power Mac G4 or G5 lines (including my personal object of desire, the dual-processor G5), it's a good bet to settle on Final Cut Pro 4.0 as your editor and effects generator of choice (see Figure 18-4).

The program offers blindingly fast performance on these machines, with some of the fastest rendering times available on a personal computer. Features like these are liable to make you faint:

✔ Easy drag-and-drop editing with real-time control over multiple sequences

✔ Support for direct FireWire DV, Beta SP, and HDTV

✔ OMF professional-level audio export

✔ Output to monitor, camera, VCR, or NTSC TV

✔ Output to streaming Web media (using Cleaner 5 EZ, which is included)

✔ Work with hundreds of layers, including text and still graphics

Figure 18-4:
Mac owners rejoice in the power of Final Cut Pro 4.0.

Naturally, a full-blown video editor like this one doesn't come cheap, but the $999 Apple price is a mere fraction of the small fortune you would spend on a professional DV hardware system.

Musicmatch Jukebox Plus

Windows/Macintosh/Linux digital audio freeware/shareware "thing" from Musicmatch (www.musicmatch.com)

Why do I call Musicmatch Jukebox Plus a digital audio "thing"? Because it does an incredible amount of stuff, all related to digital audio (see Figure 18-5).

Figure 18-5: Musicmatch Jukebox Plus is a powerful audio thing.

Naturally, it's a great player for MP3s, WAVs, and audio CDs, and that's the main function of this program. I also find myself using it at least once or twice a day, however, to take care of other audio chores. With Jukebox Plus version 8.1, you can

- ✔ Burn audio CDs from within the program
- ✔ Upload MP3 audio files to your portable MP3 player
- ✔ Rip songs from existing audio CDs
- ✔ Convert digital audio files from one format to another
- ✔ Convert digital audio files from one sampling rate to another
- ✔ Display cool light shows while your music plays
- ✔ Buy music online, either as tracks or entire albums
- ✔ Print audio CD covers and display album artwork on your desktop

You can register Jukebox Plus with all these features for $19.99, or you can use the free version (Jukebox Basic) that can handle playing, ripping, and 2X burning.

Retrospect

Windows/Macintosh backup software from Dantz Development Corporation
(www.dantz.com/en/products/personal.dtml)

I absolutely *promise* that I don't nag you again about backing up your system —
I just recommend Retrospect, as shown in Figure 18-6, to do it.

Figure 18-6:
I use
Retrospect
on both my
Macintosh
and PCs.

This program is easy and fast, and it recognizes internal and external
recorders as backup devices, including, I'm happy to say, all types of CD,
DVD, and DVD-RAM drives. Other features of this excellent program include

- ✔ The ability to create a bootable disaster-recovery disc that can restore
  your system
- ✔ Efficient software compression to reduce the number of discs you need
- ✔ An easy-to-use source selection wizard to help you specify just what you
  want backed up
- ✔ Encryption to secure your files
- ✔ Automatic launching of unattended backups
- ✔ Automatic rotation between multiple backup sets

Talk about a bargain — both the Windows and Mac versions sell for $129.95
each from the Dantz Web site.

Acrobat

Windows and Macintosh document imaging and archiving software from Adobe (www.adobe.com**)**

You may be wondering why I chose to add Adobe Acrobat to this chapter. After all, it doesn't have anything directly to do with recording or multimedia (see Figure 18-7). Ah, but what about documents? Many companies use CD and DVD recorders to archive important material, like forms, advertising materials, and even user manuals — and those documents have to be available for use not only on the Web, but also on both Macintosh and PCs.

Figure 18-7:
Acrobat
just plain
rocks —
trust me on
this one,
people.

That's where Acrobat fits in, and that's why it's now one of the most successful document standards. PDF files are very small, which explains their popularity on the Web. In the Acrobat PDF format, you can create electronic versions of your documents that look and print exactly the same on PCs, Macs, and even those rabid Linux machines (complete with graphics and special fonts). The reader is free, so anyone can view and print your documents without spending a nickel.

Plus, the standard is backward compatible. In other words, the current version 6.0 of Acrobat can read PDF files created with older versions of the program, so you can rest assured that the documents you're archiving to CD-R will be readable in the future.

At the time of this writing, Acrobat 6.0 Standard is available from the Adobe Web site for $299.

CloneDVD

Windows DVD-ROM duplication software from Elaborate Bytes
(www.elby.ch/en/products/clone_DVD/index.html)

Sometimes, you want to duplicate a copy-protected DVD movie for a perfectly good, legal reason: a backup in case of disaster or a separate disc to take with you on a trip, for example. CloneDVD is one of a new generation of DVD-copying utilities that can compress a DVD movie to fit on a single recordable DVD (see Figure 18-8).

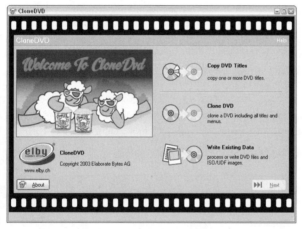

Figure 18-8: To copy the uncopy-able, get CloneDVD. (Is *uncopy-able* a real word?)

CloneDVD, however, is not a mastering program, like Easy CD & DVD Creator or Toast: You can't choose individual files or folders to record with this puppy. Its only purpose is to create exact backups of existing DVD movies.

CloneDVD can be purchased from the Elaborate Bytes Web site for about $60.

FireBurner

Windows/Linux CD recording shareware from IgD Software
(www.fireburner.com)

Cool name, right? You bet, and this extremely popular shareware CD recording program is just as cool as its name. Compared to the dozens of settings and menu items in Easy CD & DVD Creator, FireBurner is a stripped-down hotrod (see Figure 18-9). Yes, that's really the main menu! FireBurner handles data, audio, and mixed-mode CDs with ease. A Linux version is available.

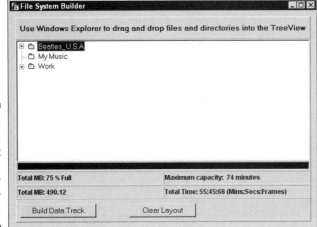

Figure 18-9:
The
minimalist
at work:
FireBurner
is a popular
favorite.

Other features include

- ✔ Support for recording from standard BIN and CUE image files (often shared on the Internet)
- ✔ Burns from digital audio (MP3 and WAV) as well as from PCM audio tracks
- ✔ Scanning of disc and track images for corruption and errors before you burn
- ✔ Burnproof recording support
- ✔ Drag-and-drop layout builder

FireBurner version 2.2 sets you back about $30.

QuickTime

Windows/Macintosh digital multimedia player/viewer from Apple (www.apple.com)

If it's multimedia, Apple QuickTime 6.4 can play it — that includes DV, MPEG, and MOV (QuickTime format) video, digital audio, still images, 360-degree panoramic images, and even Macromedia Flash animations! Plus, as you can see in Figure 18-10, this program looks like a million bucks. (That's important for a multimedia player these days, as the Windows folks in Redmond are finally figuring out.) If your recorded discs carry multimedia content, QuickTime can show it.

Figure 18-10:
QuickTime
is truly a
work of
perform-
ance art.

Along with viewing all these different types of files, I use QuickTime to watch QTV streaming video from my favorite Web sites (everything from BBC World Service to MTV and Nickelodeon).

The basic version of QuickTime is free, and the Pro version — which allows you to perform simple DV editing tasks, convert file formats, create slideshows, and resize images — is only $29.99.

Part VI
Appendixes

In this part . . .

*T*hese two appendixes include reference information that you can turn to as often as you like. (Go ahead: Dog-ear the pages. I won't tell.) You can find here a list of recorder hardware and software manufacturers and a glossary overflowing with technobabble terms, goofy acronyms, and — most importantly — the meanings of it all.

Appendix A

Recorder Hardware and Software Manufacturers

● ●

*1*n this appendix, you find contact information for manufacturers of CD and DVD recorders as well as developers of recording software of all kinds. Whenever possible, I list both the Web site and fax number for each entry. However, note that some companies do not provide direct voice telephone numbers, so you must contact them by e-mail.

Recorder Manufacturers

Addonics Technologies
Phone: (408) 433-3899
www.addonics.com

BUSlink USA
Phone: (626) 336-1888
Fax: (626) 968-8100
www.buslink.com

CenDyne
Phone: (877) 236-3963
www.cendyne.com

Compaq
Phone: (800) 752-0900
www.compaq.com

Creative Labs
Phone: (800) 998-1000
Fax: (405) 624-6780
us.creativelabs.com

Digital Peripheral Solutions
Phone: (714) 692-5573
Fax: (714) 692-5516
www.qps-inc.com

Hewlett-Packard Company
Phone: (800) 752-0900
www.hp.com

IBM Corporation
Phone: (800) IBM-4YOU
www.ibm.com

Imation Corporation
Phone: (888) 466-3456
Fax: (888) 704-4200
www.imation.com

Iomega Corporation
Phone: (888) 4IOMEGA
www.iomega.com

Memorex Products
Phone: (562) 906-2800
Fax: (562) 906-2848
www.memorex.com

Micro Solutions
Phone: (800) 890-7227
www.micro-solutions.com

Mitsumi Electronics
Phone: (800) MITSUMI
www.mitsumi.com

Pacific Digital Corporation
Phone: (888) 333-6732
www.pacificdigital.com

Plextor Corp
Phone: (800) 886-3935
Fax: (510) 651-9755
www.plextor.com

Ricoh Corporation
Phone: (800) 63-RICOH
www.ricoh-usa.com

Sony Electronics
Phone: (800) 588-3847
www.sonystyle.com

TEAC America
Phone: (323) 726-0303
Fax: (323) 727-7656
www.teac.com

Toshiba
Phone: (800) GOTOSHIBA
www.toshiba.com

Yamaha Corporation of America
Phone: (888) 926-2426
www.yamaha.com

Recording Software Developers

Ahead Software
www.nero.com

Apple
Phone: (800) 275-2273
www.apple.com

Elaborate Bytes
www.elby.ch

GEAR Software
Phone: (561) 575-GEAR
Fax: (561) 575-9315
www.gearsoftware.com

Golden Hawk Technology
Phone: (603) 429-1008
www.goldenhawk.com

HyCD
Phone: (408) 988-8282
Fax: (408) 988-8585
www.hycd.com

IgD Software
www.fireburner.com

NewTech Infosystems
Phone: (949) 421-0712
www.ntius.com

Padus
Phone: (888) GO-PADUS
Fax: (408) 370-0277
www.padus.com

Roxio, Inc.
Phone: (866) 280-ROXI
www.roxio.com

Sonic Solutions
Phone: (415) 893-8000
Fax: (415) 893-8008
www.sonic.com

Appendix B

Glossary

● ●

AAC: A relatively new digital audio file format popularized by Apple — AAC files are the native format for music downloaded from the Apple Music Store, and they can be played with iTunes or an iPod. AAC files are slightly smaller than the familiar MP3 format and provide the same CD-quality stereo.

adapter card: A circuit board used to expand the abilities of your computer. The card is plugged directly into the computer's motherboard. For example, you can add FireWire ports to a PC by installing a FireWire adapter card.

AIFF: The standard format for digital audio files for Macintosh computers. Like WAV audio files on the PC side of the fence, AIFF files are used to store CD-quality stereo, usually for transfer to an audio CD.

amorphous crystalline layer: A rather exotic name that describes the layer where pits and lands are created in a CD-RW or rewriteable DVD. This layer turns opaque when hit by a recorder's laser beam, resulting in the same effect as a pit on a CD-ROM or DVD-ROM manufactured in a factory. This layer can be cleared by formatting the disc, allowing the disc to be used again.

backup: A copy of the information stored on your computer's hard drive. In case your hard drive fails or you accidentally delete important files, you can restore valuable programs and data by using your backup. *Back up often — it's the smart power user thing to do, and I'll keep nagging you until you back up.*

binary: The language used by computers to communicate (with hardware, software, and other computers). It's not a particularly subtle language because binary has only two values: 0 (zero) and 1.

BIOS: (Basic Input/Output System) Your PC's BIOS controls basic functions, like the configuration of your hardware and the low-level functions on your motherboard. You can display and change the BIOS settings for your PC by pressing a specific key or key combination during the boot sequence.

bootable CD-ROM: A bootable CD that includes everything necessary to boot a PC or Macintosh without a hard drive: the operating system, support files, and configuration files. In the PC world, bootable CD-ROMs are recorded in El Torito format; your PC's BIOS must support bootable CD-ROMs to use one of these discs.

burnproof drive: A feature that eliminates almost all recording errors caused by multitasking. A burnproof drive can interrupt the recording process whenever you're running another program that could seriously affect the performance of your computer (like Adobe Photoshop or Microsoft Outlook). When your computer is ready to continue recording, the drive automatically resumes burning.

byte: A single character of text stored in your computer's memory or hard drive or on a CD-ROM or DVD-ROM.

caddy: A thin plastic box (rather than a tray) used to hold the disc on older CD-ROM drives and recorders. These days, drives that use caddies are considered inconvenient, anachronistic dinosaurs.

case: The metal frame that holds all the components. Like jukeboxes, all computer cases can be opened for servicing (some with a separate cover that you can remove and others with a hinged door).

CD Extra: (Also called CD Enhanced.) A mixed-mode CD-ROM with both audio and data tracks. The audio track is recorded first, allowing a CD Extra disc to be played in a standard audio CD player.

CD-R: (Compact Disc-Recordable) The standard recordable disc, typically capable of storing about 700MB of computer data or about 80 minutes of digital audio. CD-Rs can be recorded only once; unlike a CD-RW, a CD-R can't be reused.

CD-ROM: (Compact Disc Read-Only Memory) A compact disc used on a computer rather than an audio CD player. CD-ROMs can be commercially manufactured or recorded on your computer using a CD-R or CD-RW drive.

CD-ROM XA: The standard recording format for multisession discs. Note that older CD-ROM drives may not be able to read CD-ROM XA discs.

CD-RW: (Compact Disc-Rewriteable) A reusable recordable CD-ROM that can be erased. CD-RWs can't be used in most older CD-ROM drives, and they can't be used in older audio CD players.

CD-Text: A feature that encodes the disc name, artist name, and each track name when you record an audio CD. If your audio CD player (or your audio CD player program on your computer) supports CD-Text, it displays this information while the disc is playing.

data buffer: Internal memory built into every CD and DVD recorder. This memory temporarily holds data transferred from your hard drive until it's ready to be recorded. The larger the data buffer in your recorder, the more efficient the flow of data (and the less likely you are to encounter buffer underrun errors during recording).

defragment: To order files on your hard drive by rewriting them in contiguous form. After a drive has been defragmented, files take less time to read, and your hard drive's performance is improved.

digital audio extraction: (Also called *ripping.*) The process of converting a digital audio track (a song, in other words) from an existing audio CD to an MP3, WAV, AAC, or AIFF file on your computer's hard drive. Depending on the recording software that you're using, you may have to do this before you can record that track to a new audio CD.

DIP switches: A bank of tiny sliding or rocker switches you use to configure devices, like hard drives and recorders. Use the tip of a pencil to set the switches into the correct position.

Disc-at-Once: The author's favorite recording mode (can you tell?), where the recorder writes the entire disc at once (without turning the recording laser off between tracks). Using Disc-at-Once may help you avoid audible clicks between tracks when playing recorded audio CDs on some players. Virtually all recorders manufactured in the past three or four years can record in Disc-at-Once mode.

disc image: A file saved to your hard drive that contains all the data required to record a CD or DVD. Disc images are good for creating multiple copies of a disc over a long period. You should record from a disc image if you're experiencing Buffer Underrun errors while recording.

DVD authoring: The process of designing, creating, and editing an interactive DVD-ROM for personal use or commercial sale. Authoring usually involves building a DVD menu, editing digital video, and adding still images and computer programs.

DVD-A: (DVD-Audio) The DVD recording format due to replace the audio compact disc. A DVD-A can store anywhere from two to four hours of high-fidelity music along with video clips.

DVD-R: (DVD recordable) A recordable DVD that can hold 4.7GB. DVD-Rs can be recorded only once. Virtually all DVD players can use DVD-Rs, so they're popular for folks creating their own DVD-Video discs.

DVD+R: (Another form of DVD recordable.) A recordable DVD that can hold 4.7GB. DVD+Rs are very similar to DVD-Rs, but the two formats are not compatible (so you can't record a DVD-R in a DVD+R drive). DVD+Rs can be recorded only once. Most late-model DVD players can use DVD+Rs.

DVD-RAM: A reusable recordable DVD that can hold 5.2GB on each side. Only the latest DVD players can read DVD-RAMs, but they're still great for system backups and data storage. Like a CD-RW, a DVD-RAM must be formatted before you can use it.

DVD-ROM: (Originally short for digital versatile disc, and now also called a digital video disc by those with overactive imaginations.) Rapidly becoming the standard for storing movies and digital video, a type of disc that stores 4.7GB to 17GB in the same physical dimensions as a standard CD-ROM.

DVD-RW: A relatively new DVD format, DVD-RWs can hold 4.7GB on each side, and they're reusable. However, unlike the unlimited lifespan of DVD-RAMs, DVD-RWs can be rewritten only 1,000 times. On the plus side, DVD-RWs can be read in most DVD players.

DVD+RW: Another recently-introduced DVD format, DVD+RWs are rewriteable, and they can hold 4.7GB on each side. Unlike DVD-RWs, DVD+RWs can be re-recorded many thousands of times. DVD+RWs can be read in most DVD players.

DVD-V: (DVD-Video) The DVD recording format used to produce movies on DVD-ROM (by using digital video in MPEG format). All home DVD players read DVD-V. A DVD-V can hold 4.7GB of digital video and data on each side.

dye layer: A layer of light-sensitive dye in a CD-R that turns opaque when struck by a recorder's laser beam. The result acts the same as a pit on a factory-made CD-ROM. The dye layer in a CD-R can't be turned clear again, so a CD-R can be recorded only once.

EIDE: (Enhanced Integrated Drive Electronics) The interface used by virtually all PCs and new Mac computers for connecting internal devices, like hard drives, CD-ROM drives, and recorders. Most PCs have a primary and secondary EIDE connector; each connector supports two devices.

El Torito format: The somewhat silly name for the format standard used to record bootable CD-ROMs.

emergency disc eject hole: A hole that allows you to eject the disc manually even if the drive has locked up or isn't working Every recorder and read-only drive has one of these tiny holes. If you can't eject your disc, you can force it out (or force the tray to extend) by pushing a paperclip into the eject hole.

external recorder: A CD or DVD recorder that you add outside your computer. It's connected to your computer by a cable and may use a separate power supply. USB and FireWire drives are always external, and a SCSI drive may be external.

FAQ: (Frequently Asked Questions) A text or Adobe PDF file created by someone who knows the answers to the most common questions posed on a particular subject. The manufacturer of your recorder may post a list of FAQs on its Web site, answering technical support and installation questions from new drive owners.

FireWire: (Otherwise blessed with the rather cryptic name IEEE-1394.) The most popular type of connection for external devices that require high-speed data transfer, including DV camcorders and CD and DVD recorders. Like USB, FireWire devices can be connected and unplugged without rebooting the computer, but FireWire hardware is generally more expensive. All new Macintosh computers come with FireWire ports built-in, and you can add a FireWire adapter card to your PC. Two different types of FireWire exist now: the original FireWire 400 and FireWire 800, which is twice as fast. Either flavor is fine for connecting a CD or DVD recorder.

formatting: Preparing a blank CD-RW, DVD-RW, DVD+RW, or DVD-RAM for use (similar to formatting one of those old-fashioned hard drives). The disc can't be used until it has been successfully formatted, and formatting erases the existing contents of a disc.

gigabyte: A unit of data equal to 1,024MB (megabytes), usually abbreviated as GB. DVDs can hold several gigabytes.

hard drive: A magnetic storage device that provides a permanent home for computer programs and data (at least until it crashes). Most hard drives are internal, but you can also get external SCSI, USB, and FireWire models.

HFS: (Hierarchical File System) The CD-ROM file system used by Macintosh computers.

HTML: (Hypertext Markup Language) The programming language used to create Web pages. You can also use HTML to create CD-ROM menus.

HTML Editor: A program used to create or edit Web pages, which are actually HTML files made up of commands. You can edit these commands directly by using a character-based editor (like Windows Notepad or Arachnophilia), or you can use a visual HTML editor, like Microsoft FrontPage.

incremental multisession disc: A disc that adds data imported from the previous session to files recorded in a new session (effectively updating the data in the previous session).

interface: An extremely fancy engineering-style technical word for *connection* — as in methods of connecting internal and external devices to your computer. Common interfaces for CD and DVD recorders include EIDE, SCSI, USB, and FireWire.

internal drive: A recorder that fits inside your computer's case; other internal devices can include hard drives, floppy drives, or Zip drives.

ISO 9660: The most compatible CD-ROM or DVD-ROM file system around. Virtually every computer and operating system can read an ISO 9660 disc, which makes it the best choice for recording cross-platform discs. On the downside, ISO 9660 limits the length of filenames and the number of directories and subdirectories that you can use in your disc layout.

jewel box: The familiar hinged, plastic storage case that holds a compact disc.

Joliet file system: The CD-ROM or DVD-ROM file system used for Windows. It allows long filenames with periods and spaces.

jumper: A small wire-and-plastic electrical crossover used to configure a circuit board or internal device in your computer. You can change the settings by moving the jumper to connect different sets of pins.

kilobyte: A unit of data equal to 1,024 bytes, usually abbreviated as K.

land: A spot under the clear surface of a CD or DVD that reflects laser light. If the disc is manufactured, lands are the flat areas between the pits; on recorded CDs and DVDs, pits are the clear areas between the opaque pits.

laser read head: The combination of the CD-ROM's or DVD-ROM's laser lens, prism, and optical pickup. Together, they allow your CD-ROM or DVD-ROM drive to read a disc.

laser write head: A laser beam on a recorder that can be toggled to high and low power levels.

master: The setting for an EIDE device that designates it as the primary device on that EIDE cable. An EIDE recorder can be set to "single drive, master unit" (if it's the only drive on the cable) or "multiple drive, master unit" (if it's the primary drive with another device on the cable).

megabyte: A unit of data equal to 1,024K (kilobytes), usually abbreviated as MB.

mixed-mode disc: A CD-ROM with both digital audio tracks and a data track. On a standard mixed-mode disc, the first track is computer data, and the following tracks are recorded as digital audio. Mixed-mode discs are often used for storing games. Although a mixed-mode disc can't be played on a standard audio CD player, you can record a CD Extra mixed-mode disc that is compatible with audio CD players.

motherboard: The main circuit board in a computer. The motherboard is where you find the computer's CPU (or processor), the memory modules, and the EIDE or SCSI connectors. You can plug adapter cards into the motherboard to expand your computer's functionality.

Mozart, Wolfgang Amadeus: My favorite classical composer and a doggone good piano player to boot. He created the world's most beautiful music, and I'm proud to say that I've collected every single note he ever composed on audio CD.

MP3: The most popular format for digital audio on the Internet. MP3 files are very small in size, provide CD-quality stereo, and they're often used to record audio CDs.

MPEG: (Moving Pictures Expert Group) The video format used on commercial DVD-Video movie discs. MPEG is also a popular format for video transmitted over the Web.

multisession: A type of disc that stores multiple separate recording sessions. An incremental multisession disc allows access to only the latest session, and a multivolume multisession disc allows access to all the sessions (one at a time). Audio CD players and older CD-ROM drives can use only multivolume discs.

multitask: To run multiple programs on your computer at one time. If you experience problems recording a disc while multitasking, consider using packet writing recording or upgrading to a drive that uses burnproof technology (or just stop recording while using other programs).

multivolume multisession disc: A disc that stores data in separate volumes, each of which can be accessed one at a time. Audio CD players and older CD-ROM drives can read only the last session on a multivolume multisession disc.

network: A system of computers connected to each other to exchange data and share devices, like printers, modems, and recorders.

Orange Book: The international engineering standard that specifies the file structure of recorded CD-ROMs or CD-Rs.

overburn: To record more data than the rated maximum capacity of a CD-R. For instance, your drive might be able to record 76 minutes of music on a standard 74-minute CD-R. The amount you can overburn depends on your recorder and the specific brand of discs that you're using.

packet writing: (Also called UDF.) A recording method that allows you to drag and drop files directly to the recorder's drive icon just as you would copy files to a floppy drive. Virtually all CD and DVD recorders can record discs by using packet writing.

parallel port: A port usually used to connect a printer, although it can be used to connect external devices, like a Zip drive, scanner, or CD recorder.

Although some ancient CD recorders connected to your parallel port, I don't recommend them: They're as slow as an arthritic turtle and more prone to problems than USB and FireWire drives.

pit: A spot under the clear surface of a disc that scatters light and doesn't reflect it. If the disc is manufactured, pits are actual depressions within the disc. On recorded CDs and DVDs, pits are simply opaque spots within the dye (or crystalline) layer.

RAM: (Random Access Memory) The temporary storehouse for the data that your computer and its programs need to run. As you probably know, however, turning off your computer causes you to lose the data that's stored in RAM (hence the development of the hard drive, which stores that data permanently).

Red Book: The international engineering standard that specifies the file structure of audio CDs. An audio CD that you've recorded must comply with Red Book standards to be compatible with your audio CD player.

refurbished: Used or returned hardware that has been "fixed" (hopefully by the manufacturer) and resold at a much lower price. (I would say selling refurbished merchandise is also called a SCAM, but that's already in this glossary.) Let the buyer beware, as someone once said.

restocking fee: (Also called a *rip-off.*) A fee charged by most online and local computer stores if you return an item — even if it's unopened.

SCAM: (SCSI Configured Automatically) A feature that allows your SCSI adapter card to automatically allocate SCSI ID numbers to all SCAM-compliant SCSI devices. SCAM makes things easier for both you and your PC.

screen printing: A printing process that adds layers of different-color inks through a series of stencils to create a single multicolored image. Most manufactured CD and DVD labels are screen printed.

SCSI: (Small Computer Systems Interface) A popular adapter choice for high-speed internal and external devices, like hard drives, recorders, and scanners. SCSI adapters are available for both Macs and PCs. (By the way, it is indeed pronounced "skuzzy" — really!)

SCSI ID: A unique number assigned to a SCSI device that identifies it. Assigning the same SCSI ID to two SCSI devices will probably result in a locked computer.

secure connection: An encrypted connection between you and a Web site that helps prevent your personal data from being intercepted. Whenever you're buying something on the Web, frequent only online stores that offer a secure connection for your credit card number.

slave: The setting for an EIDE device that designates it as the secondary device on that EIDE cable. An EIDE recorder can be set to "multiple drive, slave unit" (if it's the secondary drive with another device on the cable).

slideshow: Just like the slideshows that Uncle Milton used to bore the entire family during reunions — only now the images are displayed on your computer monitor or your TV. The photographs are files stored on your hard drive or a DVD, and your computer or DVD player, rather than a clunky projector, does the work.

static electricity: The archenemy of any computer hardware; a type of electricity that can destroy any circuit board in a flash (pun intended, unfortunately). Always touch the metal chassis (the metal framework) of your computer before handling any internal computer device or adapter card to discharge any static electricity on your body.

terminator: Both sides of a SCSI device chain must be terminated by using a switch or small resistor pack. Without correct termination, your SCSI devices don't work.

thumbwheel: A rotating wheel that you can use to select the SCSI ID on a SCSI recorder.

track: On an audio CD, a single section of audio (typically a single song) that you can jump to immediately. On a data CD, a track is simply a section of the CD-ROM that contains data (many CD-ROMs contain only a single data track that holds all the files).

Track-at-Once: The default recording mode for most recording software. The laser beam writes each track one at a time, and the recording laser is turned off between tracks.

UDF: (Universal Disc Format) *See* packet writing.

USB: (Universal Serial Bus) A type of connection used to add external devices, like recorders and printers, to both PC and Macintosh computers. The USB port offers Plug and Play support, so you can connect a USB device without rebooting your computer. Two versions of USB devices are on the market: The older USB 1.1 is supported on most PCs and Macs (but it's not suitable for high-speed CD or DVD burning), but the new USB 2.0 standard is much faster (and works perfectly for connecting any CD or DVD recorder).

Video CD: A CD recording format that can store high-quality MPEG video for viewing on a Video CD player.

virtual memory: A method that uses hard drive space to "increase" the amount of memory available to your computer. Both Windows and Mac OS use virtual memory to run programs that would normally fail because your computer had insufficient RAM.

WAV: The Windows standard format for CD-quality digital sound files. WAV files can be played directly from your hard drive or recorded as part of an audio CD.

WYSIWYG: An absolutely ridiculous acronym that stands for What You See Is What You Get, now taken to mean a visual or object-oriented computer application. (If you know who created this travesty, please let me know so that I can send the culprit a rotten tomato.)

X factor: The author's catchy term for the figure used to indicate the speed of CD and DVD recorders (as well as read-only CD-ROM and DVD-ROM drives). It represents the multiplier of the data transfer rate for the first single-speed drives. For example, a 24X CD-ROM drive is twenty-four times faster than an original single-speed CD-ROM drive.

Index

● Z ●

Notes

Notes

Notes

Notes

Notes

Notes

FOR DUMMIES®

A world of resources to help you grow

HOME, GARDEN & HOBBIES

Feng Shui
0-7645-5295-3

Gardening
0-7645-5130-2

Guitar
0-7645-5106-X

Also available:

Auto Repair For Dummies
(0-7645-5089-6)

Chess For Dummies
(0-7645-5003-9)

Home Maintenance For Dummies
(0-7645-5215-5)

Organizing For Dummies
(0-7645-5300-3)

Piano For Dummies
(0-7645-5105-1)

Poker For Dummies
(0-7645-5232-5)

Quilting For Dummies
(0-7645-5118-3)

Rock Guitar For Dummies
(0-7645-5356-9)

Roses For Dummies
(0-7645-5202-3)

Sewing For Dummies
(0-7645-5137-X)

FOOD & WINE

Cooking
0-7645-5250-3

Cookies
0-7645-5390-9

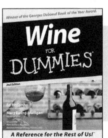

Wine
0-7645-5114-0

Also available:

Bartending For Dummies
(0-7645-5051-9)

Chinese Cooking For Dummies
(0-7645-5247-3)

Christmas Cooking For Dummies
(0-7645-5407-7)

Diabetes Cookbook For Dummies
(0-7645-5230-9)

Grilling For Dummies
(0-7645-5076-4)

Low-Fat Cooking For Dummies
(0-7645-5035-7)

Slow Cookers For Dummies
(0-7645-5240-6)

TRAVEL

Italy
0-7645-5453-0

Hawaii
0-7645-5438-7

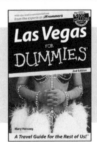

Las Vegas
0-7645-5448-4

Also available:

America's National Parks For Dummies
(0-7645-6204-5)

Caribbean For Dummies
(0-7645-5445-X)

Cruise Vacations For Dummies 2003
(0-7645-5459-X)

Europe For Dummies
(0-7645-5456-5)

Ireland For Dummies
(0-7645-6199-5)

France For Dummies
(0-7645-6292-4)

London For Dummies
(0-7645-5416-6)

Mexico's Beach Resorts For Dummies
(0-7645-6262-2)

Paris For Dummies
(0-7645-5494-8)

RV Vacations For Dummies
(0-7645-5443-3)

Walt Disney World & Orlando For Dummies
(0-7645-5444-1)

Available wherever books are sold. Go to www.dummies.com or call 1-877-762-2974 to order direct.

FOR DUMMIES®

Helping you expand your horizons and realize your potential

INTERNET

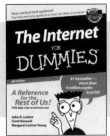

The Internet
FOR DUMMIES
0-7645-0894-6

The Internet
ALL-IN-ONE DESK REFERENCE
FOR DUMMIES
0-7645-1659-0

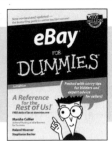

eBay
FOR DUMMIES
0-7645-1642-6

Also available:

America Online 7.0 For Dummies
(0-7645-1624-8)

Genealogy Online For Dummies
(0-7645-0807-5)

The Internet All-in-One Desk Reference For Dummies
(0-7645-1659-0)

Internet Explorer 6 For Dummies
(0-7645-1344-3)

The Internet For Dummies Quick Reference
(0-7645-1645-0)

Internet Privacy For Dummies
(0-7645-0846-6)

Researching Online For Dummies
(0-7645-0546-7)

Starting an Online Business For Dummies
(0-7645-1655-8)

DIGITAL MEDIA

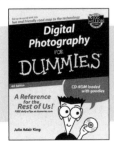

Digital Photography
FOR DUMMIES
0-7645-1664-7

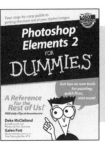

Photoshop Elements 2
FOR DUMMIES
0-7645-1675-2

Digital Video
FOR DUMMIES
0-7645-0806-7

Also available:

CD and DVD Recording For Dummies
(0-7645-1627-2)

Digital Photography All-in-One Desk Reference For Dummies
(0-7645-1800-3)

Digital Photography For Dummies Quick Reference
(0-7645-0750-8)

Home Recording for Musicians For Dummies
(0-7645-1634-5)

MP3 For Dummies
(0-7645-0858-X)

Paint Shop Pro "X" For Dummies
(0-7645-2440-2)

Photo Retouching & Restoration For Dummies
(0-7645-1662-0)

Scanners For Dummies
(0-7645-0783-4)

GRAPHICS

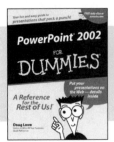

PowerPoint 2002
FOR DUMMIES
0-7645-0817-2

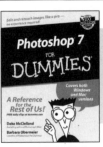

Photoshop 7
FOR DUMMIES
0-7645-1651-5

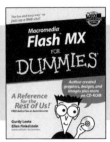

Macromedia Flash MX
FOR DUMMIES
0-7645-0895-4

Also available:

Adobe Acrobat 5 PDF For Dummies
(0-7645-1652-3)

Fireworks 4 For Dummies
(0-7645-0804-0)

Illustrator 10 For Dummies
(0-7645-3636-2)

QuarkXPress 5 For Dummies
(0-7645-0643-9)

Visio 2000 For Dummies
(0-7645-0635-8)

FOR DUMMIES®

The advice and explanations you need to succeed

SELF-HELP, SPIRITUALITY & RELIGION

0-7645-5302-X

0-7645-5418-2

0-7645-5264-3

Also available:

The Bible For Dummies
(0-7645-5296-1)

Buddhism For Dummies
(0-7645-5359-3)

Christian Prayer For Dummies
(0-7645-5500-6)

Dating For Dummies
(0-7645-5072-1)

Judaism For Dummies
(0-7645-5299-6)

Potty Training For Dummies
(0-7645-5417-4)

Pregnancy For Dummies
(0-7645-5074-8)

Rekindling Romance For Dummies
(0-7645-5303-8)

Spirituality For Dummies
(0-7645-5298-8)

Weddings For Dummies
(0-7645-5055-1)

PETS

0-7645-5255-4

0-7645-5286-4

0-7645-5275-9

Also available:

Labrador Retrievers For Dummies
(0-7645-5281-3)

Aquariums For Dummies
(0-7645-5156-6)

Birds For Dummies
(0-7645-5139-6)

Dogs For Dummies
(0-7645-5274-0)

Ferrets For Dummies
(0-7645-5259-7)

German Shepherds For Dummies
(0-7645-5280-5)

Golden Retrievers For Dummies
(0-7645-5267-8)

Horses For Dummies
(0-7645-5138-8)

Jack Russell Terriers For Dummies
(0-7645-5268-6)

Puppies Raising & Training Diary For Dummies
(0-7645-0876-8)

EDUCATION & TEST PREPARATION

0-7645-5194-9

0-7645-5325-9

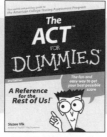
0-7645-5210-4

Also available:

Chemistry For Dummies
(0-7645-5430-1)

English Grammar For Dummies
(0-7645-5322-4)

French For Dummies
(0-7645-5193-0)

The GMAT For Dummies
(0-7645-5251-1)

Inglés Para Dummies
(0-7645-5427-1)

Italian For Dummies
(0-7645-5196-5)

Research Papers For Dummies
(0-7645-5426-3)

The SAT I For Dummies
(0-7645-5472-7)

U.S. History For Dummies
(0-7645-5249-X)

World History For Dummies
(0-7645-5242-2)

Available wherever books are sold. Go to www.dummies.com or call 1-877-762-2974 to order direct.

FOR DUMMIES®

We take the mystery out of complicated subjects